Everything to Play For

Everything to Play For:

How Videogames Are Changing the World

by Marijam Did

VERSO

London • New York

First published by Verso 2024
© Marijam Didžgalvytė 2024

1 3 5 7 9 10 8 6 4 2

Verso
UK: 6 Meard Street, London W1F 0EG
US: 388 Atlantic Avenue, Brooklyn, NY 11217
versobooks.com

Verso is the imprint of New Left Books

ISBN-13: 978-1-80429-324-9
ISBN-13: 978-1-80429-325-6 (UK EBK)
ISBN-13: 978-1-80429-326-3 (US EBK)

British Library Cataloguing in Publication Data
A catalogue record for this book is available from the British Library

Library of Congress Cataloging-in-Publication Data

Names: Did, Marijam, author.
Title: Everything to play for : how videog-
ames are changing the world / by
   Marijam Did.
Description: First edition paperback. |
London ; New York : Verso Books,
   2024. | Includes bibliographical references and index.
Identifiers: LCCN 2024014080 (print) |
LCCN 2024014081 (ebook) | ISBN
   9781804293249 (paperback) | ISBN 9781804293263 (ebk)
Subjects: LCSH: Video games – History. | Video games industry.
Classification: LCC GV1469.3 .D52 2024
(print) | LCC GV1469.3 (ebook) |
   DDC 794.8 – dc23/eng/20240411
LC record available at https://lccn.loc.gov/2024014080
LC ebook record available at https://lccn.loc.gov/2024014081

Typeset in Fournier by Biblichor Ltd, Edinburgh
Printed and bound by CPI Group (UK) Ltd, Croydon CR0 4YY

To the Jokubaičiai family — thank you for everything.
I look forward to wonderful evenings in the sun again,
on the other side, smoking fish we just caught.

Contents

Introduction: Main Menu

The year was 2018 – Vladimir Putin had been re-elected for his fourth and most influential term yet, Gazans were protesting peacefully in tens of thousands in their fight for dignity, Prince Harry married Meghan Markle and the US–China trade war began in earnest, with the US issuing tariffs against China. In the world of social media, it was the year of the explosion of TikTok and whistleblowers blowing the lid off Facebook and Cambridge Analytica. A seismic, albeit less-discussed, shift was taking place in wider mass culture and entertainment, too. That year, the global profits of the videogames* industry became greater than those of

---

* On the use of the word 'videogame', there is an ongoing debate within the gaming community (honestly, just Google it!) as to whether the term should be one or two words: 'videogames' or 'video games'. While the *Oxford English Dictionary* lists it as two words, which has made this form the more common use, I'm in the one-word camp. As I see it, the term 'video games' denotes 'games that utilise video technology', and while the medium may have begun its history as the 'video' variant of parlour games, the last half-century of growth and sophistication has brought it a long way from its origins. Videogames today are much more than 'video' in their technology and much more than 'games' in their content. The medium as a whole could more accurately be described as 'digital experiences'. Given that the old legacy name is unlikely to be re-evaluated anytime soon, I'd rather make it a portmanteau

the music and film industries combined.[1] Slowly but steadily, during its short fifty-year existence, this boundless, fascinating, grotesque industry has conquered traditional media and has become seemingly unstoppable.

Since that pivotal year for gaming, the trend has continued. When the COVID-19 pandemic hit in 2020, concert venues, film sets, and theatres closed their doors. Game developers, however, were not forced to pause entertainment creation – they simply moved their hardware from office to home and smoothly continued production. Videogames became more popular than ever. While stuck at home with few ways to entertain themselves, large swathes of the population bought videogames and consoles. The pandemic was a time where, once more, game enthusiasts could spend their evenings indoors and game without guilt, as there was little else to do. A significant number of people either remembered gaming from their teenage years and regained interest or, even more commonly, discovered the world of gaming for the first time. It is now estimated that more than two-thirds of all UK and US adults played videogames during the pandemic.[2]

The power the gaming industry holds is immense – there were 3 billion active gamers globally by 2023, and videogame sales will generate half a trillion dollars by 2028.[3] The statistics become even more staggering when one observes individual artefacts. Edinburgh-based Rockstar North delivered *Grand Theft Auto V* (*GTA V*) in 2013 and, as of the time of writing, have shipped more than 190 million copies of the game.[4] In April 2018, the game became the most financially successful entertainment product of all time, with about $6 billion in worldwide revenues.[5] Its current $8 billion revenue is larger than those of the three highest-grossing

---

word, hinting that what used to be a variant has now grown into its own unique set of qualities. Hence, videogames.

movies of all time – *Avatar* (2009), *Avengers: Endgame* (2019) and *Avatar: The Way of Water* (2022) – combined.

Despite this success, *GTA V* is not even the videogame with the most significant sales numbers or the largest gaming crowd. That honour belongs to the behemoth that is *Minecraft*. The quarter of a billion dollars in confirmed sales of this 3D sandbox game is already impressive enough,[6] but the game's playtime compared to that of other cultural media tells a staggering story. At the time of the writing of this book, the most-streamed song on Spotify, Ed Sheeran's 2017 megahit *Shape of You*, had been listened to more than 3 billion times, a length of 24,000 years. *Squid Game* – the South Korean Netflix sensation that swept the world in 2021 – boasts 190,000 years of watch time.[7] According to *Minecraft* server statistics, in China alone, the game had an estimated 597,607,200,000 hours of playtime from June 2016 to May 2020. That is nearly 70,000,000 years of playtime! In other words, the number of years back in history from now to when the very first primates appeared on Earth. *Minecraft* playtime must have hit 100,000,000 years during the pandemic. The title reigns supreme as the most-viewed game on YouTube, surpassing a trillion views in 2021.[8] One might think that children are over-represented in these statistics. Still, according to the Entertainment Software Association, in the US, 76 per cent of all gamers are adults, of whom 48 per cent are women.[9]

Electronic sports (esports) are demonstrating similar growth. The *League of Legends* (2009 onwards) World Championship in 2019 was a record-breaking esports event, boasting more than 100 million viewers.[10] Most of these fans tuned in through streaming services like Twitch and YouTube. In comparison, the Super Bowl that same year had 98.2 million viewers across the NFL's digital properties and CBS.[11] Even an event as global and commercially significant as the Tokyo Olympics in 2021 drew only 17 million viewers to its opening ceremony – a fraction of the audience numbers that esports now regularly pull in. In addition, the esports and gaming viewership is consistently growing every year. By contrast, viewership of traditional sports is flatlining. The winner of the 2021 *Dota 2* (2013 onw.) championship, held in Romania, took home just over $18 million. This is greater than the reward for the American Super Bowl that, for a few days, sucks up the entirety of the Western airways every year ($11 million). The overall prize pool for the International *Dota 2* championship is $40 million, most of it crowdfunded.

Nonetheless, given the inadequate mainstream media coverage of the development and size of digital gaming, the general public would be forgiven for thinking that gaming is a small, unserious subculture with little to no influence on the real world. The bit of televised news that comes between the daily events and the weather is still dominated by what I call old-school sports reports, which arguably cater to a shrinking audience. More worrying and consequential is that gaming seems to be of little interest to progressive crowds, even when they are convinced (in my view, rightfully) that culture is where a sizeable part of the change happens.

Beyond the worlds of sport and pure entertainment, gaming has also made serious, albeit underappreciated, strides into the realm of highbrow culture. Videogames have occasionally featured in Western high-art cultural institutions since the 1980s, but the last decade has witnessed the adoption of elements of games into multimedia collections. The Victoria and Albert Museum, MoMA and the Barbican have all organised gaming-related exhibitions. In 2019, the Game Arts International Association (GAIA) held its inaugural international summit of game curators in Argentina.

The temptation here is to describe a new dawn in game-making, some fresh spring of artistic practices that are perhaps newly

enabled by technology. In fact, games have always contained outstanding opportunities for sensual creative expression. Even as the
industry was pumping out vulgar, competitive titles barely worthy
of artistic consideration, networks of individuals enjoying a particular game found the means to break or mod the game to their
desire, bending the allocated rules and aesthetic of the game.*As
access to game-making hardware and software became more
freely available and as it became possible to store games online,
games bloomed into truly fascinating artistic inventions. Game-
influenced artists began making their way into elite museums in
the 1990s. In 1998, the Walker Art Center in Minneapolis organised the *Beyond Interface* exhibit, which featured playful web art.
That was followed in 2001 by the Whitney Museum of American
Art's *BitStreams* and the San Francisco Museum of Modern Art's
010101: Art in Technological Times.[12]

Among gamers, the most flourishing stream of creativity was
often in the modding community. Modders offer a deconstruction,
a surreal interpretation, of even the most basic, stereotype-clad
game, with fascinating results. Examples include the level design
of the legendary first-person shooter game *Doom* (1993) or a
myriad of glitches discovered in fighting games such as *Street
Fighter II: World Warrior* (1991). These mods display artistic
genius, but modding remains underappreciated. The computational, artificially augmented or sometimes unintentionally
broken elements of videogames have the potential to add greatly
to visual inventiveness, something that is essentially impossible to
achieve in other media.

It is much more usual to attribute artistic intentions only to
games harbouring some deeper narrative meaning. *Her Story*

---

* Videogame modding (short for 'modification') is the process whereby players
or fans alter one or more aspects of a videogame, such as how it looks or behaves.

(2015) invites players to experience the grimy daily grind of sub-urban English life in 1994, in a story riddled with mystery and misery. *Dear Esther* (2012) strikes an uncomfortable and ethereal note as it dissects the choices of a guilt-ridden man, isolated on an island in the Outer Hebrides. I once heard the creator of the game, and one of my inspirations, Dan Pinchbeck, reflect that in video-games, 'you get to be in a World. No other medium does that, gets even close to doing that.' Games offer opportunities for storytell-ing unmatched by any other means, but this is only one part of the medium's potential for artistic expression. Sometimes what is under the hood – the neatness of the code, the glitches, the space of dis-tribution or the creator's methods of crafting the game – presents an equally compelling imaginative argument. A myriad of approaches exists when judging a game's cultural quality, and this moment presents us with an opportunity to push gaming in a par-ticular direction.

Demanding more sophisticated, nuanced and confident output in videogames criticism may seem like a niche pursuit, particularly at a time when in the wider world, gaming is still perceived from such a narrow perspective. Every once in a while, media outlets blow up with stories of violence in videogames or of the tragic fates of gaming addicts. As in other major entertainment genres, this young industry is rife with corruption and dodgy industry practices; but few parents get worried when their child is interested in a cultural medium other than gaming. Gaming is unique in that the entire industry and its way of operating are judged by its individual artefacts and the behav-iour of single games companies or of its individual consumers. The world of gaming sorely lacks a multifaceted, refined assessment of its merits and faults. Only once this has been provided can gaming begin to transform.

And there is a lot that must be transformed! The sin begins at the moment that games are created. Game development teams are worked to exhaustion and burnout by the managerial class, which imposes tight, unrealistic deadlines on the creators. Maybe the game-making process is becoming too pricey or the team is too stretched already. No problem! To save money, even very prestigious studios outsource development to anonymised support studios in Eastern Europe and the Global South. Since the labour protections in these regions are often even lower, large AAA companies, even while reaping extraordinary profits, now employ a variety of cost-cutting measures, often at the expense of the workers.* Sexual harassment, pervasive lack of diversity and inclusion, mass firings and low salaries, especially in the quality assurance departments, are just a few of the problems chronically plaguing this massive commercial enterprise.

The homogeneous demographic of videogame writers and designers – generally, able-bodied white cis men in the first half of their lives – dictates the flavour of the majority of available titles. The tropes infusing the majority of games include women in skimpy clothes, military propaganda, fetishisation of violence and reactionary political stances. Since many use innovative and sometimes predatory and addictive mechanics to increase their popularity, it is crucial to critically assess these products beyond their narratives.

Reactionary pieces of art and literature will attract a reactionary audience, and gaming is no exception. In addition, videogames usually have a longer hold on the attention than other media. Of course, films and books are dissected ad infinitum by their most ardent fans, but the sheer length of some videogames – which can last hundreds of hours – and the varying shape of the interactions

---

* AAA (Triple-A): a classification used within the videogaming industry to signify high-budget, high-profile games that are typically produced and distributed by large, well-known publishers.

in a given game result in an increased level of dedication. Gaming, being a digital good adjacent to the internet and social media, inspires gatherings of game fans in huge online forums, subreddits and Discord channels.* Certainly, depending on the themes of a particular videogame – ones that are more progressive or artsy suffer from this less – these spaces are often unmoderated, and reproduce the worst habits of online behaviour. The slurs and insults are the least of it. Right-wing influencers create armies in these forums, with the consequences sometimes tragically spilling over into real life.

Zooming out and observing the videogames industry as a whole, we see another crucial failing, fundamental to its existence, that radically separates it from other cultural media. I call this phenomenon the dictatorship of the console. Currently, almost all videogame devices are manufactured with something close to slave labour in the Global South, from the killer mineral mines in the Democratic Republic of the Congo to the appalling conditions in hardware manufacturing plants such as Foxconn and Riteng in East Asia. The construction of this hardware is also a major contributor to climate change. According to the investigation conducted by Lewis Gordon for The Verge, more CO_2 was emitted in the creation of Sony's PlayStation 4 console over its first four years than by the entire population of Jamaica in one year.[13] All that pollution for one little videogame console, among the dozens that come out every year!

In order to imagine a new kind of politics in videogames and in the way they are marketed, perceived and critiqued, we must first reflect on the modes of production of gaming. Videogames are the future of art, entertainment, sports, and community organising,

---

* Discord: a voice-over IP and instant messaging social platform with more than 150 million monthly users as of 2021, mostly utilised by gaming communities.

no matter how reluctant some people are to accept it. They are shaping the world around us culturally, economically, linguistically, aesthetically and politically. Our mission, then, is not to opt out, ignoring this gargantuan industry and its effects on the people we love and the people we fear, but to start taking the industry very seriously. Only by injecting fresh, progressive energy into the gaming world can we truly enjoy this invigorating, sensually unmatched medium and its liberatory attributes.

A few years ago, hearing that I'd chosen videogames as a career, my father introduced me to *Homo Ludens* by Johan Huizinga. Released in 1938, the book unpacks the importance of play in culture and society. *Ludus* (play) is a primary and necessary (though not sufficient) condition for generating culture. The book is a foundational text for academic game studies. It establishes the significance of play as a cultural phenomenon and of play and contest as civilising functions, as well as the themes enveloping play and war, play and law, and even forms of play in philosophy. 'We have to conclude, therefore, that civilisation is, in its earliest phases, played. It does not come from play like a baby detaching itself from the womb: it arises in and as play, and never leaves it.'[14] Values, methods and structures for compliance and resistance are formulated, even in an abstract state of play.

Setting the politics of the vast commercial videogames industry to one side, play is essential to the general mechanics of existence and, crucially, to resistance. The unpredictable yet forceful potential of play allows for freedom and transformation, which can be found in those moments when the normal roles and rules of a community or society are relaxed and even subverted. Videogames provide countless examples of such moments; these are precious, and worth fighting for.

Are videogames a force for revolutionary good? Very rarely. Is gaming a legitimate source of joy for millions of people, from all social and economic backgrounds, in an increasingly fragmented world? Absolutely. Thus, gaming deserves not only our attention, but our efforts to build an infrastructure that improves it. At the moment, much of our play, even in the realm of videogames, can be equated to labour; by definition, gaming creates labour for the corporations that own the intellectual property of the title. But these rules are not permanent; they can and should be changed. The aim here is not to be less enthusiastic about transcendent forms of entertainment, but to re-establish how they are created, distributed, experienced and interpreted.

My father worked at a local radio station for essentially no money, but he did get a few perks with the job. Our family enjoyed free tickets to city fairs and discounts at a stationery shop, and my mum even once got a ride in a hot air balloon! The job also kept my parents close to the intelligentsia, bohemia and politicians of the town.[15] As graduates of the Saint Petersburg Institute of Performing Arts, during the collapse of the Soviet Union they were poor, but they were intellectually curious – a quality they passed on to me.

In one way, however, our home did feel wealthy: Very few households in the late '90s in Kaunas, Lithuania, had a personal computer. Yet, one day, my father brought one home from work. My brother quickly discovered how to pirate all the most recent videogames on the machine, and by the age of seven or eight, I was already slaying monsters on *Doom* (1993) fragging enemies on Quake (1996) and, soon enough, crafting a dream home on *The Sims* (2000). An entire universe of world-building, movement and pure escapism opened up to me.

Sadly, my brother was cruel to me more regularly than I would like to remember, but as I got good at certain videogames, he showed some respect for me, or at least it seemed that way. The day that I won a mini-tournament of the Windows operating system staple *FreeCell* and he had to hand me 10 litas (about €10) was one of the proudest and happiest of my young life. My father was also incapable of showing much love. Gaming nurtured my fragile relationships with the men in my life – hunting Nazi soldiers in *Return to Castle Wolfenstein* (2001) or defending our settlements in *Blitzkrieg* (2003) became a bonding ritual. While exploring a bootlegged CD copy of *Conflict: Desert Storm* (2002), my father first taught me about American imperialism. Driving around the fictional city of Lost Heaven in a taxi, we listened to the 1930s jazz soundtrack of *Mafia* (2002) for hours. Without these difficult and, at times, hurtful men, I would not have discovered the strange, exhilarating, consuming world of videogames.

Becoming a regular at our local gaming arcade in my early teenage years was a natural progression in my curiosity for digital games. 'Arcade' is a generous word for what was essentially a hideout for a bunch of young lost souls in a wooden house painted bright yellow, brimming with old consoles, PCs and messy, dusty cables.[16] I grew up in a very deprived neighbourhood notable for abandoned kids, antisocial behaviour, drugs, alcohol and abuse; the '90s were not easy on Eastern Europeans. However, sitting by a PlayStation 2, uploading *Street Fighter II* or a racing game, and competing gently allowed us to forget our circumstances for a moment. The family's financial anxieties, my parents' inevitable divorce, a terrifying sibling – all of these concerns left my body when I was on a fictional SWAT mission in downtown Washington, DC, or when I gained an advantage in a level of *Command and Conquer: Tiberian Sun* (1999).

Details aside, my early encounter with the world of videogames is a common one, an experience familiar to many – a story of bonding, the creation of social relations and healthy competition. A collection of positives, the preferable and preferred account of gaming as told by games companies themselves. It is not so for everyone, however. The tentacles of this juggernaut of an industry stretch further and are seldom discussed. Gaming is beloved for reasons that are often wrong, and may be loathed by people who are completely ignorant about it. Videogames are known for the often racist and sexist rhetoric in their narrative portrayal. At the same time, games are praised for their ability to connect people. They introduce joy and a sense of community to individuals on the margins of society. However, the brutal modes of production and imperialist propaganda implicit in the medium are rarely examined. Videogames are blamed for violence among young people and the existence of mass shootings, but the connections between the organised far right and the gaming communities are not noticed even by the progressive left. People who play videogames constantly engage in reciprocal altruism and self-organisation, expanding the horizons of what is conceivable, and yet the people making the games often suffer under unbearable conditions and work at the behest of brutal company structures.

The industry is brimming with politics, but what those politics are is in constant dispute. It is not a fixed space, although the upper hand currently lies with the powers that formulated this industry through rapacious practices. The question for this moment is, how can videogames be deployed for egalitarian purposes?

No creative medium is unaffected by capitalist modes of production. Videogames certainly have a reputation for encouraging and exemplifying the predatory, neoliberal, regressive tendencies we recognise around us. Still, to billions, gaming is a space for respite, for building lives not yet lived, structures not yet imagined. And, as such, it has to be fought for. The crossroads is clear – we can either allow this vast cultural space to be eternally entangled in the awkward nets of conservativism and financialisation that will suffocate and deform both it and the players who touch it, or we can fight to rescue it. We can battle to build a mature and potentially emancipatory digital medium that opens possibilities for worlds not yet constructed.

While frequenting messy local gaming establishments and chaotic LAN parties,* I discovered another pastime that would allow me to escape from the dark everyday – political organising. Sure, it may have been draped in punk aesthetic and youthful idealism at the time, and yet egalitarian thought, solidarity and the pitfalls of capitalism – all these concepts began to accurately explain the world around me. They began to inform much of what would become my focus for years.

Similar to many people of my generation, my political convictions formed in two waves – witnessing the atrocities of the Iraq War in 2003 and experiencing the financial crisis five years later. The latter had grave consequences for my own quiet life. My mother, freshly divorced and in her late forties, was unable to find work for a prolonged period of time. Our choices were to stay in Lithuania with no food on the table or for her to work for £4 an hour in a factory in England. The ruling class of the United Kingdom wanted cheap labour; and the inclusion of Lithuania in the European Union in 2004 certainly provided the conditions for that. For us, it was a salvation.

I was swiftly installed in a sixth form in Leyton in East London, leaving my ska-punk band and fully fledged anarchist community in my beloved Kaunas behind. A year into living with fourteen other Eastern Europeans in a tiny terraced house

* LAN party: a gathering of people with computers or compatible game consoles, where a local area network (LAN) connection is established between the devices using a router or a switch.

and staying with my mum in one tiny room, at the age of seventeen, I knew that my only alternative was squatting.*

There I was, thrown into a new country for economic reasons, with a new language, a new school, later a new, alienating service industry job and an entirely new activist milieu with its own traditions and idioms. Partially in search of a community and partially due to genuine faith, I gravitated towards these circles dedicated to left-wing political organising. This involved local housing campaigns, anti-raid and anti-fascist demonstrations, and all manner of expressions of resistance towards the oppressive state apparatus. Long days of battles with bailiffs, fascists or the police ended in exhaustion. Methods for rest and recuperation had their own rules and practices in my circles – wholesome activities such as gardening, biking and arts and crafts were encouraged and supported. Losing oneself in a digital space with a small body count of pixelated demons – that type of escapism was judged, and even prohibited. Once, my friends and I were forbidden from having a videogame console at a squatted social centre where we were volunteering, as it simply didn't fit the pure, 'healthy' aesthetics the space was attempting to emanate. Gaming became something I did in secret, rarely sharing any insights about this hobby with my fellow comrades.

Slowly I realised that gaming was not only an escape from my political life, but would become crucial for comprehending the political forces around me. Something clicked in 2016 when I read a headline that profits in videogames were about to top those of the music and film industries combined. Gaming is not a periphery of culture, unworthy of serious political examination; it is much

---

* Squatting (more familiar to UK readers) is the action of occupying empty buildings, usually for the purposes of housing. The BBC reported that in 2011, there were '20,000 squatters in the UK' and '650,000 empty properties'.

closer to the centre. At this point, I began to seriously, albeit still passively, explore the connection between videogames and social change. I was convinced that videogames are, in fact, key to identifying and perhaps even solving the current muddle of crises in the twenty-first century.

In its short fifty-year history, gaming has consistently and subtly taken over billions of people's free time. It is the largest entertainment strand there is, and yet its significance for our society is seldom noted. At least, not by the people who purport to be changemakers – members of the cultural, artistic and media communities, the activist class and academia. *Art and Agenda*, *Art and Politics Now* and *Artificial Hells* are among the numerous books written on the impact of fine art on our society. Entire university courses are dedicated to the subject. Such treatment is rarely given to gaming, although the global art industry is four times smaller. Even worse – there exists a pervasive prejudice against gaming among well-meaning progressives.

My ambition here is nothing less than to recruit an army of game-changers for this vast and influential field, which shapes so much of what is around us. And yet my approach is infused with purposeful contradictions – love and passion for this exhaustively mesmerising and charming artistic expression, alongside contempt for its exploitative tendencies and practices at the cutting edge of capitalist reproduction. 'While games tend to have a reactionary imperial content, as militarized, marketized, entertainment commodities, they also tend to a radical, multitudinous form, as collaborative, constructive, experimental digital productions,' game academics Dyer-Witheford and de Peuter point out.[17]

I was still an unbearable Goldsmiths art school kid when I discovered the writings of the academic one of the college's buildings is named after. Stuart Hall insisted that pop culture is a space of push and pull. It is a battleground. He understood that shaping popular culture is an ongoing process in which relations of control and subordination constantly shift, and specific cultural forms gain and lose support from institutions. Which cultural content and forms are preferred and which are marginalised is not fixed. According to Hall, there is a constant movement and interchange between them due to shifting power relations, the assimilation of popular content into 'high culture' and vice versa, and the use of pop culture to disseminate the interests of the status quo.[18]

Hall retained faith that culture was a site of 'negotiation', as he put it, a space of give and take where intended meanings could be short-circuited. 'Popular culture is one of the sites where this struggle for and against a culture of the powerful is engaged: it is also the stake to be won or lost in that struggle,' he argued. 'It is the arena of consent and resistance.'[19] Over his lifetime, Hall became fascinated with theories of 'reception' – how we decode the different messages that culture tells us and how culture helps us choose our identities.

He was not merely interested in interpreting new forms, such as film or television, using the tools that scholars had previously brought to bear on literature; he was also concerned to understand the various political, economic and social forces that converged in these media. It was not just the content or the language of the nightly news or of middlebrow magazines that told us what to think, it was also how they were structured, packaged and distributed – namely, by individuals with structural, institutional power. Not many know who these key players with institutional power are, who roam the gaming spaces, influencing the world around us.

Before taking a job as a political adviser at the Trump White House, Steve Bannon was running Breitbart News – a grotesque, fascist online media outlet with articles such as 'Birth Control Makes Women Unattractive and Crazy', 'Bill Kristol: Republican Spoiler, Renegade Jew' and 'The Solution to Online "Harassment" Is Simple: Women Should Log Off'. His career before Breitbart? In 2007, he was an investor in a large virtual gold mine: the hugely popular, massively multiplayer, online role-playing game *World of Warcraft* (2004 onw.).

The business model was simple – employ armies of poorly paid Chinese 'gold farmers', who played in long rotating shifts, repeating grunt tasks in the game to gain gold and rarer items. These would then be sold, with a significant added price, to Western gamers willing to pay real-world dollars to avoid the grind of *World of Warcraft*. In his own words, what Bannon found was a world 'populated by millions of intense young men', who may have been socially inept, but were 'smart, focused, relatively wealthy, and highly motivated about issues that mattered to them'. 'These guys,' said Bannon, 'these rootless, white males had monster power. It was the pre-Reddit.'[20] His venture did not succeed monetarily – following numerous lawsuits and pressure from the players, he ended this tactic. But one of the darkest public relations architects of the Western world was about to have a eureka moment. When his time in the spotlight came, less than a decade later, he was quick to utilise the tactics he'd learnt with *World of Warcraft*.

During his tenure as the editor in chief of Breitbart News, Bannon employed one Milo Yiannopoulos. According to Yiannopoulos, Bannon made him into a star. He worked for the outlet's wing in the United Kingdom, where he wrote pieces like 'Would You Rather Your Child Had Feminism or Cancer?' and 'World Health Organization Report: Trannies 49 Xs Higher HIV Rate'. The headlines say a little bit about his politics.

In 2014, this flirtation between the far right and some gaming communities reached its apogee, and with Bannon's blessing,

Yiannopoulos became a significant voice during the Gamergate controversy. Gamergate was one of the first online harassment campaign, and one of the most severe ever. Beginning in August 2014, the campaign targeted women in the videogame industry, most notably feminist media critic Anita Sarkeesian and developers Zoë Quinn and Brianna Wu, among others. The harassment campaign included doxxing them and their families and friends and sending rape threats and death threats. At least once, Sarkeesian was forced to cancel a guest lecture at the last minute as the intended venue received a bomb threat.

Gamergaters claimed to promote ethics in videogames journalism and to protect the 'gamer' identity. They opposed what they saw as political correctness in videogames. The harassers typically organised anonymously on online platforms such as 4chan, Twitter and Reddit. Yiannopoulos engineered a sophisticated numbers campaign and made contact with influential figures in 4chan and Reddit to make #Gamergate a viral success; it wouldn't be an exaggeration to call it a training ground for Trump's campaign and eventual election victory. In autumn 2014, nine #Gamergate-related articles were published on Breitbart News. In the past, Bannon had demonstrated open contempt towards gamers on the website – until the editors realised that gamers are an often malleable group of people who could be used for their political goals. They weren't wrong!

As I heard about Gamergate and its close ties to the far right, being an active anti-fascist organiser myself and by now grasping the economic impact of this industry, I knew I had to get involved. At first, this took the form of a weekly personal blog with texts about videogames and real-life politics. Although extremely imaginative, the industry tends to be relatively insular. As my tone and radical point of view stood out, the articles and my Twitter commentary suddenly got picked up – within months I was writing for *Vice*, the *Guardian* and some of the largest gaming sites, such as

Kotaku and *GamesIndustry.biz*. While still working service-industry jobs and participating in medical trials for money, I launched my own bite-sized video show, *Left Left Up*, which dissected the games industry from a historical materialist perspective. The good reception that followed allowed me to elevate the subject matter to the next level – real-life events such as *Tetris* (1984) tournaments that raised funds for progressive causes in the UK and abroad, or setting up gaming events adjacent to an anti-fascist football club. My aim was to introduce gaming as a political space for the left, whose members surrounded me, and to introduce politics in an accessible manner to individuals connected with the videogames industry.

All this didn't feel like enough, though. And then I found myself in the right place at the right time, and the stakes moved a notch higher at last. In March 2018, at the annual Game Developers Conference in San Francisco, the Game Workers Unite movement was born. A few workers, tired of the appalling conditions they often had to endure, took matters into their own hands and aired their grievances at an anti-union 'round table' organised by the business (boss) wing of the industry. After the event, they exchanged contacts, and numerous branches of the game worker network sprung up. A few comrades and I rushed in to connect the local game workers that we knew with the radical Independent Workers' Union of Great Britain. And thus the world's first legal games industry trade union inspired by the movement was born. In the meantime, I also started volunteering in delivering communications for the Game Workers Unite International network.

I saw trade union organising not only through its labour axis, but as a gateway to introducing material politics to the lost members of the alt-right. It must have worked to a certain extent: numerous people got in touch stating that they had shifted their politics from reactionary and exclusionary to more egalitarian, placing class at

the centre. Political victories aside, these were also the psychologi-
cally toughest years of my life – who knew kicking up a fuss in the
face of the most powerful individuals in the most powerful entertainment industry of all time would lead to the complete breaking
of a person? It must have meant that we were effecting change.
But this beast – the current perverse foundations of this business –
will need a stronger kicking before an alternative can emerge.

Politics in videogames stretch from the minutiae of a narrative and
activities of the title's communities to the ownership of the code
and of entire hardware factories. All that happens within those
spaces manifests itself on a spectrum that is ripe for negotiation.
It's an Overton window that has already pulled in so much of
entertainment, culture, global economics and political organisation. Is it possible to manoeuvre it towards a route of emancipation,
poise and abundance?

Or perhaps it is too late? Are we wasting our time in imag-
ining videogames beyond – dare I say the big word? – capitalism?
Hardware made from sustainable materials by co-operatives and
distributed in a sustainable manner. Accommodating videogames, made under great work conditions that inspire boundless
levels of imagination. Another world is possible, but it must be
fought for. We get enough judgement already from our mates for
playing games instead of going out. I look forward to a day where
I won't have to be embarrassed about gaming on grounds of
ethics, either.

To a keen gamer, a seasoned games industry critic or a games
professional, this book will crystallise a list of aspects to pay attention to when evaluating and scrutinising a videogame for its social
efficacy. It is structured into Levels – the reader will be increasingly challenged when exploring themes surrounding videogames

and IRL politics. The beginning of this book – the Tutorial –takes the reader through a compounded political history of the video-games industry, mainly focusing on the formation and configuration of the power players who shaped how this arena is perceived and experienced today.

Few technologies possess inherent civic agendas; they simply land in the hands of particular influence groups, which then uti-lise the technology for their own benefit. Nothing was inevitable about gaming growing into its current state: a toxic, misogynist, imperial wasteland with few, albeit crucial, saving graces. In a few short decades, distinct actors made it that way. It could easily have turned out differently, and books like this one set out to inspire the imagination needed to make gaming completely dif-ferent. But to move forward, we must understand how we got here. This introductory chapter serves as a toolbox, arming the reader with helpful terminology and concepts that will be used throughout the book.

As readers begin the journey, Level I invites them to consider the obvious – the themes of videogames. As with most cultural artefacts, viewers tend to experience and judge games according to the stories they tell. Historically, videogames have not been subtle on that front. Developers often attach politically insensitive, propaganda-laced themes and tropes onto exciting mechanics. Whether it's the story or the stereotypical portrayal of characters, or a needlessly brutal mechanic, or a particular moral to the story – narrative plays a key role in how a game is perceived. On the other hand, a growing number of socially conscious developers are crafting games with plots that they hope will convince the player of some progressive values. But is it enough? This section explores the initial surface-level representation of a particular agenda, prior to going into the ludological aspect of a videogame (ludology being the science of games and play).

Level II complicates how we understand the political intentions of the players of videogames. Gaming communities often construct relations and languages seemingly in contrast to the motifs of a given game. While game makers seem to have the power to forge the narratives of their games, communities interpreting their games may not only fail to correspond with the designers' hopes, but they may even play these games against their creator's intentions. Furthermore, not all games are linear or driven by a straightforward narrative – however, politics persist. Why is that? This chapter investigates the phenomenon of political identity-building in the expanse outside of the walls of games like *Minecraft*, *Roblox* (2006 onw.), *Fantasy Westward Journey* (2001 onw.) and *EVE Online* (2003 onw.).

Let's say a game development team has achieved the near impossible: to craft a sophisticated, deep videogame with social critique, which has not been appropriated by forces that would like to twist that message. The million-dollar question is, can videogames be of political utility, if and when directed for that cause? There are still so many obstacles facing any game developer attempting to create a piece of digital art somehow independent from the current modes of production. The very few and centralised purchasing platforms make it exceptionally hard to bring a game to an audience. The game must compete with titles backed by well-funded entities of the industry, who often prey on consumers with the latest addictive gambling techniques. Above all, developers need to deal with the highly influential members of the liberal milieu who act as gatekeepers to any material changes to the industry – be it unionisation, art that explores uncomfortable themes, or a substantial change in the reliance on the hardware that is often created under brutal conditions. Level III invites readers to ponder the efficacy of videogames with an agenda, often contrasting their techniques to similar processes used in comparable artistic media.

Level IV compels the reader to keep climbing higher, keep fighting harder. Even if a game creator has done everything right, offering a powerful, challenging theme that does not preach to the converted, attracting an empathetic activist community and using modes of distribution that introduce the creation to new audiences . . . videogames still comprise a fundamental sin. The chapter adds further complexity when discussing politics in gaming, studio structure and hardware creation issues, as well as the blood, sweat and tears of so many just to deliver us our digital entertainment. This presents a fundamental challenge to the creators who are working within this industry in good faith and attempting to promote change.

After four levels that lead the reader into various corners of this extensive entertainment strand, a Final Boss battle will commence. At this stage, the reader is armed with knowledge about the innovations and communication techniques in this extraordinary industry, the fascinating demographic groups shaping it and the deeply affecting artistic minds working in it. Additionally, they are faced with the horrifying scale and ferocity of the destruction this industry causes worldwide and the misery it brings to entire populations. The techniques and procedures practised in the privacy of gaming communities spill over into some of the darkest aspects of real-life reactionary organising. What is to be done, if anything? Is gaming worth fighting for? Can an alternative to the current state of things be achieved? What would a non-destructive games industry look like? Few, but crucial, parts of this engrossing industry can be left unchanged – what are they? Only a glimpse into the ashes after a final battle can begin to answer those questions.

While this book outlines numerous cases of gaming that cause active harm to the world around us, only someone who dearly loves this universe can offer a reasonable critique. My mission here is to rescue gaming, to overhaul it, to work towards its emancipation, rather than have it turn us into perfect capitalist subjects. Instead of accepting a dialectic of refusal and recuperation, inevitably ending in cynicism and failure, I turn towards culture as a clear political terrain, as a terrain for organisation and action from below.

There is nothing permanently determined or natural about the current state of affairs. It emerged due to power relations, an endless chase for cheap profits resulting in a chronic undermining of ingenuity. So, indeed, everything is to play for.

Tutorial: History

Many of the technological advances of today – the World Wide Web, the foundational fragments of the iPhone, the Global Positioning System (GPS) that enables geolocation and numerous others – share their roots in various publicly funded laboratories, universities and army research centres across the world.[1] Videogames have a similar origin story. In the 1950s, digital games were largely confined to research labs run by universities, corporations or publicly funded laboratories. They were not intended for mass distribution or even general consumption. This public research enables most of the inner mechanisms that allow us to spend our free time zoning out in digital universes. Semiconductors, triodes, integrated transistors, memory controllers, cache designs and so on were invented at institutions like PARC Xerox, Massachusetts Institute of Technology (MIT), the University of Cambridge and Stanford University, which are all bankrolled by taxpayer money.

The earliest public demonstration of a digital device that also contained a game took place at the 1950 Canadian National Exhibition. The four-metre-tall computer, quirkily named Bertie the Brain, was created to research the capabilities of electronic circuits.[2] It invited the exhibition attendees to play a game of tic-tac-toe against an artificial intelligence. After the two-week display, Bertie was disassembled and forgotten as a curiosity. Elsewhere, scientists programmed digital versions of games like chess and checkers. But *play* was not seen as the mission here: these pieces of software were constructed to calculate numerical probabilities and other statistics.

Tennis for Two, developed at the Brookhaven National Laboratory in 1958, is seen by many game historians as the first true videogame. Rather than being an academic project or a scientific showpiece, this primitive tennis simulator had little game design or technological innovation. Its purpose was to entertain, to encourage play and competition. Unlike any predecessors, *Tennis for Two* had a competitive element and a visual design that sought to be amusing.[3]

During the next decade, numerous similar machines were devised to run games that had an increasing level of sophistication in interaction, graphics and entertainment value. Academics and students at Carnegie Mellon University, MIT and Harvard University were experimenting in this new field of crafting playful experiences through computational contraptions. The breakthrough came a decade later.

At the other end of the entertainment product spectrum, mechanical coin-operated arcade devices were a popular staple of most amusement fairs in the first half of the twentieth century. These machines were spun into their own industry with penny arcades – entire specialised physical spaces for leisure and gambling. Coin-operated slot, pinball and fortune-telling machines brought in huge crowds, but they had clear limitations.

Building digital devices for the purpose of play, on the other hand, was incredibly expensive. But by the 1960s, a growing number of individuals with large imaginations correctly concluded that digital gaming might be the next big thing. Ted Dabney and his colleague Nolan Bushnell were shown *Spacewar!*, an early videogame developed at the Stanford Artificial Intelligence Laboratory. The pair became fixated on the idea of introducing digital games to the masses. Bushnell combined his expertise in digital engineering and part-time work at an amusement park. Dabney excelled at analogue and hardware engineering. Together, they worked out how to make a digital arcade device economically feasible. After a few trials and tribulations, the pair formulated ways to manipulate a video signal on the screen without a computer controlling it. Later, they removed the expensive part – the computer – altogether. By using discrete logic circuits instead, Bushnell and Dabney manufactured a system that was reliable, less complex and, most importantly, much cheaper than computers.[4]

In 1971, *Computer Space*, a coin-operated arcade device, became the first videogame to be released commercially. The game was presented in a curvy, futuristic fibreglass cabinet, which had been designed by Bushnell with modelling clay, built by a swimming pool manufacturer and painted in bright, glittery colours. *Computer Space* sold 1,000 units (a non-digital arcade game at the time might have sold around 2,000 units), which did not give Bushnell and Dabney the overnight success they had hoped for. Still, they felt sufficiently encouraged to incorporate themselves into a company called Atari and hired their first employee, computer scientist and engineer Allan Alcorn. Their destinies were about to change forever.[5]

Vast technological advances in the digital gaming arena rapidly occurred during this period. Numerous actors got involved; the race was on.

In 1972, an arm of Magnavox, a hardware electronics company, released their version of 'the new electronic gaming field of the future', or a 'closed-circuit electronic playground'. Their technical solution was Odyssey, the first commercial videogame home console, which took a different approach to what a console ought to be. What if, instead of trying to source all the computing power necessary to run a game from a separate machine, they used the inbuilt capabilities of a television set? Most people who were interested in playing games were likely to have one already. This new home console also allowed consumers to purchase separate cartridges with chosen videogames on them. In contrast to Atari, which banked at the time on shared spaces and separate devices, the home console market began to shape up.

The development of Odyssey moved gaming closer to the kind of experience we are familiar with today. The home console sold around 70,000 units, slightly below the projected performance. This was mostly due to its steep price of $99.95 (the 2024 equivalent of $740) and the unfamiliarity of the whole concept. Many assumed that the device worked exclusively with Magnavox brand television sets. Still, the high customer satisfaction reports in surveys convinced the company to continue investing in the console.

Although consumers who played Atari's *Computer Space* said they enjoyed it, they also voiced frustration about the complexity of the instructions. Bushnell and Dabney understood that their next game had to be much more elementary. After witnessing a demonstration of the *Table Tennis* game played on the Odyssey console in early 1972, Bushnell directed Alcorn to produce a table tennis game fit for an arcade.

Developed swiftly in three months, the result was the now-legendary *Pong*, and the rest is history. The controls were indeed simple this time: an in-game paddle could be moved vertically across the left or right side of the screen, while players bounced the ball (a dot on the screen) back and forth from one side of the screen to the other. The goal was for one player to reach eleven points;

points were earned when one player failed to return the ball to the other. The players could compete against each other or against the game itself. During a trial at a bar near Atari, the *Pong* cabinet drew in huge crowds, with a queue of players forming in the street.[6]

Atari knew they had a winner on their hands. To avoid competition snapping at their heels and, even worse, a complete replica of their game, they sped up the production process of the physical arcade cabinet. By 1974, an estimated 100,000 coin-operated gaming machines were in place in the United States, bringing in half a billion dollars that year.[7]

Videogames were now global, with Japan and Europe launching their own industries and establishing customer bases. The Japanese game market, mostly focussed on export, produced timeless consoles such as Super Nintendo Entertainment Systems (SNES). With origins in analogue playing cards and toys, Nintendo entered the digital games market in the 1980s with the first handheld mini console, called Game and Watch. The device sold 43.4 million copies and became the company's most popular product in its 100-year history.[8] The mini console's neat, minimal look, quality build and ease of use revolutionised the market for handheld game hardware and shifted the games industry eastwards.

From then on, Nintendo pivoted specifically towards gaming and became a cornerstone of the global games industry. Until Game and Watch, the company had been mostly known for their electronic toys, such *The Love Tester* (1969), a novelty that measured the 'love compatibility' between two people holding hands and touching the sensors on the device, and *The Ultra Machine* (1967), an automatic baseball pitching toy. Today, Nintendo is a giant of both games hardware and software. The company has sold more than half a billion devices in the forms of Game Boy (1989, 1996), Nintendo Switch (2017), the Super

Nintendo Entertainment System (SNES; 1990) and Nintendo DS (2004), and they own some of the most profitable IP products of all time.[9] *Pokémon* (1996 onw.), *The Legend of Zelda* (1986 onw.) and *Super Mario* (1985 onw.) are all major staples of pop culture, and their new releases are surrounded by enormous hype.

A few key players emerged in Europe as well. The British BBC console paved the way for the UK to become a creative power-house in contemporary game development. The Cambridge-based Sinclair Research developed the ZX80 computer, which was successfully exported across the continent. In the mid-1980s, British game studios such as Rare created games that became big local hits, and the Scottish DMA Design eventually became the giant that is Rockstar North – the makers of the *Grand Theft Auto* series.

The former Yugoslavia became another European capital of game making: for example, Galaksija was a modular, DIY computer product designed in Belgrade that offered a cheaper gaming alternative to the consoles of the time. Game studios were also established in Croatia, Slovenia and Slovakia, among other countries.[10] The lack of access to hardware in the Soviet Union hindered its progress on the game-making front, but it was still home to one of the most famous videogames of all time – *Tetris*.

Nonetheless, it is almost impossible not to locate the political history of videogames in the United States. In the process of developing gaming, Western technological powerhouses actively stifled innovation elsewhere. Capital and research power were concentrated in the US in this crucial period, inducing a snow-ball effect, with subsequent discoveries in technology taking place within similar circles. Those discoveries were then advertised and semi-imposed onto the rest of the world with heavy proprietary guards.

On the other hand, the 1960s and early 1970s were also a unique time in the US, when large sums of public funds were diverted into scientific research. Many individuals forming private companies wanted to be close to the action. Silicon Valley became a hub for the exchange of ideas and iterations, and sometimes straight-up idea theft, all with the aim of funnelling publicly acquired knowledge into privatised industries.

Who Gets to Play

The process of making games was inaccessible to most, which solidified a stratified cabal of change-makers in this field. Their mission was to advance specific technologies and a new commodity market, rather than interrogate the cultural and political significance of this new terrain. As the history in the following section demonstrates, the demographics of the people behind these innovations also proved to be significant and, unsurprisingly, a point of contestation.

The conscription of men during the Second World War resulted in the technology, manufacturing and research sectors becoming dependent on women workers. During that period, women were responsible for coordinating ballistics computing, a task seen by the remaining male engineers as below their level of expertise. In the 1940s, way before the time of videogames, almost all the people employed as computers (yes, that was actually the term!) were women. According to MIT professor Jennifer S. Light, even men acknowledged that 'programming requires lots of patience, persistence and a capacity for detail and those are traits that many girls have.'[11]

Grace Hopper was one of the first women to earn a PhD in mathematics from Yale in 1934. One of the first three modern 'programmers', Hopper is best known for her trailblazing contributions to the development of computer languages. She volunteered as a lieutenant in the US Naval Reserves during the war. The Navy assigned her to the Bureau of Ordnance computation project at Harvard, where her assignment was to program the Mark I computer. She even coined the term 'computer bug', after a moth shorted out the Mark II model.

Similarly, in Britain, Joan Clarke worked closely with Alan Turing on the all-important Enigma machine, built in Bletchley Park. Many of the men who developed methods increasing the speed of double-encrypted messages had the techniques named after them. That was not the case with Clarke, whose contributions have been largely forgotten by history.

In 1962, three Black women – Katherine Johnson, Mary Jackson and Dorothy Vaughan – worked as NASA mathematicians and helped calculate the flight paths that put John Glenn into orbit. An award-winning Hollywood movie, *Hidden Figures*, celebrates the influential and inspiring trio. But the period when women headed tech and, by extension, games, was short-lived. In the aftermath of World War II, the percentage of women programmers in the United States collapsed: only around 40 per cent of computer programmers were women in the 1950s, and 25 per cent by 1960. Today, around 8 per cent of programmers in the United States are women, and the statistics don't look better elsewhere in the world. While women occupy a rising number of positions in art, design and human resources in videogames companies, they are still a rarity among coders.

What were the conditions that prompted this dramatic demographic shift? By 2017, a male programmer at Google was confidently circulating a memo that used gender stereotypes to argue that women were inherently worse at programming than men. 'Women, on average, have more: Neuroticism (higher anxiety, lower stress tolerance). This may contribute to the higher levels of anxiety women report on Googlegeist and to the lower number of women in high-stress jobs,' the memo reads. What was the path to this state of affairs?

In her 2018 book, *Brotopia: Breaking Up the Boys' Club of Silicon Valley*, Emily Chang describes this transition insightfully and in great detail. While her findings focus on the tech industry at large, they can be readily applied to the games industry, too. As this exciting, brand-new field of tech began to boom, and thousands more employees were required, large companies used technical aptitude tests to identify and recruit programmers. These tests filtered for traits that were thought to be essential to good programming, such as logical thinking and abstract reasoning. In 1967 alone, 700,000 people took the IBM Programmer Aptitude Test, which at the time was the gateway into the vocation.

However, aptitude tests were not enough for some, and a more 'psychological' evaluation was required to pinpoint not only good programmers, but 'happy' programmers, who might stay in the profession and in the workplace long-term. In the mid-1960s, a branch of IBM called the System Development Corporation commissioned two psychologists, William M. Cannon and Dallas K. Perry, to define a vocational interest scale for programmers, a personality profile that would predict which types had a good chance of becoming happy programmers. Cannon and Perry profiled 1,378 programmers, only 186 of whom were women, and used their findings to build a scale that they believed could predict satisfaction and therefore success in the field.

Based on their survey, they concluded that people who liked solving puzzles of various sorts, from mathematical to mechanical, made for good programmers. That made sense. Their second conclusion was far more speculative. Based on the data they had gathered from mostly male programmers, Cannon and Perry decided that satisfied programmers shared one striking characteristic: they 'don't like people'. In their final report, they wrote, specifically, that programmers 'dislike activities involving close personal interaction; they are generally more interested in things than in people'.

The limitations that this characterisation entailed for women's careers was immense. However, it is worth noting that the birth of the stereotype of the reclusive, socially inept, nerdy man was also detrimental to men's perceptions of themselves. Out of such framing, subcultures are formed and within them, margins where radicalisation can happen. At that point in history, these practices not just reflected, but actively constructed and determined much of how gaming looks today.

Cannon and Perry declared that their new Programmer Scale was more 'appropriate' than existing aptitude tests and that it would help schools, vocational counselling centres and recruiters across the country screen for the best programmers. The use of their personality test became widespread, which meant that people were being recruited not solely because of their talent or interest level but, at least in part, because of dubious assumptions about what type of personality made for a happy and productive programmer. This was the beginning of an enduring stereotype that has limited opportunities in the field for generations of women and people of other marginalised genders or otherwise affected demographics.[12]

Another reason for this steep decline in acceptance could have something to do with how and when children were learning to program. The advent of personal computers in the late 1970s redefined the pool of students who pursued computer science degrees at American universities. Until that time, computers were a scarce and costly commodity, found mostly within research facilities or corporate environments that provided a level playing field – coding was new to all students. This shifted with the introduction of personal computers, such as the Commodore 64 and the TRS-80. Families that could afford these machines gave their children a head start in programming skills. By the mid-1980s, students embarking on their courses were already proficient programmers.

Technology was beginning to be marketed to a certain population, predominantly white men, and this was reflected in the students who enrolled. Clive Thompson wrote in the *New York Times* feature 'The Secret History of Women in Coding': 'Boys were more than twice as likely to have been given one as a gift by their parents. And if parents bought a computer for the family, they most often put it in a son's room, not a daughter's.'[13]

Thompson interviewed Jane Margolis, an academic from Carnegie Mellon University, who painted a revealing picture. 'Unless one had been coding obsessively for years, they were not welcome in the classroom.' Margolis continued: 'While it was okay for the men to want to engage in various other pursuits, women who expressed the same wish felt judged for not being "hard core" enough. By the second year, many of these women, besieged by doubts, began dropping out of the program.' According to a 1983 study of MIT students,

> Women who raised their hands in class were often ignored by professors and talked over by other students . . . Behaviour in some research groups 'sometimes approximates that of the locker room', the report concluded, with men openly rating how 'cute' their female students were.[14]

Of course, in the late 1970s, the need to possess and know how to work a personal computer excluded not only women from the tech industry, but people from working-class backgrounds. In North America, this disparity disproportionately affected Black, Latino and indigenous populations. The international effect was stark as well. While the United States was racing ahead in computer literacy and building its own infrastructure, other regions were slower due to a lack of active investment at first, and then to the need to adhere to expensive patents and software licensing fees. A certain tech monopoly, geared to the interests of Western hegemony, emerged.

These conditions would only begin to be challenged by decoupling the locations of software and hardware development a few decades later. While America was home to a lot of intellectual property, the later decision of many US companies to outsource a hardware building would change the balance of power. The mass adoption of digital devices in offices and homes in the rest of the world lagged behind until the 1990s, when a shift was largely enabled by the more accessible (that is, more pirateable) Windows operating system.

The phenomenon of women and girls being pushed out of computer work occurred in parallel with what was happening at Atari. *Pong* brought enormous success to the company, but the real money came with the decision to tap into the home console market, instead of exclusively manufacturing arcade cabinets. Turns out they were pretty good at that, too. By 1975, Atari was posting $3 million in profits and $40 million in sales (the 2024 equivalent of $17 million and $230 million, respectively). In 1976, the company banked a whopping $28 million when the brand was sold to Warner Communication. The themes of videogames had yet to turn overly gory (give it another fifteen years or so), and their late-1970s titles, such as *Gotcha* (1973), *Tank* (1974) and *Breakout* (1976), appealed to young boys and girls as well as to men.[15]

However, Bushnell's corporate culture showed all the signs of a boys' club gone wrong, further excluding women from the industry. A 1985 ad by Apple depicted how much a computer could help a boy named Brian, while also demonstrating what fun Brian could have by teasing a girl who was attempting to use a computer. The videogames industry had already mastered this type of exclusionary advertising. In a 1973 Atari advert, a tall woman in a see-through dress stood next to their *Computer Space* arcade machine. It is astonishing that such abstract games, which had few explicit themes, had already been deemed to appeal to a single gender.

In 2018, after Atari's founder Nolan Bushnell received the Pioneer Award at the Games Developers Conference in San Francisco, multiple people finally spoke out about what went on inside their offices in Sunnyvale, California.[16] Reportedly, board meetings took place in hot tubs (naturally, all the board members were men), with junior women employees sleazily coaxed to join in the fun. Cocaine and marijuana were freely passed around during work hours.[17]

In a 2012 *Playboy* profile of Atari, Bushnell, who often proudly wore a T-shirt with 'I like to fuck' written on it, recalled that prototype machines were named after attractive female employees.[18] The home version of *Pong* was given the name Darlene – she 'was stacked and had the tiniest waist, just like one of our employees'. It should be noted that this was not Atari's first profile in a soft porn magazine. A reporter for the French *Oui* magazine – which in the '70s was the name of an adult porn magazine on the tackier end of the spectrum – was invited to spend time at Atari's offices for the September 1974 issue. 'If profitability were water,' wrote Robert Wieder, 'Atari could hold the Sixth Fleet.'[19]

Reports suggest that after work hours, professional porn movies were shot at Atari's offices. While supporting the local porn industry with its resources may be commendable, little is known about the labour practices being supported here, other than what's implied by the imagery itself; presumably the filming went ahead without the knowledge of Atari's women workforce. While desperately attempting to appear sexy, Atari's culture was unambiguously sexist. No doubt the acts described were the norm at most early tech company hubs, but such a work environment could never substantially improve the numbers of women in the burgeoning games industry; indeed, it likely solidified a certain status quo for quite some time. As Kotaku's Cecilia D'Anastasio wrote ruefully, 'It's a culture where bragging about "stacked" secretaries as late as 2012 garnishes Atari's mythos instead of muddying it.'[20]

This demographic of white men soon began to define not only how this new entertainment genre was created, but its content as well. The consequences would be far-reaching.

The Crash

A pivotal moment in the early economic history of the global games industry was the videogames crash of 1983, which took place mostly in the United States. The reasons for the crash were multiple – mismanagement, market saturation in the number of game consoles and available games, many of which were of poor quality, as well as waning interest in console games in favour of personal computers. The numbers are staggering – home video-game revenues peaked at around $3.2 billion in 1983, then fell to around $100 million by 1985. That is a drop of almost 97 per cent![21] Widespread stories exist about hundreds of thousands of Atari videogame cartridges being buried in a New Mexico landfill site, as it was impossible to sell them.

The crash, which lasted from 1983 to 1985, bankrupted numerous game development and console production companies. Some thought the shift was permanent and that the viability of a popular global industry was a pipe dream. While the North American market eventually bounced back, that was largely due to the widespread success of the Japanese export Nintendo Entertainment System (NES). Rebranded as Famicom for Western audiences, this 1983 console rebooted the North American games industry market. Other countries weathered the storm much better: Europe was much less dependent on the console market and so was less polluted by low-quality titles. Videogames were here to stay, but how they were to be made and marketed was about to enter a new era.

Apart from realigning the geographical centre of the video-games industry, with Japan now taking the lead, the crash also pushed games companies to adopt more extreme marketing techniques.

Before this time, apart from a few notable exceptions like Atari's 'efforts', videogame advertising was not that explicitly divisive. In the 1970s and early 1980s, *Adventure* (1980), *Combat* (1977) and *Space Invaders* (1978) were being sold through family-friendly toy channels. The creator of the Japanese 1980s sensation *Pac-Man*, Toru Iwatani, also wanted to expand the game's audience beyond the typical demographics of young boys and teenagers. He had noticed that arcades were much less frequented by girls and women and wished to change that. *Electronic Games* reported in 1982 that *Pac-Man* was 'the first commercial videogame to involve large numbers of women players'. Director of sales for Midway, the company holding the North American licence for *Pac-Man*, Larry Berke recalled: 'Women kept calling us and saying it was "adorable".'[22] It turned out that a game that avoided violence and did not have a purposefully high barrier to entry sold tons of copies among casual players, women among them. Many couples, groups of friends and entire families played these games.

After 1983, the focus on a certain type of consumer sharpened. In the Polygon article *No Girls Allowed*, journalist Tracey Lien unravelled the story behind the stereotype of videogames being for boys and obtained this enlightening quote from a games marketer of that time:

Knowing that you have limited funding, you can't just market a shot-gun. You can't just go after anybody, you need to have a very clearly differentiated and specific brand because that's going to play into where you're running your ads and what kind of ads you run. That niche-ing, that targeting makes it easier for marketers to have a very succinct conversation with their target without overspending and trying to reach everybody. So the industry put all of its efforts on catering to boys.[23]

And cater they did! The videogame crash of 1983 marked the creation of a certain hegemony: in the United States, games were now made almost exclusively by young men to please an audience of almost exclusively young men. Games companies were explicit – during the September 1983 Boston Computer Society event, an executive for the Adam computer clearly stated that that their target audience were 'boys aged eight to sixteen and their fathers. We believe those are the two groups that really fuel computer purchases.' When audience members booed during his speech, the executive simply added that the marketing strategy was based on consumer research.[24]

The later expansion of the Japanese gaming industry did not particularly help matters. Titles followed many of the objectifying and often misogynist tropes found in some anime comic book culture. Furthermore, 1985 megahit *Super Mario* used the damsel-in-distress trope that became a staple of videogame themes.[25] Polygon's Tracey Lien highlights the story of *Myst* (1993) – a game that was released in the same year as *Doom*, but made more money, attracted a strong audience among women and yet failed to garner the same cultural significance. 'Why? Because video game developers didn't have to care. Targeting men worked . . . Industries tend to look beyond their existing target demographic only when the market has become totally saturated.'[26]

In *Myst*, the first-person adventure puzzle game, there is no dialogue, no enemies, no time limit and no way of dying. Thanks to that, it still holds the official Guinness World Record as the least violent adventure videogame ever. Awards aside, *Myst* was the best-selling PC game throughout the 1990s but, bizarrely, it achieved nothing near to the canon-defining honours that were attributed to *Doom*. Similarly, *Barbie Fashion Designer* (1996) nurtured an entire generation of gamers and outsold *Doom*, with half a million copies shipped.[27] The game makers' desire for violence somehow trumped even the market logic of sales.

The 1980s brought about another foundational transformation in the global videogames industry. While the axis of power in fields like intellectual property, hardware design and software creation still stayed firmly in the West, manufacturing and resources were about to shift that balance. It was during this decade that East Asian countries entered the world of games from an unexpected angle.

On 23 February 1983, in the wake of the crash, the *New York Times* reported that Atari was transferring the bulk of its manufacturing plants from California to Hong Kong and Taiwan. The move was intended to reduce costs. The consequence, however, was the firing of nearly 2,000 workers in the United States. In a statement, the company said it 'deeply regrets the hardship that this necessary step to achieve manufacturing cost reductions may cause affected workers in the community'.[28] Citing competition from other companies, such as Commodore, as well as the growing market for personal computers, Atari forever changed the ethics of the creation of their hardware and arguably, by extension, the ethics of all gaming of their devices. Even though some of the workers responded with inspirational defiance and briefly occupied the Atari manufacturing facility in Limerick, Ireland, withholding stock and machinery, the move to lower-wage territories appeared to be permanent.[29] Other companies followed.

This was probably the most significant shift in the global video-games industry – a cost-cutting, profit-raising, environmentally disastrous decision. As a result, videogames became completely dependent on the manufacturing lines in the Global South. This move is inseparable from any discussion about politics in digital games. Unlike most other entertainment and cultural practices, gaming is centrally tied to this circumstance. All hardware used for gaming – personal computers, home consoles and lately mobile phones – are assembled in factories riddled with labour abuses in East Asia and utilise natural resources extracted in Central Africa under conditions of mass displacement, slave labour and enormous corruption.

The Takeover

Post 1983, lessons were learnt and entire new centres of the universe emerged. Some companies went bankrupt, and those that persevered focussed ruthlessly on savvy marketing and outsourcing. The profits started trickling in again. The next defining moment in the story of videogames development came not from large market or economic fluctuations, but from a single technique, a single title: the first-person shooter. A group of young goth kids, who until then had been selling their creations to a monthly magazine that gave out free CDs with games, were about to change the industry forever.

Up until this period, technical limitations allowed only a few gaming genres to emerge: top-down, left-right views and movement were a real constraint on creativity. Platform games, puzzle games and top-down management games were available and popular, but no company had succeeded in crafting a game that enabled players to truly immerse themselves in an environment, rather than manage it.

In September 1990, American computer programmer John Carmack developed an efficient way to rapidly side-scroll graphics from the first-person perspective on a personal computer. This meant that a player could actually stand in a room in the game and survey their surroundings, as well as move forwards, backwards and sideways. Never before had such a realistic perspective been possible. Players could finally feel like they were walking around a particular space.

Working with other members of what would become id Software, programmers John Romero, Tom Hall and Adrian Carmack knew they had something special on their hands. To test the capabilities, they decided to create a remake of *Castle Wolfenstein*, which had been developed by Muse Software for the Apple II computer in 1980. The concept was pretty radical – a Nazi shoot-em-up! The aptly named 2003 book *Masters of Doom: How Two Guys Created an Empire and Transformed Pop Culture*, by David Kushner, explains this moment in detail. The team was interested in the idea, as Romero, Hall and John Carmack all had fond memories of the original *Castle Wolfenstein* and felt that the maze-like shooter gameplay fit well with Carmack's 3D game engine. Encouraged by the reception of the idea from his colleagues, Romero proposed a 'loud' and 'cool' fast-action game where the player could shoot soldiers before dragging and looting their bodies. The core of the gameplay would be simple, since Romero believed that due to the novelty of a 3D game and control scheme, players would not be receptive to more complicated, slower gameplay.

Now called the grandfather of shooters, *Wolfenstein 3D* showcased this new concept very well and earned id Software $2.5 million in revenue, selling 250,000 copies. However, the team knew they could push the first-person perspective mechanic even further. To prove it, they went for a gore extravaganza with distorted Christian symbolism, images drawing on Hieronymus Bosch and demons galore. *Doom* was a game based in Hell, and it changed everything. The legacy of this game cannot be overstated. It revolutionised videogames in a variety of ways. What are now called first-person shooters, which for many gamers is their understanding of what a videogame is, for years were titled *Doom*-clones.

Doom became a ritual for the youth of the day, myself included: sharing the diskette (floppy disk), playing it in school classes. It brought the popularity and perceived social impact of gaming to a new level. In the age of grunge and the Satanic panic, popular culture items such as *Doom* were blamed for the ills of the youth. Alienation, economic and social insecurity, and mental health crises were all dismissed in the popular media in order to denounce the perceived true culprit – videogames.[30]

In fact, *Doom* brought to many a sense of community and belonging. Qualities associated with being an outcast in other settings were celebrated here. The game inspired conversations and hours of socialising. Even though its gory aesthetics became a catalyst for some of the more toxic traits in gaming that would become difficult to shake, primarily the insistence that a videogame is defined by an encounter with violence, it also introduced the art of creative gaming and game making to millions.

The 1983 title *Lode Runner* had originated the concept of modding. The game supplied a level editor in which players could craft their own levels and share them with other players on the same computer. But the release of *Doom* allowed modding to truly flourish. The developers deliberately made the game's engine separate from the assets, meaning that digital enthusiasts could design their own 'look' for the game – redefining levels and wrapping them in various skins, reimagining the product, enhancing character art and manipulating the mood of the game.

The results were staggering, with many extraordinary pieces of digital art conjured up. Now each user could give the title a new look and a new feel, making it their own. For the first time, some of the pieces coming out of these more abstract attempts to reimagine a game, including machinimas,* were showing up in makeshift real-life fine art expositions and digital showcases, exhibited simply by exchanging a floppy disk.

The release of *Doom*, therefore, was a crucial milestone in the narrative about videogames. The abstract mechanics prevalent in gaming before *Doom* were capable of creating a story – lines of dialogue and a degree of character formation were certainly utilised. But immersion, the heart of gaming as it is perceived today, made *Doom* the standout. Due to that first-person perspective, an alternative world transported the player into the game and was now sufficiently sophisticated to be truly immersive. And the world into which players were drawn offered a variety of options. The game opened itself to a reimagination of its own limits. This success also had its downsides – the innovative mechanics of *Doom*, when wrapped in its violent aesthetic, sadly solidified in many people's heads what gaming overall looks like. An image that is still difficult to dislodge even today!

Finally, it was the first game with the potential to be truly viral. *Doom* was very well optimised, tiny in digital size and, as a result, effortless to pirate. It could be passed around and played on a variety of devices, which endowed it with worldwide cult classic status. Before this time, games were relatively locked into isolated infrastructures. Since this golden age of easy distribution, the walls have gone up again, with hardware options for gaming limited by strict

---

* Machinima is the use of real-time videogame graphics engines to create a cinematic production. The word *machinima* is a portmanteau of the words *machine* and *cinema*.

subscription services and extremely proprietary hardware. The sense that this medium can be almost limitless began with this generation of videogames.

And yet, social gaming communities as we know them today were arguably established at a slightly earlier stage. Same story, different game – the mechanics were once again genre-defining. Two hit boxes have their health chipped away as they interact with each other;* two opponents press buttons at an arcade cabinet in a unique combination, competing to reduce said health. To this day, *Street Fighter II* has one of the most loyal and devoted fan bases in the global videogames arena, with annual competitions drawing in thousands of fans of all generations. This 1991 creation by the Japanese developer Capcom is not subtle on the aesthetics – buff men and women and characters wrapped in every racial and gender stereotype imaginable violently settle scores in various geographical locations. For professional players, the graphics or plot of the game are absolutely irrelevant; all they see are the speed and the size of their hit boxes. John Romero thought similarly about *Doom* and some other shooters – they can be seen as screen-cleaning exercises, harnessing the inherent satisfaction in clearing a level of messy enemies, revelling in the hygiene and precision of it all.[31]

Fighting games exposed another inequality brought about by the industry: who even gets to play or win at videogames and how? In most other videogame formats, the time and money that players invest ultimately lead to their advantage. A competitor can invest coins to practise against AI bots, which are likely to mimic most of another player's moves. Fighting games do not really work that way. Of course, practising, and practising a lot, is important, but what is

---

* Hit box: an invisible shape outlining all or part of a model (such as in a videogame) used to determine whether another object collides with the model.

crucial is practising the game in a live context, against other, better players. No amount of playing online will resemble the moves and the mind games that players encounter when competing against current champions. This phenomenon, along with issues of latency,* results in the necessity of live tournaments and sessions in real life.

The demographic of the Western fighting games community is working-class, often hailing from ethnic and racial minorities. They cannot spend days practising, but even if some can, practice is not really rewarded with any serious advantage. There is a historical precedent for this classless meritocracy — arcade culture. According to research by the historian Carly A. Kocurek, most players insisted that the money they put in the arcade machines was not given to them by their parents, but was earned through doing household chores, collecting bottles and cans for return deposits or working newspaper routes or other odd jobs.[32] But even if players had more coins in their pockets, if they lost, they went back to the end of the queue.

Much of the early arcade culture has been deliberately dismantled: these spaces were undermaintained and overpoliced. As is sadly common, urban areas that attract young people without parental supervision often also attract a disproportionate negative reaction by the state. Gaming arcades were swiftly viewed in the same way as gambling arenas. Local officials feared that arcades 'would become a hang-out for teenagers who would cause problems for police'. Neighbourhood groups feared that 'video game arcades located near residential neighbourhoods might introduce undesirable elements into the community.'[33]

The spread of the home console moved much of gaming to people's living rooms, but we have to thank the arcade culture for

---

* Latency: the time between pressing a button and it registering and displaying the effects in the game.

one of the most fascinating aspects of gaming – IRL communities. The fighting games community is the outstanding example of organic affiliation building, a precursor to much more heavily manufactured, but still powerful, current electronic sports fandoms. LAN parties hosting *Doom*, *Quake* and *StarCraft* (1998 onw.) tournaments also emerged as the precursors to the kind of gaming communities in existence right now – self-reliant, complicated, sometimes exclusionary, incredibly precious to those involved. The state of gaming as we know it today was shaping up, both with its creativity and its ills. Everything was up for grabs.

State Actors Enter the Ring

By the 1990s, videogames were mainstream, both as a creative product delivering new and profound moments of joy and as a space for political actors to create political realities. As profits soared, this creative industry succumbed to the claws of financialisation and corporatisation.

It was a decade of bursting creativity and the calcification of business practices. Games like *Cosmology of Kyoto* (1993) or *Vib-Ribbon* (1999) were revered by art critics, and even acquired by institutions such as the Museum of Modern Art for their profound aesthetic and conceptual aspects. On the flip side, studio sizes grew, leading to a bloated managerial class, with their lingo and auditing of certain creative ambitions. The orientation of games as products, or artefacts of popular entertainment, along with the mechanisation of production and marketing processes, rendered the games industry homogeneous in terms of both output and cast of creators.

At the same time, game distributors clamped down on pirating, tightened their grip and increased their share of the pie for offering their shopfronts to game developers. Thrown to the margins, many smaller game developers could not keep up. Any potential ambition for a mass movement of artistic game development guilds or cooperatives, fair trade hardware solutions and diverse themes and mechanics in videogames was buried here . . . for a while.

Many kids who grew up with games between the 1970s and 1990s became important players in this new billion-dollar industry. By the time the new millennium rolled over, the technology in games had become sufficiently advanced to focus not only on the exciting mechanics of the game; storytelling could begin to truly take centre stage. What kind of stories were to be told, of course, was up for debate. At the same time, a certain stratification was underway, too.

A few popular game genres could be trusted to release a significant dose of endorphins. Shooter games like *Duke Nukem* (1991 onw.), horror titles like *Resident Evil* (1996 onw.), platformer games like *Super Mario World* (1990 onw.), racing games, sports games, strategy games, role-playing games or horror games all had significant fan bases and ever-growing production teams, and produced healthy revenues. The technological advances accommodated not only singular, linear stories with two-dimensional characters, but also entire worlds, side quests and labyrinths of plot devices.

Players could now focus not just on the plot, or the mise en scène of a game, but also on the broader message. What type of values or narratives did this produce? Videogames were now sufficiently sophisticated to build a chronicle of persuasion. Those eager to popularise a particular ideology – be they opinionated game developers, publishers courting a particular demographic, political spin doctors funding the projects, or other cultural influencers wishing to diversify their storytelling techniques – wasted no time getting involved in this innovative medium.

Strategy games like *Freeciv* (1996 onw.) or *Sid Meier's Colonization* (1994 onw.) and shooters such as *Tomb Raider* (1996 onw.) were already independently peddling colonial or jingoistic fantasies. In these games, the plot usually unleashed tropes of imperial land grabs, white supremacy and racist depictions of non-Western populations, ranging from 'primitive' to full-on terrorists.

By the late 1990s, the United States Department of Defense was beginning to sense the power of the games industry over adolescent men – the Department's main audience – and created a campaign of recruitment and manipulation around gaming. Serious institutional power underwrote the move to tie the global videogames industry to the Western military complex. The Pentagon spent more than $150 million on military-themed games or simulations in 1999 alone, with another $70 million injection in 2008 and still more since, all on projects with their own, very particular political agenda.[34]

America's Army, released in 2002, developed and published by the United States Army in the wake of the post-9/11 military boost, was the starkest and priciest example of this practice – with a ten-year development and marketing budget of $50 million, on top of the investments mentioned before.[35] This round-based team tactical shooter with realistic combat scenarios was described in a review of the time as 'the most realistic portrayal of weapons and combat of any game'.[36] The game has collected a number of awards over the years and has managed to attract several million players, on both personal computers and consoles. This so-called 'strategic communication device' was 'intended to inform, educate, and recruit prospective soldiers'. On the official Frequently Asked Questions page, the developers confirmed that one of the reasons people outside the United States can play the game is that they 'want the whole world to know how great the US Army is'. Not subtle, then. Nonetheless, videogames were a perfect vehicle for the purpose of state propaganda. When the franchise was eventually discontinued, a total of forty-one versions of the game had been released between 2002 and 2014.

Themes around militarisation and armed resistance were instilled in games to build narratives around a variety of conflicts. *Jane's IAF: Israeli Air Force* (1998) was clearly intended to raise publicity for the Israel Defense Forces. The content of the game included two types of campaigns. The first covered historic operations of the Israeli Air Force in the 1967 Six-Day War, the 1973 Yom Kippur War, and the 1982 Lebanon War. The second type included fictional futuristic operations in Iraq, Syria and Lebanon.[37] A Syrian game studio released the action game *Under Ash* (2001), which recreated moments from the history of Palestinian resistance to the Israeli military occupation.

This attention and the seemingly popular acclaim military-themed games received in the early 2000s inspired an entire generation of neo-colonial videogames that underlined Western military agendas and values as a prime moral objective. Developers of the *Conflict: Desert Storm*, *Medal of Honour* (2002) and the now-infamous *Call of Duty* (2003) franchises found it relatively easy to secure funding during this moment. The revolving door of consultants going back and forth between the organised military complex and the enormous *Call of Duty* franchise is well documented, albeit hardly spoken of. A colonial narrative can be transmitted through the story plot and the cast of characters featured or, sometimes even more significantly, omitted. Bias can be transmitted through choices as simple as the colour grading for different settings: yellow for Africa and the Middle East, signifying 'dusty', 'historical'; blue for the West, that is, 'modern', 'civilised'. Other choices include what languages players hear spoken in the background and the tone of voice used.

All these aspects invite an interpretation that often reflects a certain ideological affiliation. In gaming, the introduction of such narratives alongside the development of technology strong enough to support them presented a double victory: a moral judgement and a desensitisation towards massacring anyone deemed to be a state enemy.

Today, the modern military complex uses experiences that are styled to look like videogames to train soldiers. More disturbingly, they apply an aesthetically pleasing user interface akin to that of a videogame in targeting machines for real-life remote bombing action. A 2007 video, which WikiLeaks titled 'Collateral Murder', depicting US soldiers engaged in a helicopter strike that killed two Reuters employees and a number of civilians, has a distinct video-game look to it. The user interface in today's drones was in fact designed to replicate that of a videogame.

Electronic sports events and gaming conferences are now regularly funded by local state military bodies. It's a win–win strategy. Games companies represent governmental organisations and boost their own public image in the process. An image of being close to the state allows studios to receive lucrative tax breaks, too. And the military outsources the building of cumbersome training simulators and attracts new recruits in the process. Critics of such arrangements and the tight relationship between the military and games companies are rarely listened to. While these camouflage-tainted collaborations may benefit one side of the global games industry, more progressively minded studios suffer when they're drowned out by these slick and bombastic displays of aggression.

Gamify Everything

As the arms industries got involved, the propaganda and profit-making got bolder and more cynical. Weapons companies, including Colt's, Barrett Firearms, Kalashnikov Concern, Zenitco, Remington Firearms, Daniel Defense, Troy Industries, Insight Technologies, Aimpoint and Eotech, have their guns actively licensed by numerous games companies in order to appear in videogames; details of such deals or the money changing hands are undisclosed.[38]

Arms companies and various advertising agencies were not the only ones beginning to sense that digital games were worth investigating. The dopamine hit that reaches the brain after a correctly solved puzzle or a well-placed shot could be applied to areas other than mere entertainment. In 2008, the concept of *gamification* began to surface in the entrepreneurial and corporate worlds.

Other fields had already adapted elements from videogames – for instance, some work in learning disabilities and scientific visualisation comes from user interface inventions in gaming. Venture capitalists soon started to experiment with incorporating social, rewarding aspects of games into their software. Elements of game design that were originally intended to increase the satisfaction of a player experience, such as points, badges, leaderboards, performance graphs and slick button design and audio effects, could be extended to other digital implementations.

In their 2014 book, *The Gameful World: Approaches, Issues, Applications*, editors Steffen P. Walz and Sebastian Deterding chronicle the wide adoption of gamification. According to the authors, with the rise of Web 2.0 business models in the mid-2000s, web start-ups were increasingly faced with the challenge of how to motivate users to sign up with the offered service, invite people they know, and interact with their products regularly. They needed new tools for raising engagement. For instance, in 2007, IBM contracted communication researcher Byron Reeves, who published a white paper on the role of online games for business leadership.

In 2008, a question-and-answer platform for software developers titled *Stack Overflow* was launched using a reputation system with points and badges inspired by the gaming experience of its developers. It quickly gained cachet in the technology industry. In March 2009, the iPhone app Foursquare debuted at the South by Southwest (SXSW) festival and demonstrated that game design elements can drive the initial adoption and retention of users. The following August, Bunchball's Rajat Paharia registered the domain gamification.com. The video-sharing site Vimeo added a 'like' button in November 2005, and Facebook followed suit four years later. Adding a calculus, a playful interaction into the interface, increased the sites' engagement rates.[39]

Today gamification is a widely adopted technique that is almost seamlessly incorporated into how we engage in various digital scenarios, such as organisational productivity, self-help apps, knowledge retention, employee recruitment and evaluation, physical training, traffic rules learning and more. Naturally, the biggest adopters of gamification have been marketing agencies; 70 per cent of Forbes Global 2000 companies surveyed in 2013 said they planned to use gamification for the purposes of marketing and customer retention.[40]

Gamified shopping experiences are now common online, but companies have also added videogame visual components to their brands. Games theorist Ian Bogost writes:

> Gamification is reassuring. It gives Vice Presidents and Brand Managers comfort: they're doing everything right, and they can do even better by adding 'a games strategy' to their existing products, slathering on 'gaminess' like aioli on ciabatta at the consultant's indulgent sales lunch.[41]

On the other side of the spectrum, many videogames now offer a 'labour' angle: complete tasks, collect points, solve problems and grind your way to the next high score. From the 2009 farming simulation sensation *FarmVille* to the modern cult classic *Euro*

Truck Simulator (2012 onw.), game companies now unapologetically invite the player to labour all day, and this toil has been embraced by the player base. In November 2022, *A Little to the Left*, where players tidy shelves or cleaning items and do other organisation tasks, was released to rave reviews and branded as the 'cosy' game of the year.

The highly successful social simulation series *Animal Crossing*, launched in 2001, was praised by players for providing them with a sense of security, no matter how unreal. Many reported that completing the tasks gave them a feeling of accomplishment, stability and safety, and that they found the tasks impossible to resist. To players, this game personified the promise that capitalism made to them: that there will be rewards for their labour.

It is tempting to judge these players as capitalist subjects, doing laborious profit-making exercises for somebody else's gain. Nonetheless, fans of *Stardew Valley* (2016) – another staple of the genre – would probably argue that in a world filled with so little certainty and sense of control, the predictable, repetitive results of the actions in these games have a calming effect. And who am I to argue with that?

Grandma Picks Up a Console

Videogames became an increasingly powerful apparatus, not only in the realm of digital entertainment, but as a pioneering space in private advertising, public cultural discourse and national and international propaganda. After seemingly selling a gaming device to every middle-class adolescent boy in the world by the mid-2000s, gaming companies began to look around for a new demographic of consumers. The unexpected success of doll-house social simulator *The Sims*, released in 2000, once again broadened the purpose of videogames and the emotions they are capable of eliciting.

Inducement of fear and anxiety, resource management and distribution are game design tricks as easily attached to a lifestyle and relationship management game as to a military one. The only thing that changes is the setting.

Japanese gaming giant Nintendo had always been a bit more expansive in the pool of players they marketed their hardware and games to. Their 2006 Wii console had something special going for it – the accelerometer chip inside the wireless hand-held 'Wiimotes' that detected motion in three-dimensional space. Without the restraints of messy cables, players could freely move around the room. Most importantly, their hand gestures and movements were registered in the game! The Wii games also provided Nintendo an opportunity to sell a range of accessories for the controllers, so that many households in the late 2000s had white plastic racquets, guitars or golf clubs cluttering up the living room.

Crucially, the marketing of Nintendo Wii, whether on billboards, TV adverts or public relations documents, had one central message: this console is for everyone; it is for the entire family, for every generation, for dedicated gamers and newbies alike. An iconic poster featured an old lady with silver hair and a bright smile holding one of the Nintendo Wii controllers. This message, combined with a lower price, allowed Nintendo to sell 135 million copies of the console.[42] Even retirement homes, not widely known as active digital gaming communities, bought them in droves.

During the same time, as mobile devices began to reach the pockets of millions, digital games were tailored for them, too. The total global revenue from mobile games was estimated at $2.6 billion in 2005. Three years later, that figure doubled to $5.8 billion.[43] Mobile gaming revenue reached $50.4 billion in 2017, accounting for almost half of total global gaming revenues.[44]

The model for acquiring such profits has changed, however. At first, games were embedded within the phones themselves – think *Snake* and *Space Impact 2* on the Nokia 3310, which were beloved by many. With the introduction of the WAP, or wireless internet access on mobile devices, many owners could now access browser-based games and, later, purchase new apps. In an attempt to merge the two markets, Nokia released the N-Gage in 2003, designed as both a handheld console and a phone. However, separate consoles were still technologically superior at the time, and the unit was a commercial failure.

When it arrived in 2007, the iPhone changed the game. Apple's touchscreen product, with intuitive user experience featuring a strong wireless connection, crucially came with an integrated App Store. Users could download various applications, and naturally, digital games, for free, or for a unit price. The free games often contained advertisements that brought in profits for the developers. Later, in-game purchases for specific features or aesthetic add-ons would become a goldmine.

Candy Crush Saga, which debuted in 2012, is considered the most successful use of the freemium model (a free game with money-making bloatware). The gameplay consists of swapping two adjacent candies among several on the board to make a row or column of at least three matching-coloured candies. Incredibly basic! While the game can be played without spending money, players can also purchase special actions that will assist them. This option earns King, the developers of the game, eye-watering sums. At its peak, the company reported that gamers were spending more than $4 million per day.[45]

Around 2014, more than 93 million people were playing *Candy Crush Saga*, while the revenue over a three-month period, as reported by King, was nearly half a billion dollars.[46] Five years after its release on mobile, the *Candy Crush Saga* series has received a staggering 3 billion downloads.[47] Such profits incentivise predatory practices, and many of the addictive facets of certain videogames were conceived in the mobile game market.

Today that market is plagued with malicious operational networks that have made products akin to digital casinos. Methods of endorphin stimulation are studied as science and implemented into products in nefarious ways. Deceit, false advertising and various psychological tricks that keep the player engaged are all integral to this enormous industry, which has overtaken PC and console games sales and is projected to bring in one-third of a trillion dollars in sales by 2030.[48]

On the brighter side, the rise of mobile game development also enabled the birth of a videogames industry in the Global South. Local developers in countries like Kenya and Nigeria, in territories where fast broadband was less available and console games were expensive, leaned into the strength of burgeoning mobile game markets and became active developers of them.

Recently, a game developers association in Africa was launched, encouraging this growing community of consumers and creators. The Pan Africa Gaming Group (PAGG) is made up of ten studios from Cameroon, Ethiopia, Ghana, Kenya, Rwanda, Senegal, South Africa, Tanzania and Tunisia, with more expected to join soon. The association will bring together games developed by its members for publishing under Gara, an African game store, and Afrocomix, a content hub for Afrocentric creative work.[49] The African videogame market was worth $3.9 billion in 2023, and revenue is expected to reach $5.8 billion by 2028.[50]

The Indian videogame industry is centred in Bangalore, Mumbai and Pune, with mobile games again dominating the $2 billion market. While the existing studios are slowly beginning to make a case for developing their own intellectual property (IP), the region is still a major space for outsourcing of more manual tasks from large Western companies. Similarly, in my native

Lithuania the industry grew from being a space largely for out-sourcing and building relatively simplistic mobile titles to forging a growing number of its own IP and experimental artistic projects.

The Indie Game Revolution

High-end, story-driven AAA videogames like *Grand Theft Auto III* (2001), *Mafia: City of Lost Heaven* (2002) and *Max Payne* (2001) were thriving by the early 2000s, transporting games into the mainstream. Consoles such as PlayStation and Xbox were a common item in middle-class living rooms, and game development teams had grown their numbers from dozens to hundreds, while budgets scaled into multiple millions. The emerging and astonishingly popular mobile games market proved something new, however: a project does not need overtly complex graphics or profoundly elaborate mechanics to be popular. A different way of making games had emerged.

As the price of hardware decreased, reaching larger swathes of people who could now play games, the software required to make games likewise became more readily available. By the mid-2000s, cross-platform game engines, such as Unity or Unreal Engine, and tools such as Adobe Flash were easy to obtain or license, meaning that anybody could potentially make their own videogame on a personal computer. Entire communities crafting smaller games and mods had been in existence for a while, but for the first time, physical copies of the game were not the only medium for releasing one – the internet allowed players to fully access large digital files from anywhere in the world. Game makers were no longer depend-ent on external publishing deals and the business of imprinting of the game onto CDs and cartridges and distributing these physical copies to game stores. Now, they could either cook the entire thing and release it online themselves or approach publishers, who might invest in them and release the game on their digital platforms.

For the first time, the tools required for entering the global games industry were not entirely in the hands of a few publishing conglomerates and increasingly enormous games companies with dozens of departments. Anybody with some experience in coding, digital sculpting and marketing could generate sales with their own creation. These conditions expanded the pool of who could make games. Whereas games companies were by and large populated by young, middle-class men, now anyone could have a go at making their stories relevant in gaming. A new range of authors resulted in a new wave of subjects and methods of gameplay.

In fact, many independent game developers of this time saw their mission as providing an antithesis to contemporary gaming choices. Women, people of colour, trans, queer and non-stereotypically masculine people could finally have stories made for them, by others who wanted to share their experiences. Progressive social and political causes, which hitherto had seldom been explored in gaming, had finally found a voice.

Size, it turned out, was not all that mattered. Indie developers found substantial revenues by simply releasing their game straight to the audience and advertising it online.

The success of the indie games revolution can partially be ascribed to the tendency of leaders in other other media – notably the legendary film critic Roger Ebert – to dismiss gaming as an inferior cultural realm, driving game makers to prove otherwise and seek to have their digital oeuvres recognised as fine art. Some institutions agreed: in 2012, the Museum of Modern Art purchased a version of *Pac-Man* and *Tetris* for their permanent collection.

With the help of the burgeoning social media, indie game developers created brand and marketing campaigns by themselves and for their own tiny companies; they acquired direct access to their audiences and became adept in nurturing these communities, forging loyal customers out of them. Now, any person with the financial means to put in the time could spend days in their bedroom tinkering with a small game that had the potential to become a huge best-seller.

Gamergate

Some failed to see the expansion of narratives in games, and the diversification of the people making them, as a pie growing larger. To many long-term gamers, these changes felt not only like their share of the pie was decreasing, but as something even more personal. As feminist and racial justice causes altered the everyday realities of marriages, workplaces and even mainstream entertainment, gaming zones had felt exempt from these shifts, in a 'safe space', if you will, from the cultural turn towards the 'woke'. No longer, many gamers feared.

This pent-up tension was released in forums and message boards, expressing all the discontent over what gamers perceived as a major shift of attention from small and big games creators towards more politically correct, inclusive content. Gamers would not allow these changes to take place without a fight. The breaking point came unexpectedly: 2014's Gamergate exposed these resentful communities, to very unsettling effect. Encouraged by far-right organisers such as Steve Bannon, Milo Yiannopoulos and Ian Miles Cheong, legions of gamers went after a few game developers, journalists and commentators who were deemed to be the enemies of gaming as it should be.

As with any harassment campaign, Gamergate needed a trigger to justify the participants' cruelty. In this case, it was a blog post penned by a disgruntled ex-boyfriend of a game developer named Zoë Quinn, including copies of personal chat logs, emails and text messages that dissected their failed relationship and subsequent break-up. Crucially, the post implied that Quinn had received a favourable review of her game *Depression Quest* in exchange for a sexual relationship with Nathan Grayson, a reporter for the gaming websites *Kotaku* and *Rock Paper Shotgun*. *Depression Quest* was of a genre typically detested by the right-wing gaming milieu – an indie game, exploring themes of mental health and loneliness, made by a woman. It did not matter that the accusation of a lapse in gaming-journalism ethics was false. Nor did Gamergate have a leg to stand on with the plea to leave 'political intrusions' out of their games (videogames have always been political). The #Gamergate crowd now had the numbers, the organisational infrastructure (4chan, Breitbart and Internet Relay Chat (IRC), among others) and, most importantly, a target.

As a consequence, Quinn was subjected to severe online harassment, including rape and death threats and doxxing that subsequently led to her fleeing her home. Anyone who dared to defend her – journalists, other women game developers and various online activists – also became targets of a coordinated online assault. And why not settle some old scores in the meantime? YouTuber and activist Anita Sarkeesian, who had already tasted some of this harassment back in 2012 after she released a YouTube video about the tropes that plague women characters in most videogames, also appeared in the firing line. Sarkeesian was forced to cancel an October 2014 speaking appearance at Utah State University after the school received numerous anonymous bomb and shooting threats, all of which claimed affiliation with #Gamergate. The threats were not subtle. The gaming sphere was the training ground for a form of online harassment that today seems ubiquitous.

After a relatively quiet period of acceptance by the mainstream media that videogames are a legitimate entertainment field, stories plastered across the *New York Times* and the *Guardian* once again warned about the dangers of gaming communities. By the time the dust settled in 2016, the professional games industry was split into two – those who justified the behaviour of #Gamergaters and those who vehemently opposed them. Even all these years later, it is not easy to determine who had won – yes, the industry is much more open to diverse casts in videogames and their themes have certainly branched out to include all manner of underdog stories. More people of various backgrounds are working in games than ever before. On the other hand, there has been an upturn of conservative and regressive content in games and other digital media, too.

Participants in Gamergate provided an environment that encouraged and applauded numerous real-life acts of terror. The perpetrator of the shootings in Dayton, Ohio, that killed ten people; the 2019 Poway synagogue shooter in San Diego; and the attacker in the Christchurch mosque massacre, which killed fifty-one people, all referenced gaming memes in their manifestos.

In 2019, a twenty-seven-year-old neo-Nazi stormed a syna-gogue in the German city of Halle before attacking a nearby kebab shop, killing two people and injuring two more. The perpetrator broadcast the attack on the gaming streaming platform Twitch, repeatedly calling himself a loser for failing to kill more people, as his gun kept on jamming.[51] Grotesquely, his fascist manifesto included a 'score sheet of achievements' for the attack, including goals for the numbers and methods of killing.[52]

Recently, the husband of the Democratic party leader Nancy Pelosi was attacked at his house just before the 2022 midterm elections. Again, the attacker named Gamergate as his moment of radicalisation.[53] It was another merging of the gaming world and real life.

Game Workers Rise Up

And yet, it is a sad reality that the people who can afford to have discussions about representation and those who land top jobs creating the games are already lucky enough not to be employed in manufacturing the tools that are paramount to the industry. With this in mind, I ventured into this scary, problem-ridden, utterly fascinating industry. My sense was that a material inquiry into the ethics of the games industry may help us discern the real enemies who dictate and formulate our everyday experiences.

The enemies were clearly not women and other minorities. Perhaps it was the asset owners, the proprietors of these products, who deserved our ire. If gamers really cared about the level of political correctness in their games and the demographics of the people who made them, they would also show interest in the well-being of these developers. Developers who are well looked after produce better games and, for the most part, the consumers understood that.

The loud collective voice of gamers has sometimes become a tool for organising, uniting various political factions among video-game enthusiasts. Bobby Kotick, the former CEO of one of the biggest game companies in the world, Activision Blizzard, is now almost universally disapproved of, regardless of the commentators' political affiliations. Under his leadership, games were rushed or unfinished, to the irritation of the players. His tenure also exposed masses of labour violations, including discrimination, sexual harassment and union busting.[54] The internet, and people of all political inclinations, were united, and #FireBobbyKotick regularly trended on social media. With their proximity to fans, numerous game developers could tell their stories on digital forums first-hand.

The notion that not all was perfect for the workers in the games industry was now a subject for action. While most games studios seek to curate a public relations image of a relaxed workplace, with ping pong tables and afternoon beers, the reality is much grimmer. In 2004, as people began posting public messages on the internet, a spouse of an Electronic Arts (EA) employee penned a passionate letter about the constant anguish of her husband.[55] The anonymous post detailed the declining mental health of a worker who was struggling to meet increasingly brutal deadlines with a decreasing sense of job and material security. The worker experienced numerous nights at the office, 'crunch',[*] depression and anxiety and difficulty connecting with family back at home – and many of his colleagues were seemingly in the same situation.

EA has amassed extraordinary revenues developing and publishing popular franchises such as *The Sims*, *FIFA* and *Need for Speed*. The letter kindled a sense of solidarity that had not been felt before. Three class action cases followed, and in 2007, the plaintiffs were awarded $14.9 million for unpaid overtime.[56]

Predatory tactics were rife not only within the production of videogames, but also in the way they were marketed, structured and sold. Free-market economics surely had a hand in the debilitating circumstances in both work and leisure. Game developers, often nurtured by entrepreneurial Silicon Valley ideologies, knew that their will, attitude and discipline might not guarantee a safe, comfortable and secure work environment. The priority was making money, and caring for workers was not a useful tool in

---

[*] In the videogame industry, *crunch* is a word for worker overtime, usually occurring close to the completion of a project or its milestone. Crunch can lead to sixty to 100 hours of work per week, for extended periods of time, and is often uncompensated. While it is often perceived as a failure by management in planning the workers' time, crunch is commonly used as a planned part of the videogame development cycle.

meeting that goal. Games industry execs, in tandem with those of tech, saw unionisation as an outdated practice, limiting innovation and growth. Accepting the necessity for those structures felt to developers almost like looking backwards, admitting some kind of defeat. Luckily, they did not have to look back, they could just observe what was taking place in parallel to them.

In 2016, the Screen Actors Guild-American Federation of Television and Radio Artists (SAG-AFTRA), which represented voice actors and motion capture artists in the videogames industry, organised a strike against eleven American game companies, including giants such as Activision, EA and Disney Character Voices International. SAG-AFTRA advocated for better compensation for their members at a time when studios were making hundreds of millions. Traditionally, voice actors and motion capture artists received a flat-rate payment for their work. The union held that residual payments should also be considered. Other issues raised included more safety precautions, oversight to avoid vocal stress for certain roles and better safety assurances for actors while on set.[57]

After 340 days of strike, the longest-ever for the Screen Actors Guild, a settlement was reached. The action received broad support among the player base as well as from equivalent international guilds and unions. While strong unions and worker protection are historically a common feature of Hollywood movie studios, the games industry had never received that support. The success and the energy of the strike generated a lot of buzz among the game-dev community. All this momentum needed was a spark to ignite it into a full-blown movement. Game company bosses visiting the 2018 Game Developers Conference (GDC) in San Francisco were about to provide just that.

The International Game Developers Association (IGDA) is a US-based lobbying body for the industry, mostly advocating for the needs of the management of companies – tax breaks, governmental funding, anti-censorship, business and legal issues and student and academic relations. Few can comprehend why, during such a delicate moment in the games worker–management relationship, they thought it was a good idea to host an anti-union round table talk at the GDC. The talking points in the event blurb were familiar – Human Resources departments would take better care of workers than unions could, unions curb innovation in industries, the games industry is uniquely unsuitable for broad unionisation.

Nevertheless, the room for the round table was packed with game workers challenging the misleading notions about unions. Furthermore, the event inspired the gathering of individuals determined to take active steps towards broad unionisation in the videogames industry – Game Workers Unite International was born.[58] In the preceding months and years, numerous networks as well as actual games industry unions were founded in dozens of countries. Support for these movements was universal – even the reactionary crowd of the games industry saw the necessity of these institutions. Few expressed fears of some sort of Marxist takeover of their beloved 'anti-woke' videogames. The legal processes of setting up a union, and the issues that need to be confronted, vary from country to country, but broad coalitions have been established and are doing incredible work thanks to the dedicated activists involved.

Labour issues in the videogames industry in the Global North are extensive, pernicious and well documented. Crunch, sexual harassment, insecure wages, mass layoffs and union-busting are problems that most people working in the videogames industry have experienced or heard about. Still, many of these workers can use their voice to hold their employer accountable, either via unions or other networks. On the other hand, outsourcing for software development, as with the destructive but lucrative instrument of hardware outsourcing, had become an option, thanks to the World Wide Web. In game-development facilities in Eastern Europe and the Global South, a race to the bottom determined workers' pay and conditions.

Dozens of prestigious game companies in the Global North are holders and planners of intellectual property that is often completed by outsourced staff in India or Belarus, creating tremendous savings on labour costs. The mobile games market relies heavily on underpaid and overworked staff in Asia-Pacific and South America. Furthermore, the in-game economies of many free-to-play titles are artificially inflated by click farms in the Global South. In click farms, workers are assigned a display of up to 100 mobile devices, where they are instructed to manually click on particular prompts, commands, rewards – anything that creates currency that can then be sold off to wealthier gamers in the Global North.

Click farming was, in fact, the business that Steve Bannon dabbled in before running Donald Trump's election campaign. The right recognised and used spaces of gaming for their own ends, allowing the industry to be shaped into an integral part of the contemporary capitalist system, rather than offering an alternative to it.

The Game Is On

Today videogames affect the world on both micro and macro levels. On a granular level, practices of gamification have seeped into a host of everyday activities – language learning, Human Resources activities, mental and physical health tracking and more. Apps such as PACT, HealthyWage and Nexercise have gamified a way to pay the user for exercising! Billions of people now enjoy casual videogames, and more ardent gamers have entire clothing, furniture and esports industries dedicated to them. Rivalled by Twitch, Netflix is now considering setting up its own live-streaming service.[59] There are games informing us about news and elections, educational games on history and others on science or medical research. Celebrities have their avatars in videogames, famous musicians are creating soundtracks for them and fashion giants such as Balenciaga are setting up exhibits of their clothes in game engines. Communities of particular videogames stretch beyond continents and provide friendship groups, solidarity and support systems for millions. The organisation Games for Peace has even demonstrated how gaming can bring torn communities together, in this case young Israelis and Palestinians. Videogames are therapeutic for children with chronic illnesses, and they can improve preschoolers' motor skills and help individuals with dyslexia.[60] Some studies have even shown that first-person shooters can improve players' eyesight.[61]

Artificial intelligence – almost certainly the future of most technology – also shares a long and intimate history of evolving alongside gaming. While AI is currently mostly used for graphics efficiency, non-playable characters or enemy behaviour, the future of integration of AI in games may affect not only their content, but also how they are made. If not opposed, the tools will be utilised in game production, with entire departments replaced by AI bots that instantly generate desired work with a few commands. This is an upcoming labour issue that will require adaptation and creativity from the newly formed global videogames industry trade union movement.

Recently, dodgy financial speculators also flooded gaming zones with non-fungible tokens (NFTs) and other crypto schemes, scamming many in the process. The economies of many popular videogames are lamentably filled with encouragements to gamble, amid various shades of fraud, deceit and tactics that prey on customers. The FIFA World Cup Qatar 2022 demonstrated the consequences of depoliticising an entertainment medium for too long, leaving it to metastasise into a corruption machine that cannot be stopped and costs numerous lives. Arguably, games already produce such an outcome, with the aforementioned production of devices necessary for games hardware. What nefarious, unchecked repercussions can be awaiting in this industry, which morphs into new phases and stages every few years?

Videogames are everywhere – in people's living rooms, in their real-life and digital ad space. More passively, they are also propping up many side industries that contribute to the current neoliberal order. Within that, there are also wonderful pockets of resistance. These range from union organising to studios forming themselves into cooperatives, and are manifest in games so eclectic, elegant and thought-provoking that they surely provide a respite from the homogenisation of culture. Despite the efforts to strip the soul from this artistic medium, serving only the darkest parts of our society, game makers continue conjuring up pieces that reimagine how lives could be lived.

Level I: The Theme

The history of videogames production has always been mired in politics but, for most, one aspect of politics here seems to overshadow the rest. Digital games are perceived as primarily a representational medium; crucially, mainstream media prefer to fret over the content, the theme of games, as opposed to focussing on how they are made. Gameplay footage tells a speedier story than the context for these depictions. Critics rarely pass up an opportunity to scrutinise and sensationalise the distasteful narratives of average videogames, the crude and hackneyed characters in anime digital trends and the brazen mechanics of shooter games.

Communities that support them, which are examined in Level II, provide their own, often more inventive, interpretation of these concepts. The mechanics or, as some researchers would describe it, the ludology of a game, present a whole other dictionary for analysis. Just as the editing techniques of the legendary French–Swiss director Jean-Luc Godard are assigned political meaning, simply through his use of jump cuts, games too consist of design systems, mechanics and interfaces to instil affect.[1]

As long as a narration, a plot, is key to describing a videogame
and its moral or ethical values to the masses, this inability to look
beyond the theme infantilises the medium, warps the capacity for
critique and, as a result, weakens the prospect for making more
sophisticated games.

Upon its release, the creator of *Super Columbine Massacre RPG!*
(2005) was dragged through the mud for depicting the violent
aspects of the shooting in a game so soon after the 1999 tragedy.[2]
The game was not refined or subtle; at times, the killing aspect was
explicit, and the graphics seemed crude. It felt juvenile and jarring
for a game that deals with such a serious issue; and the attempt to
humanise the perpetrators – risky. Still, Danny Ledonne's main
objective was to create a piece of art that utilised games to understand the thought process of the killers and society's reaction to
their crime. Flashbacks, haunting audio design and gameplay
tricks luring the player into making uncomfortable choices are
all thoughtfully curated to produce an unsettling, multifaceted
societal critique.[3]

Ledonne, himself an avowed loner subjected to intimidation and
bullying when he was young, felt an urge to understand where the
point lies when one crosses from normal life to the dark side. After
seeing the 1971 film *A Clockwork Orange* and hearing of the school
massacre, Ledonne reflected on how close he had come to becoming
like the shooters: 'It was a bit scary, once I learned more about these
boys, because it was like I was looking in the mirror and I didn't
want the same fate for myself.' He began taking martial arts classes,
studying film and seeing a therapist. He graduated from school with
high grades and was voted Most Likely to Succeed by his peers.[4]

The release of *Super Columbine Massacre RPG!* a few years later
nearly destroyed Ledonne's life, as he was publicly vilified and
rejected by gamers, artists and activists alike, many of whom had
probably never loaded up the game and experienced its depth of

soul-searching, exploration of atonement and commentary on the American media landscape. The game's creator was inundated with hatred for daring to touch the theme. The game was banned from traditional envelope-pushing industry events, and Ledonne was accused of fetishising and profiting from the Columbine tragedy. A piece of art that would have probably received acclaim if it had been executed in any other medium proved to be too controversial as a videogame. As the prominent games critic Ian Bogost pointed out in his book *Newsgames: Journalism At Play* (2010), two years before the release of *Super Columbine Massacre RPG!*, Gus Van Sant's film *Elephant* (2003), a fictional account of a school shooting inspired by Columbine, won the Palme d'Or at the Cannes International Film Festival.[5]

At the other end of the spectrum, games that feature powerful women or cute objects are hailed as a progressive victory, ignoring the sometimes militaristic undertones of the women heroes or the deeply conservative nature of ostensibly wholesome narratives. Deconstructing videogames purely on their narrative risks losing much of their civic and cultural meaning, yet this is the space that commands most public interest. Violence, sexism and other politically charged meanings become the primary lens through which the products are viewed. Although this is only the first layer of necessary enquiry, its potency and weight in the discourse dictates that it become the first obstacle we encounter in our journey.

To progress to Level II of this book, readers must be capable of answering the following questions. What are the limitations of considering politics in games through the consideration of narrative alone? Can violence in videogames ever be progressive? Are more powerful women characters the answer to sexism in videogames? Can anti-colonial videogames even exist, given the current modes of production? How are game creators widening political literacy through the stories they write, and is it working? Just how much correspondence exists between players' political affiliation and the politics of the media they consume? And can that relationship be changed?

Violence

Most parents will avoid encouraging their kids to game, presumably due to the fears about the influence of violence on young minds. Many progressives sneer at gaming spaces, seeing them only as vulgar digital products where macho men enact their most brutal fantasies or, even worse, project them onto real life. Railing against gaming is a cyclical event that often occurs when attention to the medium is most concentrated. This suspicious characterisation, although for the most part misguided, is not entirely misplaced. Politicians, wishing to signal some basic care for the well-being of families, denounce videogames and call for regulations on how games are packaged and sold. Notably, though, in almost all the instances of attackers professing to be gamers, it was the player communities of the cited title that encouraged the actual violence, not the games themselves.

Relatively innocent compared to the games of today, violent videogames were developed even during the time of very primitive graphics. Spaceships downed each other, tanks collided and aliens prepared to colonise the Earth, even in a very low count of available pixels. *Mortal Kombat*, launched in 1992, pulls no punches – broken bones, gore, pools of blood and scenes that are brutal to the point of exhibitionism glamorise violence. Governments around the world rushed in to condemn the game and attempt to ban its sale.[6] Meanwhile, movies with similarly violent content were becoming cult classics.

But this assumption that we have to judge games by their violent properties requires a closer look. A competitor game to *Mortal*

Kombat, Street Fighter II, was released around the same time with analogous fighting game mechanics. However, its community members challenged the idea that they were there for the violence. Other aspects of the game were of greater interest to them. Professional fighting games players report that an aesthetic of a game, namely that two individuals are engaged in a virtual fight, fades away as soon as they begin to take the battle seriously. All the player sees and perceives are hit boxes – the invisible rectangular space inside and around the character that determines and represents whether an attack was successful or not. Characters with larger hit boxes are more vulnerable, but stronger. Smaller hit boxes mean weaker characters who are substantially nimbler and speedier. It is the battle between the two hit boxes, rather than the aesthetic of their characters, that is of significance here. Yes, the design of these characters and their interactions employs over-the-top shock-value imagery, but for the players who spend the most time with these games, all of that becomes invisible.

Similarly, *Under Ash* (2001), created by a Syrian games studio, invites a rethink on whether the presence of violence or the purpose of it is more significant. The game sheds light on the Israeli occupation of Palestinian lands, also through the strong use of violence.[7] The player takes the role of Ahmed, who, through the course of the game, progresses from throwing rocks at Israeli soldiers to destroying Israeli military positions with real weapons. The design of the game's use of violence tells a story, too. It is very easy to be killed; hence, the game is actually very hard. If the player shoots a civilian, the game ends automatically. In the end, similar to the reality for Palestinians living with the existing imbalance of power, it is not possible to achieve victory. The goal here is not education or a bid to inform or project a meticulous moral judgement; rather, the game is a cathartic, fantasy-fulfilling exercise.

There is nothing inherently evil about the mechanic of shooting or hitting. After all, videogames in which the main character is invited to shoot Nazis or other baddies are rightly revered. What is of significance, then, is the identity of the body receiving the blow or the bullet. Here, the direction many game creators have taken is clear. Sadly, many of them hold abhorrent views that justify or positively encourage game themes which subject already marginalised and brutalised populations to violence. Women, racialised characters, and entire demographics that are deemed expendable in life are violently killed off to advance the hero's storyline.

Historically, comic books, television and hip-hop have all been unjustly blamed for inspiring violence. But, in contrast with other media, games offer an opportunity for truly enacting certain manoeuvres, actively pursuing the objective of destruction, rather than merely observing it. Instead of being a target of the projection, a videogame player becomes an actor in it. Despite this property, numerous studies have shown that violent videogames do not intensify a player's relationship to violence. However, it would be naive not to acknowledge the games' ability to be the perfect tool for someone to indulge an earlier desire for a violent action.

Virtual violence in isolation is not necessarily a radicalising force. One can play the most brutal shooters (guilty as charged!) and retain a sense of empathy, or even find it strengthened. How boring would the arts be without violence! The Viennese Actionists in the 1960s used violence in performance art to underline the desperation of the human spirit. Damage and visceral pain were moulded into poetry. The American artist Chris Burden had himself shot in a white cube gallery. The English artist Jeremy Deller orchestrated a lavish re-enactment of the Battle of Orgreave, a violent confrontation between strikers and police that occurred in

1984 during the UK Miners' Strike. Violence in the arts is a necessity, but how it is sold must be closely examined and, in certain cases, regulated. When used as a tool for terrorising already marginalised populations, the content is hateful and must be called out as such. But when violence in a piece of art is handled with maturity, it has the potential for bringing about sublime experiences.

The indie game *Hotline Miami* (2012) became a sensation upon its release. This high-octane, top-down-view shooter did not refrain from depicting blood and violence; even in its minimalist pixel-art graphics, gore was ample. Spoiler alert: there is even a nuke at the end of this intense and surreal action game about the fight against the Russian mafia in Florida. The game is also laced with extraordinary, melancholic, exquisitely produced music, and offers rich character development.

Hotline Miami exposes the banality of violence, instead of glorifying it. In isolation, violent imagery may be perceived as an instinctive reactionary tool, unless engaged with by the right people, of course; but artistic decisions can also turn this inherent gore into a tool for reflection. Few things illustrate this better than a simple comment on a YouTube video of one of the songs from the score of *Hotline Miami*:

> My eyes were drawn to a random gangster I had shot earlier, lying still on the floor in a pool of his own blood. He was clutching his chest and, despite the pixel graphics of the game, I could tell that his face was scrunched up with an expression of agony. I took a second and wondered; who was this guy? What was his name? Why was he a part of this gang? . . . Then, I realized that I had done this very thing to about thirty-five other gangsters just a few moments ago. I finished the level after that, but I didn't feel happy or victorious after I shot the last enemy; I felt awful. I still absolutely love this game to death, but goddamn, I still sometimes think

about all of the people that you have to kill in order to complete just a
single level of it.[8]

All this underlines that we must continue to challenge and question
the purpose of violence in a given videogame. If violence is an apparatus to further entitle people in positions of power – imperialist state
militaries, fascists, misogynists and so on – then as with to all reactionary propaganda, it must be called out. But otherwise, violence
should not scare the progressive left. There is a lot of it in the
world, and more of it will come our way before we feel like we're
winning. While videogames are a space for escapism, they do not
have to be sanitised of the discomforts of life to be radical or politically useful. One can be sure that the political right will employ
the gaming space for any and all themes; instead of blindly censor-
ing violence, we must come up with egalitarian alternatives.

Misogyny

Another depressingly correct suspicion of videogames is that most
of them are sexist. It turns out that when horny, lonely game devs
are given free rein on how women should be depicted in their
games, if at all, their assumption is that other lonely, horny men
will only buy games that present women in a disparaging or
sexualising light. The Tutorial describes the methods by which
women were essentially pushed out of the tech and games industries for a good while.

This expulsion allowed for the festering of sexist portrayals of
women; they were hardly the target consumer audience here, any-
how. As per the stereotype, there are indeed abundant examples of
misogyny in videogames – women NPCs (Non-Player Characters)
in tiny bikinis who can be brutally beaten and murdered by characters or, alternatively, saved from danger – only by muscular

strong men, of course.[9] Women characters until recently had no representation other than subordination and a need to be rescued.

Countless franchises, such as *Grand Theft Auto* (1997), *Dead or Alive* (1996) and *Duke Nukem* (1991) share brazen misogynistic attributes. These games contain endless references to fellatio and lesbian sex (not for queer audiences), and dress women in underwear thin as dental floss. The depictions often border on the surreal – the women's breasts are so large that they have entire animation physics systems dedicated to them, their improbable bounciness calculated to look just rubbery and elastic enough to not seem liquid. Of course, mechanics exist for men characters to slap said breasts.

The one-sidedness of the gender portrayal cannot be overstated. A famous meme illustrates this beautifully. An astonishingly muscular Black man is wearing a hat that conceals his eyes and a white cape that covers most of his oiled-up body, except for his torso, pubic area and thick thighs, which are covered in stringy lace. His abs are so defined, one could grate cheese on them. A penis half the size of the model's arm is sheathed in white silky fabric and tied with a string. The text above the picture reads, 'If male video game characters were dressed like female characters'.[10] Needless to say, male characters are not often sexualised in this way in videogames. Heterosexual men game devs would never.

Sexist videogames and their success send a message which, in effect, asserts ownership over the entire medium. Enthusiasts of games without explicitly sexist elements, such as *Halo 3* (2007) or *Fortnite* (2017), exploit the chats systems to communicate misogynist views just to repel non-men gamers from joining these spaces. The message that videogames are not for girls is thus entrenched, even when sexism is only in the heads of the people playing rather than in the games themselves. According to studies, in game chats, women are subject to three times more derogatory or offensive remarks than men receive.[11] Many women gamers report that they now prefer to simply hide their gender online, a move rarely reported by men. The bullying experienced by LGBTQ+ players is undoubtedly even worse – homophobia and transphobia are devastatingly rampant among gamers.

This dynamic further seeps into the way the industry carries itself overall – scantily clad 'booth babes' are a common sight at many gaming conventions, and reports of scores of sexual harassment incidents still plague the industry. It's a closed circle – as long as videogames are sexist and their public relations exude misogyny, women will not want to be part of the industry. All this is changing for the better, but very slowly and with various degrees of success around the globe.

The trends and structures of sexist videogames are horrifying, reflecting the worst of humanity. Even people who know next to nothing about digital games can tell you one thing: for the most part, and until relatively recently, videogames were a boy's world. Instead of listing examples of these egregious practices, I prefer to dig into the reasons for and results of such tendencies.

Many credit the Proteus effect when explaining the inclination of swathes of game players to act out their misogynistic fantasies online. The term describes a phenomenon whereby, within the walls of a virtual world, individuals inhabit the characteristics of their avatar. Borrowing its name from the shape-shifting Greek god Proteus, the effect theorises that this online personality switching is the result of an assumed expectation by other users of the virtual environment towards the avatar. So, if the avatar that the gamer has adopted is a buff, emotionally unavailable macho guy, then their actions are likely to reflect that stereotype.

A recent study investigating the relationship between avatar design and real-world behaviour supports the existence of the

Proteus effect. The study compared the appearance and behaviours of avatars in the virtual world of *Second Life* (2003) to the reported real-world behaviour and appearance of their users. It found that participants who had designed their avatars to be more physically attractive also reported engaging in more confident and extroverted behaviour when interacting through their avatars, in comparison to their typical real-world selves.[12]

Seemingly, then, people go into titles with already existing prejudices and simply have an opportunity to enact their desired tendencies without guilt. That, of course, shifts the responsibility to game makers to avoid providing platforms for destructive acts, to create limitations for certain behaviours. In a study conducted by Edgehill University in Lancashire, England, researchers concluded that game studios should consider implementing systems that encourage more constructive, cooperative forms of social interaction among players, such as allowing players to collaborate on tasks while still remaining part of their said groups. The authors propose that such set-ups would mitigate the negative and aggressive attitudes frequently expressed towards women players.[13] Perhaps through this encounter with other players, and with a suitable representation of themselves, gamers could engage in self-actualisation and, by extension, exhibit kinder behaviour. The task, then, is design, not narrative.

As more marketing executives woke up to the lack of women characters (and potential women customers) in videogames, an effort was made to bring some 'bad-ass', brave women into the casts. Yet the results were at times less than politically affirmative. The authors of a phenomenal book on videogames and capitalism, *Games of Empire*, point out the following:

> The new mainstream game 'sheroes' are corporate – military professionals, death-dealing, punishment-absorbing exemplars of . . .

women that kill – avatars for an era of a female national security adviser and an equal-combat opportunity US Army. The protests of 'Girl Games' and 'Grrrl Gaming' had been captured in the virtualities of imperial feminism compatible with militarised capitalism.'[14]

The quintessential example is *Tomb Raider*'s Lara Croft, a figure that crops up in every piece examining the burgeoning representation of women in games. Sure, she may be a woman, but that is just one of her characteristics; the others are much more problematic. Her daddy issues compel her to visit a number of the world's archaeological wonders. Somehow, after thousands of years of existence, these historical sites are destroyed as a result of her stopover. This descendant of an aristocratic family ferries herself around the world, asking for help from poor indigenous people, who almost always certainly meet their death. Not exactly a progressive hero to emulate.

Similar typecasting was given to Chun-Li from *Street Fighter* – an expert martial artist and Interpol officer who relentlessly seeks revenge for the death of her father at the hands of M. Bison. Tifa Lockhart from *Final Fantasy VII* (1997), another strong pin-up shero, runs after Sephiroth, who became her archenemy for murdering her father, Brian Lockhart. One can guess the writers' gender from these storylines. In the mid-2010s, women were typecast again as traumatised, self-centred teenagers, as portrayed by *The Last of Us* (2013) and *Life Is Strange* (2015). Violence against women is a vestige of women's historic status as property: a product of the division of society into exploited and exploiting classes. Far from solving the historic inequality of women, capitalism incorporates violence against them into its business practices and its imperialist military strategies. It is unambitious and politically ambiguous for women to support the exact same systems.[15]

Only quite recently, and entirely thanks to the energy of creators of marginalised genders, have we begun to enjoy videogames with women characters who are complex, flawed and empathetic. The protagonist of *Dead Pets Unleashed* (2022) is a woman named Gordy, trying to manage her punk band and life in her early thirties. In *Immortality* (2022), a story about the demons of Hollywood reminiscent of the work of David Lynch, actress Manon Gage puts on a tour de force performance in the role of Marissa. In *Night in the Woods* (2017), Mae, a twenty-year-old college dropout, deals with the effect of economic stagnation in Rust Belt America. We have come a long way from the egregiously sexualised, dumb female characters in other videogames. Not that there are fewer of those – as the videogames industry expands, the breadth of characters is simply expanding, too.

There are still plenty of two-dimensional sex symbols to choose from, they are just not all that exists. Trans characters such as Birdo in *Super Mario Bros. 2* (1988), Tyler in *Tell Me Why* (2020) and Lev in *The Last of Us Part II* (2020) are allowed to simply have their story play out, without their gender identity driving the narrative.

Lately, though, videogames have pushed the envelope on expectations of more diverse characters. In 2023, critics lined up to praise the third episode of HBO's *The Last of Us*, a TV adaptation of the famous videogame, featuring a gay couple named Frank and Bill. Set in a post-apocalyptic, fungal-infection-ridden world, the game portrays a passionate, but fraught relationship between the two, with Bill being particularly unlikeable. The TV show, however, wishing to positively represent these characters, went for a sort of Romeo and Juliet story, with little friction apart from the circumstances Bill and Frank found themselves in.

Although the two scripts had the same writers, they felt that TV audiences would struggle with a more nuanced approach to gay characters. All this underlines the way games are now entering a truly mature chapter in their existence where, depending on which direction we press the industry to take, they can either concentrate the vilest impulses of our society or provide a space for experimentation and make a real positive difference in pop culture. The goal is for complex and empathetic characters to become mainstream, not just part of progressive games. Pushing the Overton window wide open is important.

Colonialism

Perhaps less discussed in the mainstream media, but no doubt very visible to the players themselves, are the racial and colonial undertones of many games. The birth and expansion of this digital space is intimately linked with the perspectives – or, more to the point, the limitation of perspectives – of the creators and audience of the Global North. The United States in particular tends to dictate much of the political tone in games. Videogames have seen it all: violence, expansionism, orientalism and outright racism, laced with jingoism, the white saviour complex and straight-up state imperialist propaganda.

Numerous small, independent far-right productions tout white supremacist and Nazi paraphernalia or attract game communities building fascist monuments in existing, massively multiplayer online games. But racism in games is not just a phenomenon on the margins: multi-million-dollar franchises, backed by major corporations, are also more than content to peddle similar narratives.

The scholar Stefan Schubert reminds us:

Video games relate to constructions of empire narratively – as it is broadly understood – in a number of ways, and this is often how they most obviously engage with the topic: series like *Age of Empires* (1997–) or games like *Empire: Total War* (2009, part of the *Total War* series) signal this interest already in their titles, and the way in which such strategy games, and others like the *Civilization* series (1991–), represent the history of colonization and imperialism is highly significant for judging whether they assume a critical, postcolonial stance on their subject.[16]

A 2009 study analysing the portrayal of racial identities in videogames revealed that the racial depiction of characters largely resembled the demographics of the game development industry, which is predominantly composed of white men. Until recently, African-American men were depicted accurately only in games simulating real-life sports leagues. In contrast, African-American men in non-sports games tended to be shown as gang members or individuals living in poverty.[17] Latino, Hispanic and Asian characterisation in games is also plagued by tropes and often gives these characters little to no agency.

Outright white supremacy and casual racism are peddled by major franchises, such as *Call of Duty 4: Modern Warfare* (2007), *Resident Evil 5* (2009), *Gears of War* (2006) and *Grand Theft Auto: Vice City* (2002). In contrast to films or other artistic media, the racism evident in these worlds is barely critiqued. The profits roll in with minimal scrutiny. Freedom of speech is certainly a worthy principle, but more often than not, this argument is used simply as an excuse or a means for inflicting a violent rhetoric on marginalised communities. As usual, money talks first. There is not a particularly interesting story here – the game creators know which side their bread is buttered on and are attempting to match the games' politics with their expectations of the audience. When game budgets are so large, challenging the audience with a progressive agenda is seen by many as a money-losing exercise. Recent surveys by Deloitte and other large consultancy agencies, which are beginning to make their mark in gaming, suggest there is profit to be made from inclusiveness, so things are changing.

As in the case of of misogyny in games, it is often even more useful and interesting to dissect games that are attempting to present a more complex picture, often failing in the process. Consider *BioShock Infinite* (2013), the last of the first-person shooter trilogy *BioShock*, which has earned a spot in the history of videogames for merging clever combat mechanics with a sophisticated plot. The first two instalments of *BioShock* took place in the underwater city of Rapture, a place with pristine art deco aesthetics and Norman Rockwell–style paintings building an eerie, enthralling atmosphere. *BioShock Infinite* moves the action to the floating steampunk city state of Columbia.

Institutional racism and elitism are widespread there, embodying the essence of American exceptionalism. The conflict arises between the Resistance and the ruling class of Columbia, culminating with the leader of the Resistance, a Black woman called Daisy, threatening to kill a young boy. This is a plot twist heightened by a liberal, centrist ideology – both sides of extremism are to blame. Instead of framing the conflict as one between oppressor and oppressed, the white ruling class somehow gets to keep the moral high ground, as they are merely ruining the lives of a mass of children rather than ordering the elimination of one. Daisy is then killed by the protagonist Elizabeth – a white woman. Another twist awaits – in fact, Daisy arranged to have Elizabeth kill her in order to teach Elizabeth to make hard decisions and because she may have not survived long after the revolution anyway.

In the end, Elizabeth's growth, her story, is the more significant, while those of Daisy, the Vox Populi resistance movement, and the liberation of Columbia's subjugated people are of lesser importance. The white hero's path and her mounting strength trump any collective anti-racist effort. This is a failure of storytelling, but also of game design, which relies heavily on the established hegemony of a singular hero – an individualist who destroys, manipulates, conquers and accumulates power – gameplay habits dictated by a form of imperialist ambition plaguing many game devs.[18]

The self-proclaimed progressive wing of the game development community is not itself free of semi-colonial tendencies. In early 2010, Lucas Pope, a white American independent games developer, noticed that he felt uneasy going through passport checks in airports. He thought this would make a fun game! The result was the 2013 hit puzzle simulation game called *Papers, Please*, which sold around 2 million copies in three years (5 million copies by 2023), bringing huge revenue and fame to the sole developer.[19]

The gameplay of *Papers, Please* involves assuming the role of a border agency officer in the fictional country of Arstotzka. The player is invited to scrutinise the documents of various individuals seeking entry into the country. The task is to identify expired or fraudulent documents and other irregularities in the migrant's paperwork. The overall aim of the game is to illustrate the often-mechanistic bureaucracy involved in determining life-or-death outcomes for many people in real-world border control situations. While the game's intention to shed light on modern border control practices is commendable, it ultimately ends up preaching to the converted, and may even be deemed self-congratulatory. The game was catnip to the liberal class of the videogames industry – an indie game with political undertones! It wiped the floor at pretty much every games awards ceremony that year.

The UK continues to proudly implement harsh border controls and operate detention centres that have been accused of human rights abuses, such as Yarl's Wood, Harmondsworth and Dungavel. The British government's appalling treatment of migrants arriving on the country's shores is well known, but their plight did not feature in Lucas Pope's speech when collecting his BAFTA. In fact, Pope made no mention of his subject matter at any point while on the accolade-collecting tour. Pope had spotted a theme that earned him millions, yet he made little to no connection with the real-life devastation caused by these issues during the promotion and publicity of this game. Some critics have suggested that Pope was not consciously making an overtly political game, so it should not be judged as such. This heightens our suspicion of such practices: creators are universally acclaimed precisely for their edgy, antagonistic thematics, but when challenged, they choose to take a more apolitical stance in order to appease potential buyers of the product.

The danger of falling into mediocrity when making 'politically engaged' games is enormous. It is not sufficient to claim that a work possesses anti-racist and anti-colonial content while blithely using these forces yourself. Instead, creators must actively evaluate their own practices and their connection to oppressive systems in a genuinely just manner.[20] Of course, it is almost impossible to achieve such ambitions, since videogames rely entirely on technology that perpetuates brutal exploitation in the Global South. I long for a day when political games don't stop at merely critiquing the status quo but provide tools for destabilising it.

To be generous, *Papers, Please* can incite a sense of guilt and empathy through its mechanics of moral dilemmas. As the game progresses, the player is faced with decisions such as whether to allow an immigrant with incorrect documentation through, potentially risking the entrance of a terrorist, or accepting bribes to provide for the player's own family. The narrative here suggests a commentary on individual and systemic responsibility and action.

However, humanising the plight of a border agency official also suggests a certain shedding of responsibility. Such institutions, like the police, thrive on corruption, and the border of Arstotzka is not inefficient or flawed, but rather a prime example of how such systems are designed to function.

Few people in the gaming industry are honestly prepared to acknowledge that one of their primary rewards is a sense of superiority, particularly when associated with the status of being a 'political' game developer. Producing actual cultural or social change can be much harder and more isolating.[21] As such, self-prescribed artistic practices calling for social change may fall into the category of mundane preaching, leaving the player feeling guilty rather than empowered. In the worst case, they may be co-opted and used to endorse oppressive structures and ideologies.

The practice of shedding such narratives from videogames is beginning to grow. In a recent conversation published as 'How to Design Games That Promote Racial Equity', Lai-Tze Fan, Kishonna Gray and Aynur Kadir 'consider responsible theories and methods towards racial equity, racial justice, and anti-racism in game design'.[22] As well as hosting a conversation helping people grasp the intricacies of these issues, the scholars also released a handbook, *How to Not: A Guide to Avoiding Worst Practices*, which offers advice to game makers on pursuing anti-racist game design. Together, they facilitate a network of creators learning from each other about how to design games in a manner that is inclusive, but also, crucially, not ashamed to revisit and reiterate. One exercise consists of going through various perspectives and asking how different populations would receive the narratives they are designing. Gray explains that

Black Card Revoked (2015) is rooted in mainstream Black culture and knowledge [which] epistemologically is really recognized in the game.

I brought it into a classroom and a white student talked about the fact that they felt at a disadvantage to playing the game but, after sitting with the discomfort, realized that this game doesn't have to be for them. That student used it as a learning process and enjoyed learning about Black culture from the game and the people in the space with them. *Black Card Revoked* is an example of designing a game by us, for us, but it's also a way to educate other folks about Black culture.

Similar to the representation of women in games, stories from and about characters who do not fit the usual 'hero' story are crucial, made even more powerful when negating, or moving beyond, the imperialist fantasies of conquest and pillage as a source of power. In 2015, the British studio The Chinese Room's *Everybody's Gone to the Rapture* depicted the experience of a Black lead character in a small English village. This is only a small part of the devastating post-apocalyptic plot, but the game captures beautifully the minutiae and mundanity of the everyday racism experienced by the protagonist. *Pentiment* (2022) by Obsidian Entertainment also achieves something unusual. The writers conducted substantial research to recreate the true diversity of sixteenth-century Bavaria; Ethiopian missionaries and Jewish characters play a role in the tapestry of the cast here.

In 2021, the indie sensation *Hades* also offered a brilliantly diverse Mount Olympus. Both Athena and Eurydice are Black women, with Eurydice's Afro styled with tree branches and leaves. Dionysus is of South Asian descent and Hermes is East Asian. *1870: Cyberpunk Forever* (2018) by Santo Aveiro-Ojeda, an indie title that received rave reviews, asks fascinating questions about the aftermath of colonialism. Numerous BIPOC game creators, such as Michelle 'Missy' Senteio, Derrick Fields, Cara Hillstock and Andrew Augustin, are developing much-needed games reimagining the audience and the purpose of videogames in an industry so often built by white people for other white people. Even the largest franchises are now adding an option to change the hero's skin colour, something that was unheard-of as recently as the early 2010s.

Still, it will take much more than diverse characters and storytelling for games to truly shed their colonialist impact and practices, especially in the manner of their making. Moreover, the bulk of the white supremacists organising in gaming are purposefully targeting abstract massively multiplayer games, meaning that the fight to get rid of racism in games must go beyond themes and narrative.

Escaping Political Narrative

Videogames occupy an odd space; they are the most influential and profitable entertainment strand there is, but at the same time they are exempt from any serious cultural criticism. The liberal media overall treats gaming as an infantilised space with a negligible impact. The Met Gala, the Oscars and the discourse around the latest tour of a pop star receive many more headlines. This, in effect, creates a vacuum and a vicious cycle, where gamers and game makers feel misunderstood and fall deeper into their own exclusionary languages and alienating subcultures. But challenging this dynamic seems like a very tall order when the general adherence to the cross-pollination of games and politics is mostly confined to the previously mentioned discourses. Political narrative, or the lack thereof, continues to play a crucial role in our understanding of gaming, even when it is not overly offensive.

Multiple subgenres of politically inclined games also exist. Sometimes they educate players about a particular historical or political event – *1979 Revolution: Black Friday* (2016) fits the bill. Sometimes they're satirical, like *Liberal Crime Squad* (2004), or derivative – war survival simulator *This War of Mine* (2014) leads the charge here. Then there are games that value simplicity and relaxation and purposefully avoid conflict and tension. That, in itself, signals a certain political stance. There is no escape: even the rejection of politics is political.

An online event titled Wholesome Direct, showcasing a burgeoning genre known as 'wholesome' games, has attracted tens of thousands of viewers since 2021. Wholesome Direct also sparked an active online discussion about the goals and limitations of wholesomeness as an artistic practice. In case the name is not self-explanatory enough, here are a few examples from the event: a puzzle game set against the backdrop of a rainy afternoon, with a lo-fi soundtrack and Bob Ross-style paintings (*Behind the Frame*, 2021); a girl running around a warm-toned pixelated world completing tasks with animal companions (*Yokai Inn*, 2021); and even a game in which the player simply takes pictures of cute dogs (*Pupperazzi*, 2022). It is easy to see the appeal of these games. Cute animals, cosy tasks and warm pastel colours are the standard fare of this subgenre.

Wholesome games represent an entirely justified sentiment of resistance against mainstream gaming products, so often marketed towards adolescent white men with an interest in violence and competition. We should be glad that now thriving spaces exist for game developers concerned with different audiences, and that their aesthetics are now being celebrated. After all, how many more exhausting, grimy, frustrating post-apocalyptic games can we really handle?

But the concept of wholesome escapism warrants examination. 'Cute' here is equated with the good, positive and democratic; the ethos is reminiscent of the cults of *hygge* (the Danish word for 'cosy') and positive psychology, which may seem grotesque and unattainable to anyone experiencing increasing material anxieties or the erosion of actual freedoms. It is understandable that game makers would wish to stick to safe, sanitary and accessible themes when crassness, complication, intensity and awkwardness can be classed as punishable crimes.

The inbuilt contradiction in wholesome games' desire to represent a sort of 'games for good' comes into sharp focus when, halfway through the Wholesome Direct stream, the presenters introduce their appeal to donate to the International Rescue Committee – an organisation that helps victims of global humanitarian crises, including in the Democratic Republic of the Congo. This region is gravely affected by conflicts related to the mining of the minerals needed for electronic hardware, including those used for playing wholesome videogames. Needless to say, the connection was not mentioned, and the brutal irony of the situation appears to be lost on the organisational team of Wholesome Direct.

In the art world, the term *kitsch* refers to aesthetic qualities that are cute, quirky and sentimental, rather than controversial or unsettling. Some might argue that all videogames can be considered kitsch, as they are mass-produced commodities that often prioritise accessibility and appeal over intellectual or mechanical challenge. However, critical practitioners of kitsch in the art world, like Takashi Murakami and Jeff Koons, have used this aesthetic with self-awareness and an understanding of their art's place in the larger cultural context. In contrast, the wholesome games movement seems to lack this self-reflection, and it remains to be seen if it will be able to produce a digital equivalent to Koons's work.

As Liz Ryerson, musician, writer and theorist of the videogame industry, notes,

> Wholesome Games come out of the same collective lack of imagination that AAA game tropes come from. Either we have to have meaningless violence as mass spectacle, or we have to be pure and

stripped of anything too troubling. It is two sides of the same coin. They are both unchallenging! People want to read 'conservative' as politically conservative and not as 'without risks and defined by market trends', which is also what 'conservative' means.[23]

It is important to recognise that, while games can provide temporary escapism and relief from everyday stress, their true potential lies in their ability to foster solidarity and promote learning and activism. By focussing on creating wholesome, meaningful experiences, the videogame industry has the opportunity to make a positive impact on the world. However, it must not shy away from feelings of discomfort, irritation, struggle – all of which are often a reality for people closing themselves into the digital realms.

Chasing Utility

Finally, games can reach beyond their echo chambers when they are consciously designed for educational purposes, especially when they purport to be politically useful. Examples include titles that centre on political events or assign particular civic functions to them – to inform, research and present information in innovative ways. The practice is nothing new. *Tax Avoiders* (1982) was a title that garnered praise when it was released on the old-school Atari 2600 console. Currently, small-scale propaganda games often accompany any election or other significant political event. While games are mostly crafted with moralistic or grotesque stories, this final grouping of political games seeks to effect civic change by curating information in an inventive and surprising fashion.

In 2003, in preparation for the US presidential primary elections, the campaign for progressive Democrat Howard Dean presented a novel way to send a message: *The Howard Dean for*

Iowa Game. The purpose of the first-ever official game for the US presidential election was to encourage people to participate in pre-caucus campaigning in Iowa and other states. The game clearly did not move the needle enough to secure Dean the nomination (ultimately John Kerry won the Democratic nomination but lost the election to Republican George W. Bush in 2004), but it was a good example of diversifying the methods for reaching an audience.

Institutionally, left-leaning activists may have been too slow to recognise gaming as a space for political negotiation and dissent, but these dedicated projects prove that they were always there at the margins. Still, while the political right has had tremendous success in moulding much of how the games industry is understood and organised, the left has yet to gain similar influence, even with its own propaganda games.

Election games vary in form. Most often, they are constructed to stage comical encounters between politicians, while also informing the player of the policies of both sides. In *Corbyn Run* (2017), the player is cast as Jeremy Corbyn, the British Labour Party's socialist leader at the time of the game's release. The player's task is to chase the Conservative politicians Boris Johnson and Theresa May and the ghost of Margaret Thatcher, who are attempting to stymie the player's run. How long can you escape these attacks? In more ways than one, as Corbyn found out, not for long.

Bernie Sanders, the progressive senator of Vermont, also commissioned a game for his 2016 primary campaign against Hillary Clinton. *Labour – Elections 96* (1996) invited Israeli players to control a jet fighter piloted by the politician Shimon Peres in order to change poll results in different cities. It's an entire industry now: Persuasive Games is an Atlanta-based consulting company developing tools in persuasive game design as well as titles worldwide that would fit the category. The efficacy is still debatable – while presenting information through a variety of methods makes sense, just how much these games actually change people's minds remains to be researched.

Videogames have also been found useful in the realm of digital humanities. Stella Wisdom, digital curator at the British Library, talks about collaborating with game creators to bring historical documents to life. Pudding Lane Productions, mostly staffed by students at Leicester's De Montfort University, crafted an interactive environment of London before the Great Fire in 1666, based on the detailed street surveys and maps by John Leake. These visualisations include the Old London Bridge, which existed between 1209 and 1831. There are also modular houses with different tops, middles and bottoms that can be arranged in various manners to assemble very different-looking streets.[24]

In 2014, a team of three students from the University of South Wales crafted a virtual reality experience of rebuilding Fonthill Abbey. There is no trace left of this once-stunning Gothic revival mansion, as it was demolished in 1845 after the collapse of its gigantic ninety-metre tower. For this digital reconstruction, the game makers used detailed illustrations of the building from the British Library.[25]

Although the mainstream associates videogames with mental health issues for their tendency to cause addiction or induce isolation, research has shown that games can also work as a form of therapy. One example is the *SPARX* (2012) videogame, developed as a treatment for depressed adolescents. The acronym *SPARX* stands for 'Smart, Positive, Active, Realistic, and X-factor thoughts,' crucial for combating depression. The study included 168 adolescents, with an average age of fifteen, who were suffering from depression.

Half of the participants received 'treatment as usual', typically consisting of five one-on-one counselling sessions, while the other half played *SPARX*, a fantasy game in which players created avatars to eliminate 'negative automatic thoughts' and restore balance in the virtual world. Each level of the game educated players with facts about depression, strategies for managing intense negative emotions, and relaxation techniques. The results of the study were particularly promising for the group that played *SPARX*, as 44 per cent of those participants fully recovered from depression, while only 26 per cent of the control group were no longer depressed.

PlayMancer (2009) was a project funded by the European Union aimed at creating a videogame to treat specific mental health conditions, including eating disorders and impulse control disorders. The game, called *Islands* (2009), introduces players to an interactive scenario with the goal of improving their emotional self-control skills and helping them manage impulsive behaviours. A team of clinicians, engineers and programmers designed the game based on the needs and emotional responses of the target patient population, as well as their personality profiles.

Short-term effects of the game have included the development of new coping strategies for managing negative emotions in response to everyday stressors, more generalised patterns of improvement, and increased self-control when faced with challenges. Crucially, the game has been found to be highly patient-friendly, with 85 per cent finding it comfortable to use for these purposes. This high usability may make it more likely that certain groups of people, variously resistant to other forms of mental health treatment, may work to improve their mental health by using the game.[26]

Multiple studies reveal a variety of benefits of gaming. Videogames are therapeutic for children with chronic illnesses, and improve preschoolers' motor skills.[27] They can reduce loneliness among older people, and they help doctors refine their dexterity and develop their knowledge of anatomy.[28] Computer games help dyslexic kids to read and can even alleviate pain.[29] The uses and benefits of games, especially when developers set their eyes on this goal, are vast, and specialists are only beginning to tackle the potential utility for the body and mind. Gaming is a potentially persuasive medium that can have many civic implications. Yes, the theme of the game can be hugely instrumental here, but this is only one element of the connections between digital gaming and real-life outcomes.

Beyond Representation

There are limitations and even pitfalls in hoping that representation alone will achieve all victories, that if only games were endowed with a certain theme or mechanic, they could be rehabilitated as instruments for change. In fact, this idea formed the basis for two prevailing schools of thought dominating the games academic discourse. Which is more important: narratology (roughly, the plot) or ludology (roughly, the gameplay)? The framing of this argument already reveals a lot about the type of stakeholders involved in defining the rules of game studies, and indicates a certain politics through what it excludes. A more critical perspective would involve a study of production and marketing elements. The efficacy of social relations, of which play is a fundamental part, can only be reflected, then, by paying attention to the circumstances in which they are situated.

To that end, framing games studies as pivoting only between narrative and mechanics exposes a dissonance with the world outside the enclosed spaces of games media and parts of games academia. So much of how a game is played, perceived and utilised for ideological means depends on how it is located in the commodity market, meaning that its proprietary value, accessibility and marketing techniques can have an infinitely more significant role. Anthropological, ethnographical and, crucially, material methods of games research are emerging and ought to be encouraged.

Still, for people less versed in the intricacies of how video-games are situated in global class relations, judging a game in terms of its overarching themes is a predictable and popular approach. Doubtlessly still influential, and capable of providing insight into our social reality, the subjects of games are more varied every year. At the same time, games marketers are more insistent on classifying them within a specific genre. Whether a first-person shooter (albeit with a moral story about the shooter), a role-playing game (albeit with a surprising location), a racing game (albeit with a character arc for the driver) – games sell better when they stick to familiarity.

This circularity of what is permitted or what is deemed to be unprofitable (and hence not given the production time and resources to be achieved) both classifies games and gives them stringent limitations. While noticing more intricate stories with more complex characters and granular settings, we also observe a distinct stratification.

The late academic Mark Fisher wrote extensively about the narrowing of culture and, by extension, pop culture, and his findings can most certainly be applied to videogames. Under a consolidation of political systems (i.e., semi-democratic state market economies), the boundaries for citizen expression are predefined, reducing the plurality of cultural expression as well.[30] By retaining a definitive outline within which creativity is pursued and articulated (in this case, IBM- or NVIDIA-chipped Microsoft or Sony machines), we are forced to curtail our imagination and, by extension, our ambitions regarding the conditions of our collective livelihoods. So games convey the notion that all significant ideological debates have concluded, portraying politics as mere administrative tasks. If economic discourse is off the table, the focus inevitably shifts to allocating the leftovers.

This is not to fetishise abstraction, which can also lead to inter-pretations formulated by the powerful. However, an upsurge of abstract tendencies is not a current problem for gaming, whereas its reliance on aesthetic tactics tends to underline, overexplain and align ideologies according to the consumer base. This impulse should be interrogated, if only to encourage better techniques of propaganda for egalitarian ends.

Avant-garde art, art that challenges, surprises and is unortho-dox, implies possibilities and the urgency of social, political and economic reform. Instead, many games are conservative and formulaic, a source of stability for the status quo. There would be little wrong with that if the medium were not actively harm-ful while also dependent on the processes of destructive forces. But non-challenging structure coupled with nefarious modes of production leave a lot to be desired. These problems must be addressed if games are ever to serve a broadly egalitarian agenda.

Even the voices of resistance, games that are made with the best of intentions and actively support the mental and physical well-being of numerous groups of individuals, are still commodities under the capitalist mode of production. And, as discussed in the Tutorial, games are especially susceptible to becoming dependent on fundamentally antagonising logistical tools.

Focussing too much on the content may leave us feeling helpless, overloaded with imagery, overstimulated and incapacitated as to how to change the conditions enabling that imagery. There is an overwhelming feeling, rooted in much of our everyday experience, of being stuck in the prison of digital baroque.[31] Powers beyond our control are pumping dozens of immaculate, high-octane images into our daily existence at an incomprehensible speed. This makes us feel disorientated and leaves little space to consider action beyond spectacle. Just as the overwhelmingly baroque and rococo styles were chosen to reflect the interests and desires of the ruling classes, much of today's digital depictions also fight for our attention. Jean Baudrillard assists here:

> It is often said that the West's great undertaking is the commercialization of the whole world, the hitching of the fate of everything to the fate of the commodity. That great undertaking will turn out rather to have been the aestheticization of the whole world.[32]

Baudrillard was of the view that 'we have lost the secret'. Everything is said, everything is exposed; everything acquires a meaning and nothing is said at the same time. To borrow Marshall McLuhan's gospel, not only is the medium the message but crucially – the selling is the message.

We do not have to be sceptical to this extent, but it is important to underline that advocating for decentralised, democratised and egalitarian systems can only take place when the actors fighting for these goals are themselves engaging from within democratised and decentralised systems.[33] We must update Baudrillard's critique to account for the vertigo of the internet and other vast digital realms.

As an old punk at heart, I am also conflicted – what about the incredibly explicit punk aesthetic, our brash, loud pronouncements of our politics? We were clad in pins and patches signalling our political beliefs. I felt at home at political punk gigs and benefit concerts for various causes, organising anti-fascist events under various banners. Following my critique, are these worth little, too? The crucial difference must be at the level of the mode of production, as always. At its most visceral and material, the best of punk is executed by DIY means, reaching for something authentic. What would that mean in games?[34] It would mean repurposing existing objects by withdrawing them from the commodity market and changing their aesthetic to something anti-thetical to the habits of consumption.

Mods, free games and non-commercial projects created with free software such as Bitsy and Twine all come close to that ideal. It would involve the creation of games to be played on devices built under decent labour conditions, with components that did not cost lives in the Global South. It would somehow publicise that it did not rely on the internet, with servers owned by asset management firms who landlord our communication networks. In this particular age, I can hardly imagine how all of that might work, but this has to be our ambition. (Of resonance in this framing are the words of liter-ary critic and theorist Fredric Jameson: 'It is harder to imagine the end of the world than the end of capitalism.') Anything less does not a decolonised videogame make, and influencers who attempt to claim the contrary are only building their own social capital. To be clear, I'd absolutely love to play a Tatar farm simulator of my grandfather's bee hives in the Urals Mountains, but I also know that currently it would not be the most efficient method to tell his story and would not honour the anti-consumerist ethos he lived by.

Jen Pan, in her video essay for the magazine *Jacobin* brutally titled 'Why Liberals Lose Their Minds over Hollywood Movies', brilliantly encapsulates the deliberate and limiting choice of focussing on representation above all else. She points out how tempting it is to call the recent burgeoning of diversity in Holly-wood products a political win. After all, when we control so few of the actual outcomes of our lives, observing victories in pop culture may indeed feel empowering. Pan cites two novels that arguably prove political pop literature can bring about mate-rial change: *Uncle Tom's Cabin* (1852) by Harriet Beecher Stowe, and *The Jungle* (1905) by Upton Sinclair. She then reminds us that these cultural artefacts were in fact complementary to the political struggles of the time, rather than instigators of them.

Neither Stowe's nor Sinclair's books themselves catalysed political change or led to the creation of new movements. Rather both novels came out of political movements that were already underway. The abolitionist movement in the case of Stowe and the socialist movement of the early twentieth century in the case of Sinclair. Cultural production can only ever complement, not stand in for the work of politics.[35]

Pan then aptly quotes the political scientist Adolph L. Reed Jr: 'Nothing could indicate more strikingly the extent of neoliberal ideological hegemony than the idea that the mass-culture industry and its representational practices constitute a meaningful terrain for struggle to advance egalitarian interests.'[36]

The interests advanced are usually ones reflecting what already exists; real political victories are harder to achieve and involve real risk. These critiques must be applied to videogames, or should at least be addressed by self-described political videogame makers. At best, the authors should stress that their work broaches only the themes that can be tackled due to practical political organising. At worst, the exploitation of certain themes, while offering little to no material help to the people who live in that struggle, should be seen for what it is – a marketing ploy. The message of the director of the *Crazy Rich Asians* (2018) franchise, who claimed, 'It's not a movie, it's a movement,' illustrates the need of the liberal class to envisage emancipatory politics within representation, even if it is one of obscenely rich individuals, who in all probability acquired that wealth through the oppression of individuals of the same race but lower social-economic rank.[37]

On an institutional level, however, it seems that games will continue to receive support predominantly for their themes, while their other special traits continue to be ignored. The storytelling aspect of games seems to be the safest bet in securing future investment from parallel industries, too. The success of *The Witcher* (2019) adaptation for Netflix and the critical darlings that are HBO's *The Last of Us* (2023) and Amazon Prime's *Fallout* (2024) are helping gaming reach the final frontier – Hollywood.

In the public sector, narrative is also valued seemingly above all else. Cultural heritage organisations in the United Kingdom, for instance, have divided their support for games into the following categories: the Victoria and Albert Museum is interested in the art and design aspect of games; the British Film Institute is focussed on film and animation; Tate Modern on digital art; and the British Library on narrative and storytelling. One can pin the highest hopes on the Tate here, as it is most likely to next investigate some lesser aesthetic parts of a videogame, such as mechanics, communities and impact, but, to date, they have done nothing with the field.

Videogames have promising political uses, but their current limitations must be clearly outlined, if only to abolish them soon. Games critic and writer Samantha Greer, mostly known for her exploration of the marginalisation of working-class voices in the games industry, released a poignant video on YouTube reflecting on the scope of empathy in computer games. 'Games Are Not Empathy Machines' investigates the lessons to be learnt from *The Last Guardian* (2016) – an action adventure game centred on the relationship between a little boy and a half-bird, half-mammal creature who becomes his companion. Greer concludes that the narratives of videogames are mirrors.[38] If a player possesses qualities that lead them towards empathy, then, with most probability, they will feel it. If not, empathy for the characters in game will fail to materialise. Games with an intrinsic political theme can be evaluated in a similar fashion – other properties must be mobilised in order to achieve a change in consciousness, rather than just supporting an already existing inclination.

The idea of games as mirrors is supported by studies, too. One conducted in Germany from 2012 to 2015, with 824 participants, found no correlation between the amount of time spent playing videogames and sexism.[39] The study, which followed a theory called cultivation, did not, however, demonstrate that sexism is not present in the gaming industry and culture. Certainly, most popular games depict women in a stereotypical or sexualised manner, and sexism is a common issue among players, particularly as experienced by women players. There must be another power that turns people into political actors. The theme is imposed by the creators, but what the players themselves do with the games can become much more subversive, creative and, at times, dangerous.

Level II: Communities

The year was 2015, and I was in my safe cocoon of an anarchist lifestyle – political struggle day and night, more tranquil, private moments of partying and gaming in between. I fell in love with an English lad who was moving to London at the time. Like me, he also found temporary housing security through squatting. I was a political person with a niche interest in gaming. He was a fighting games influencer and YouTuber, known online as TheoryFighter, with a lefty heart.[1]

We started exchanging thoughts, ideas and life experiences, and an entire world opened up to me. It was TheoryFighter who first told me about the Goonswarm versus Band of Brothers struggle in *EVE Online* (2003), probably with some Polish beer in hand, during a cosy bohemian street drinking session in Hackney Marshes. As clearly as I can identify, this was the moment that broadened my conception of what gaming spaces are capable of. And opened my eyes to the possibility that all of us are living in a reflection of the customs of these spaces.

To those who have not spent years in it, *EVE Online* appears like a glorified spreadsheet. Playing this space-themed MMORPG (massively multiplayer online role-playing game) involves a lot of counting and organising while dispensing a finite amount of resources among the characters within the game. Set more than 21,000 years from now, when Earth's resources have been exhausted, *EVE Online* imagines humanity seeking to colonise the rest of the Milky Way. Players control a fleet of ships, the size and powers of which depend on the skill and social or material capital of each player.

However, by the late 2000s, this monetary inequality became glaring. While some players were investing tens of thousands of hours to upgrade their fleets, others took a short cut by acquiring in-game enhancements with real-life money. The so-called Band of Brothers was a small group of spaceships that used the latter tactic – outsourcing, or straight-up buying, power over the virtual environment – and soon dominated the galaxy of *EVE Online*. A group of poorer, but more skilled, players grew fed up with this dynamic and began scheming and coordinating on ways to reverse this trend, which they believed had wrecked the game.

In 2006, thousands of these players formed the group Goonswarm, and commenced an epic battle against the Band of Brothers. It took an incredible amount of gameplay, unity and coordination, but eventually Goonswarm secured the victory in this modern David and Goliath story. The destruction of the Band of Brothers' virtual fleet cost its players around $6,000 actual real-life dollars.[2]

The key to Goonswarm's success was their number, their anonymity, and their inventive communication techniques. Their members infiltrated the private forums of the Band of Brothers, leaking information to their teammates and sabotaging any counter-attacks. Their large numbters and dedication to the mission allowed them to gain the upper hand over their affluent adversaries. The turning point came when the chairman of Band of Brothers, Haargoth Agamar, defected to Goonswarm because he, by his own account, preferred the group's more horizontal organisational structure. To add to the beauty of this marvellous act of resistance, it thoroughly undermined the business plan of the game's developer – CCP Games. The company had introduced microtransactions to boost profits, a move seriously challenged by this legendary fight.

Such activities by gaming communities exhibit the potential for game spaces to be sites of political expression. Unlike the narrative imposed from above by the game maker, the actions of communities are self-defined and self-motivated and reflect the active will of hundreds, sometimes thousands, of players. This expression adopts many different forms: explicit political organising in games, consumer organising, cooperative disruptions and online meetings where players enact various functions in real life. This constitutes, perhaps surprisingly, an activation of otherwise passive individuals into political subjects.

Advancing to Level III will require readers to examine how and why players regularly behave as publicly engaged beings. What are some key examples of civic engagement in games? Why is it barely recognised as a form of political expression? At a time of general political malaise and nihilism, what is it about videogames that ignites a sense of belonging and what makes this space ripe for meaningful action? What is the spectrum of this expression, and who controls of it?

Some of us recognise our role as consumers in videogames and learn to effect change as active entities in this role. Having achieved our goal or enjoyed trying, we move on to attempting to affect real-life politics. Some succeed; in other instances, the results are devastating. From in-game experimentations with various models of self-organisation to political actions and straight-up radicalisation, the intensity and techniques represent an assortment of aims. While players like me simply admire clever storytelling tricks and engage in relatively basic sportsmanship, other players were creating entire civic systems in game. Sure, some of it arose from a spirit of competition, but as I started digging into the world of gaming communities, it became clear that much of it lay somewhere between power grabbing and seeking a sense of belonging. And if those are not politics, I don't know what is.

Gamers as Civic Entities

While some players assign political meaning to gamer communities, many do not. In fact, many participants in the epic Goonswarm versus Band of Brothers fight might shrug or even shudder to hear their struggle described as reflecting leftist tendencies. Gamers do gamer stuff, they would retort, and it's nobody else's business. Nonetheless, many of them engage in activities that are altruistic, such as coordinating and agitating; they canvas, form and self-select into distinct factions. MMORPGs provide a platform that is abstract and relatively light on narrative which can become a rich space for self-expression, civic or otherwise. There, consciously or unconsciously, players compose slogans and languages that mimic existing power structures and the struggles between them. In an age of fears over declining civic participation and a widening gap between governmental bodies and the people they are meant to represent, it is fascinating to observe populations building communal structures and experimenting with various forms of management and administration, all this voluntarily!

Similarly to *EVE Online*, *World of Warcraft* (*WoW*) is another massively multiplayer online game that is hugely popular. It is home to an array of groupings with their own traditions, expressions and forms of unity. For almost twenty years, it has captivated audiences with its huge, lore-rich universe, plentiful customisation and progression options and epic high fantasy, including mythical creatures and diverse kingdoms. Famously, the game contains the Horde and the Alliance, which have a long history of conflict – the player is thrust into being a soldier in battle, looking for associates to gain the best result. The relationship between the two powers are grounded in complex loyalties, according to the game's lore. But even within those flowing communities, distinct organisational formulas emerge.

In his YouTube video 'DKP Is Market Socialism', the artist and streamer Joshua Citarella explains in detail how *WoW*'s virtual loot system, called dragon kill points (DKP), demonstrates a level of sophisticated horizontal trading that should be analysed and admired by progressive thinkers. A standard *World of Warcraft* raid involves forty or so players attempting to defeat a boss together. Once defeated, the boss usually throws only some four or five collectable items, not easy to share among dozens of players. 'So the guild is tasked with the distribution of scarce resources among a group of angsty nerd rage gamers. Each player is a worker in a cooperative system of a guild, it incentivises playing the best and sharing the loot equally,' Citarella says approvingly.[3]

Fifteen years of practice, habit, and care have turned these presumably chaotic groups of digital participants into members of some of the most trustworthy, horizontal and fair mass economic distributions in existence. Some guilds democratically appoint 'loot councils', who represent the players and make decisions about resource distribution. Other guilds assemble themselves under elite clan monarchies that keep the spoils. Some decide the beneficiaries of the loot with a dice roll, but these groups are often unstable, and the tactic rarely yields winning results. None of this is suggested or encouraged by the game creators (Blizzard Entertainment); all these structures come from the players themselves. One can only conclude, therefore, that in the proven economy of *World of Warcraft*, reciprocal altruism, cooperation and an equal distribution of wealth results in the most consistent victories and player happiness.

Another example of gaming communities organising for a single issue is the 100th anniversary commemoration of the armistice that ended World War I, in the online first-person shooter *Battlefield 1* (2016). Players coordinated to temporarily cease their eternal hostilities at 11 a.m. Australian time on 11 November 2018 – exactly a century after the Allied powers and Germany ended fighting on the Western Front. The gameplay footage depicts something truly and strangely powerful – a huge battle on a beach between dozens of people, with explosions and bullets flying in every direction, and then . . . nothing.[4] Peace.

The players observed a moment of silence, remembering those who fought in the real battle. This kind of ceasefire could never be officially mandated by Electronic Arts, the game's publisher, because their business model relies on the agreed ceaselessness of war and on customers endlessly duking it out across their privately owned perpetual battlefields. But the players themselves had no such obligations. In typical gamer fashion, however, the two-minute period of eerie silence was shattered by an opportunist launching an attack from a plane.

A sense of collective coming together, of this beautiful, sensitive melancholia, was also recently displayed by the China-based players of *World of Warcraft*. After a licensing dispute between the US developer Blizzard and its local partner NetEase, it was announced that the game would go dark in China for good at the end of January 2023. 'It was not just a game. It was also the memories of a whole generation,' a Chinese player wrote.[5] In its more than fifteen years online, some had given their entire lives and built their entire livelihoods on the platform.

In the final moments when the servers were available online, the stages were filled with devastated, yet crucially, hilarious and kind players, all collectively commiserating in chat, while their virtual avatars were gathering, shooting out sparkles and fireworks and, most heart-wrenchingly, gifting each other expensive and rare items that would have taken years to obtain.[6] It was the last carnival of a group of friends who had seen each other through so much – weddings, birthdays, divorces and funerals.

Numerous stories exist on the internet forums describing how groups of players finally met IRL, after having spent years playing together online. Mostly, they are joyful stories and sometimes utterly tear-jerking. This was the case with Joe, who in 2018 finally met the five pals he had gamed with for the past five years. After hearing about his diagnosis of Ewing sarcoma, they all met at a New Jersey oncology clinic. Speaking to the BBC, one of Joe's friends, Davi, said: 'Wet played pretty much everything. Even if we weren't playing games we would be just hanging out talking about anything. We just hung out like we had done it a thousand times before.'[7]

In *Elite Dangerous* (2014), another player with cancer was trying to reach a Dove Enigma station. He wished to make this his last journey. As he was getting near it, he found that the station had been taken offline. Some troll had exploited a glitch that made it possible to shut down stations by overloading them with unknown artefacts. But when a bunch of gamers found out about this, they all got together and beamed meta alloys, an item that counteracts the interference. So, the station was brought back in time for Brandon Keith, the cancer patient, to reach it before his passing.[8]

This game is also known for its crew of Fuel Rats, a dedicated group of players who spend thousands of hours catching up with other players stuck in the outer regions of the game's universe and delivering fuel to them. There are also beautiful stories of gamers organising in-game funerals, vigils or just hype campaigns for their playing colleagues who are struggling, shooting little beams into the air in solidarity or engaging in other kind-hearted theatrics.[9]

After player organisation for gameplay purposes comes the consumer protest. Players can utilise game mechanics to convey their frustration with the game's developers and publishers. By demonstrating a threat to their profits – the only language the CEOs of most gaming companies understand – gamers can bring about real change, affecting the course of a company or sometimes even an entire industry.

Ultima Online (1997), one of the first MMORPGs, suffered persistent problems upon launch, having amassed hundreds of thousands of subscribers within its first six months. A year into the game's existence, players organised a 'peasant revolt' to protest the unrestrained killing of novice players, lagging servers, lost progress and catastrophic world crashes. During the action, scores of serf avatars invaded the virtual castle of Lord British – the character created and voiced by Richard Garriott, self-made millionaire and creator of the game, who was investing vast sums of money into the game to maintain his advantage. In an exhilarating display of chaos, destruction and the joy of protest, the crowds of gamer protesters virtually drank their master's wine and ate his food, danced naked in the halls and vandalised his chambers, while loudly airing their grievances in the chat.[10]

Archived screenshots from this protest look like a surreal, beautiful mess – much like many real-life protests – and its organisers should be hailed for their innovative usage of the new medium. The power imbalance, the fact that Lord British got to rig the rules of the game simply by virtue of his wealth, turned what could pejoratively be called a mob into class warriors. Deliciously, this also sent a message to the developers – the huge corporation Electronic Arts – that the players would resist the company's reliance on in-game currency for financial gain.

In another instance of disappointed players taking things in hand, Chinese players of the MMO *Fantasy Westward Journey* (2001) were not pleased with what they perceived to be its pro-Japanese sentiment and content. The stakeholders of the game had been recently bought out by a Japanese company, which sparked nationalist distrust among the players. The administrators then locked the account of a player with an anti-Japanese username, who was also the leader of an anti-Japanese guild with 700 members. On 7 July 2006 – the anniversary of the beginning of the Second Sino-Japanese War – an astonishing 80,000 players simultaneously mounted what is perhaps the biggest political demonstration ever held in a virtual world. Since there was no active real-life conflict taking place, it is hard to conclude that this was anything more than a consumer protest; but it also clearly demonstrates how early networked game players were able to bring nationalist views to this burgeoning medium. Predictably, the action attracted little to no interest from groups studying the development of nationalist ideologies away from the screen.[11]

While some types of consumer activism are lauded by liberals, it is generally overlooked when undertaken by gaming communities. Twelve-year-old Maddie Messer, a fan of the hit mobile game *Temple Run* (2011), noticed that it was free to play as the default character, Guy Dangerous, whereas playing as a girl character cost extra. Not cool, Maddie thought, and she decided to publicise it. The *Washington Post* agreed to publish her complaint, which was retweeted by people at the *Financial Times* and then reached the creators of *Temple Run* – Imangi Studios. To Maddie's delight, and no doubt to clear up the PR mess caused by her complaint, the developers emailed her that same day, confirming that they would make the Scarlet Fox character free. They also promised a cast of diverse characters in the future.[12]

In another expression of protest towards a game creator, Russian players of *The Sims* spoke out loudly against the developer Electronic Arts's decision to comply with the law passed by the Kremlin regime, outlawing any mention of what is deemed to be LGBTQ+ propaganda in the country, by turning off the ability of same-sex individuals to marry inside the game. The slogan #WeddingsForRussia was endorsed by many gamer communities on Twitter, and an online petition attracted over 10,000 signatures. The protest worked, and EA announced their decision to market the 'My Wedding Stories' game pack unaltered to their player community in Russia.[13]

With the progressive politicisation of gaming communities in the wake of Gamergate, players on the left are attempting to effect real-world change. In this nascent stage of lefty gamer activism, the preferred technique thus far is boycotts. In 2023, swathes of internet communities campaigned for a reduction in sales for the *Hogwarts Legacy* (2023) action role-playing game, in response to the franchise author J. K. Rowling's transphobic views and the antisemitic tropes portrayed in the game.[14] The social online pressure to not engage with the game was so strong that mainstream gaming media outlets, such as IGN and Kotaku, were running their reviews with large disclaimers about the politics of the game, or outright refused to review it.

Where were these activists when the new *Call of Duty* was released? Where were they during the glamorous launches of one Islamophobic videogame after another? Why am I seeing so few calls to boycott *Atomic Heart* (2023) – a game created and funded in Russia during its invasion of Ukraine, which glorifies the imperial violence of the Eastern Bloc? Why are we not collectively skewering the huge investments into gaming by Saudi Arabian princes, or other dictatorships?

But I recognise I am seeing the glass half empty. In practice, we are witnessing an increase of left voices within the gaming space and of progressive activism in the industry. One boycott turns into many boycotts, and that fuels political awareness and the drive to get involved in action with higher stakes. Instead of playing an ever-satisfying game of whataboutism, I am choosing to celebrate this collective political awakening. Culturally, the *Hogwart's Legacy* protest had clout, with many media outlets following and reporting on the community's refusal to buy the product and urging others to follow. Monetarily, it was less effective – the game recouped the expenses to its reported $150 million budget in the first week of release, hitting a $1 billion revenue three months after its launch.[15]

Techniques such as review spamming, public shaming and boycott have, after all, been weaponised by the right for quite some time, with equally limited success. *Buck Up and Drive!* (2022), an innocuous driving game inspired by arcade classics, offended some whose experience of the game was apparently affected by a few Pride flags on the side of the digital track. An attempt at lowering the game's review scores failed when the game creators pushed back and justified the flags. The subsequent media coverage ensured a wave of positive reviews, protecting the game's status on the all-important Steam game publishing platform.[16]

Still, this is another example of gamers organising politically to effect change beyond the game's own walls. The question of what is a useful political action can sometimes grip the left to the point of paralysis. It took many of us too long to recognise the rebellion of the summer 2011 rioters in the UK as a righteous cause against systemic racism, not just an angry, violent mob (as the media described it at the time). Protests in digital playgrounds are in these cases way less consequential – incurring none of the brutally harsh sentences meted out to protesters in Tottenham and elsewhere that year – but their methods are equally misunderstood. The aesthetics of protest can be varied as well. What constitutes its righteousness or usefulness must be calculated, taking into account the reasons for protests, the power balance, the aim, and the technique. A Gamergater is closer to a 2021 Capitol rioter than to an *Ultima Online* looter, who is closer to a Tottenham rioter, who is closer to an anti-fascist demonstrator.

Gamers Turning into Actors

Besides organising within games, players also organise en masse to effect change outside of the game arena, without explicitly declaring or perceiving themselves as political agents. Let's touch briefly on three cases – review bombing, charity streams and Gamergate – before diving into the depths of a fourth one, the 2021 GameStop short squeeze.

The attempt to rally conservative forum members online into leaving negative reviews for the game *Buck Up and Drive!* is a classic case of the practice known as review bombing. This tactic is commonly used by gamers to express their disgruntlement with aspects of a game or the politics of its creators. Average user review scores matter a lot – digital distribution services like Steam and the Apple App Store are the main avenues for game sales, and their design highlights aggregated user review scores much more prominently than other metrics, such as reviews by professional critics. Moreover, their algorithm employs user review scores to choose which games to promote on the store's front page. So, a successful review bombing can seriously harm a game creator's business.

For many gamers, this is their first experience of activism, such as it is. Forming into large affinity groups, strategising on tactics and implementing them is something gamers are good at – in-game, structuring themselves into an outward-facing online force comes relatively easily. Affinities and networks built in games, with their own language, 'memeology' and traditions, can spill out of game chats and forums and into very tangible, material consequences on the outside.

On the positive end of this spectrum, gaming communities are responsible for some of the largest fundraisers online. A 2022 charity games bundle raised more than $12 million for the victims of the war in Ukraine.[17] Games Done Quick – a fascinating organisation of gamers who play on live stream and attempt to get through a game as quickly as possible, sometimes by the ingenious use of glitches – have raised nearly $100 million for the Prevent Cancer Foundation. Jingle Jam, which focuses on the mental and physical well-being of young people, has raised more than $40 million for charities over a decade.[18] These are just a few of hundreds of such endeavours, not to mention the thousands of individual Twitch and YouTube streamers who have their communities raise large or small amounts for various causes all the time.

On the darker end, one can find #Gamergate and similar gaming communities, who instigate and support what amounts to acts of terror while still claiming to be apolitical. The Verge ran a brilliant piece outlining the themes of some of Ubisoft's games, which their executives insist are politically neutral. The themes include an island compound in the South Pacific owned by a rich tech CEO, who made his fortune through autonomous drones and AI; a rogue group of former US soldiers, Mexican drug cartels and huge civilian populations destroyed by US-government special agents; a white supremacist–glorified Americana takeover; and a Washington, DC–based shooter in which the player is tasked with clawing back control of the capital's government buildings. The community's response to these games was predictably reactionary. 'Not political', insisted Ubisoft's spokespeople.[19] Strangely and for obviously different reasons, this denial was a distorted mirror of the views held by many self-proclaimed progressives.

There are many stories online of girlfriends and mums who have witnessed their partners or sons become radicalised to right-wing communities in the wake of Gamergate.[20] No doubt these men already harboured poisonous opinions, but crucially, in Gamergate they found a community that justified those thoughts.[21] Members of the Gamergate community gathered in online forums such as 4chan, where they formed an identity out of geek culture and resolved to protect it, perceiving diversity in games as a threat.

At the time, the Gamergate movement was walking a tightrope, calling their campaign a consumer protest against what they regarded as ethics in games journalism. They demanded that media and creators alike not 'politicise' games, while at the same time using starkly political language and methods that extended into real-life action. The 'leave politics out of our games' crowd was, in fact, highly politicised.

Huge communities met on spaces like 4chan and grew up together. These message boards are filled with requests for brotherly advice and mentoring. Technological advances have barely reduced the working week and, in many cases, made it more all-encapsulating. Widening class inequality forces many to work longer days, leaving them lonelier and more alienated. Communication devices provide the easiest method for social encounters. Patriarchy and other prejudiced belief systems underpin these forums, the opinions shared by a majority curdling into the extreme when members meet enough like-minded souls.

Progressive ideas countering this extremism are innovative and require change. If put forward by only a very few people, these ideas can hardly compete. So forums like 4chan, reflective of broader trends, have simply become spaces where individuals can find unfettered support for their darkest instincts, having to prove themselves with the most exclusionary attitudes. The left can sometimes neglect giving personal advice for a call to action for the many, and individuals can fall through the cracks, forming into masses at the bottom. The GameStop short squeeze phenomenon of 2021 provided an opportunity for a rambunctious, productive and, once again, outward collaboration between these communities.

The relationship between the internet cesspool of 4chan and the videogaming communities is a complicated one – people who are 'very online' congregate around these forums, looking for like-minded souls. If someone spends so much time on their computer that they reach these depths of the internet, it is safe to assume that the activity they are engaged in online is gaming. Sure enough, 4chan is filled to the brim with gaming memes, much more than with memes on books, fine art, music or literature. Many of the original internet memes can be attributed to videogames, such as the mother of all memes, 'All your base are belong to us'.[22]

The short-squeezing of GameStop made sense in the logic of these spaces. GameStop is an American brick-and-mortar video-game shop chain, the largest of its kind worldwide. As the world of media, games included, moves rapidly into digital distribution, physical storefronts like GameStop suffering financially. GameStop's demise was predicted by major capitalist conglom-erates, Goldman Sachs among them, who began investing in bets against the company. The COVID-19 pandemic only accelerated its seemingly inevitable fate. However, the gamers had other ideas.

The subreddit WallStreetBets, self-described as '4chan finding a Bloomberg Terminal', is a congregation of 4chaners with bank accounts (or, more accurately, with Robinhood accounts) which the app utilised for the short squeeze. In mid-2019, investor Michael Burry, of *The Big Short* fame, had acquired a 3.3 per cent stake in GameStop and wrote to the company's board of directors, urging them to buy back shares due to identifying overlooked value in the company.[23] The guy who predicted the 2008 subprime crash and made billions from the mainstream banks' collapse was urging the company to invest in its own shares? That was enough to pique interest, and the Canadian activist investor Ryan Cohen joined GameStop's board in January 2021 with a 9 per cent investment.[24] This was the key to triggering the stock rally.

Hundreds of Robinhood account holders, organising on Wall-StreetBets, decided to jump on this 'troll with potential'. Artificially inflating the price share of GameStop was a golden cocktail of righteousness, opportunity and banter; it also offered the chance of profit. They were sticking it to the big guns of the traditional financial market, sending a financial crisis their way. Crucially, it was, in the view of WallStreetBets, very funny. A fictitious campaign of money and power utilising the sort of absurd, egregious procedures that usually cause financial disasters such as the 2008 crash, working for the benign purpose of saving an early millennial shop.

Mainstream media outlets were running meme-filled live feeds reporting on the hot frenzy of investing by regular folks. From the outside looking in, the picture was that of a beautifully formulated, hilarious direct action, getting one up on the corporations while creating enormous profits for the players of the game. Regulators eventually barged in to introduce an extraordinary ban on Robinhood trading. This fuelled further indignation and the impression that procuring money through stock trading by a mass of average Joes is somehow illegal, though the big trading conglomerates are allowed to demolish each other in such exchanges all the time.

The aftermath and the impact of this financial and media phenomenon was, in the end, a sad one for the little guy. WallStreetBets broke the page view records due to the short squeeze, receiving 73 million page views in twenty-four hours.[25] It became the fastest-growing subreddit at the time. The community surged by more than 1.5 million users overnight (to a total of 6 million members) on 29 January 2021.[26] Millions wanted to get in on the action after reading the accounts of people who had invested in GameStop early and were urging others to join (increasing their profit in the meantime). At the peak of the trading, this effectively defunct business was worth over $30 billion: as much as the hugely profitable videogames conglomerate Electronic Arts or the leisurewear giant Adidas. It wiped out billions from sophisticated investment management firms, notably Melvin Capital and Citadel LLC, and the former shut down operations entirely in May 2022.[27] Executives at GameStop cashed in $22 million in stock, greatly increasing the personal wealth of the board of directors.[28]

Although the short squeeze was initially believed to have been instigated by individual investors, it was later revealed that large hedge funds played a significant role in the market activity revolving around GameStop and its associated securities. Wall Street's giant asset management firms, such as Morgan Stanley and BlackRock, reaped massive profits from their holdings, as well as by lending stocks to short sellers.[29] Institutional investors had a significant hand in the trading activity related to the short squeeze. The internet ended up littered with heartbreaking stories of the meme-affected latecomers who bet their life savings and lost most of them to the large funds in the process. The house always wins.

The choice of the name Robinhood for the platform alludes to the mischievous legendary character who took money from the wealthy and distributed it to the poor. There's a reason why. In the McCarthy era, there were calls to ban Robin Hood from the schoolbooks for perceived communist connotations. The self-righteous use of this rebellious imagery, pitting David against Goliath, is remarkably effective, even among individuals who espouse socially conservative views. Co-opting a figure that was indeed rallying against the capital-owning class to make him a 'disruptor' who not only fits within the capitalist means of production, but enhances their worst traits, is a tactic all too familiar to seasoned activists.

The speed and deceptive nature of the GameStop short squeeze illustrate how an influencer class of the subreddit sold a profit-making exercise as the communal experience that so many are craving. As the media reported on this financial meme, probably themselves lost in the weeds of the numbers and the strange language of it all, they convinced many, myself briefly included, that some sort of redistribution of wealth was taking place. The idea that a small group of gamers was taking on the big guns of capitalism was a story too good not to tell. The reality, however, was the opposite of the myth of Robin Hood.

Gamers as Activists

Gamers are transforming themselves into political subjects in a variety of ways and with differing levels of intensity. They forge in-game alliances, invest in advancing their allegiances, and sometimes turn that energy into attempting to influence the architects of the platforms that occupy them. Bolstered by their successes, or simply having found a community in what is an increasingly alienated world, they direct their powerful swarm towards real-life issues and subjects.

In December 2018, a *World of Warcraft* player wrote a post on the game's official web forum titled 'When Did the WoW Community Get So Political?'[30] The post itself reads: 'It's on Guild Chat, it's on Trade Chat, it's on Group Chat. It seems everyone is complaining whatever is headlining that week or going back to the old classics like Feminists, SJW or Political Correctness. What is going on?' In the hundreds of comments underneath this post, passionate players offered their explanations for the politicisation of the game, blindly refusing to acknowledge the political subjectivity they have had all along.

Games are now bursting with politics. Some expressions are subtle and have more to do with self-organisation, but increasingly, these spaces are filled to the brim with people of varied ideological beliefs. That is a lot of kinetic energy available to be directed and charted. In contrast to members of the right, who are fully awakened to this fact and are engaged in active manipulation and exertion of that energy, the left is late to the party. Individuals doing the serious political work for social change – electoral politics, non-governmental organisations or organic, alternative forms of activism – are apt to rule games out of the realm of progressive activism. Some nerds, possibly in their parents' basement, typing away on their keyboards in order to move animated pieces in the virtual world? The aesthetics may seem less than inspiring, but to disregard this massive activity and dismiss its potential eliminates a powerful tool and limits the left's range of tactics. After all, the same techniques are notoriously used for political activism and gains on the opposite side of the political spectrum.

The ability of gaming communities to form into potent political groups is well noted by the neoliberal forces that build them. This swarm of consumers, enticed by the possibility of changing the world beyond their favourite game, is a powerful tool for shaping policy.

In Brazil, influential industry figures understood that power. So, when in 2017 a bill was proposed to regulate multibillion-dollar esports, the stakeholders knew that their one means of resistance was the crowd. In 2019, the #TodosContraPLS383 campaign ("All Against Bill 383") began trending, driven by regional gaming influencers and led by their employers. The new policy threatened to create an official association to supply the kind of governance and compliance found in real-life sports. Citing fears of a reduction in future investment, the profiteers of Brazil's multibillion-dollar games industry rallied the industry actors and the players them-selves to oppose the legislation.[31] The hashtag began appearing on social media and the streams of regional gaming stars. The lobby-ing and the pressure succeeded in delaying the ratification of the bill until its final approval in mid-2023 by a new left-wing government led by Lula da Silva.[32] Admittedly, the legislation was not perfect, with few insiders consulted. But its opponents' attempt to move the conversation from industry corruption to state corruption was deeply disingenuous to say the least. Executives in their boardrooms, anticipating a loss of profits, passed on talking points to gaming influencers, who in turn rallied gamers to put political pressure on legislators. A barely regulated market, squeezing every last penny out of the players, convinced those same players to become its foot soldiers. In this case, strong regulation by the state reined in a market usually able to evade oversight. Still, the political fight put up by the masses against their own interests was notable and is important to acknowledge.

Videogames are an arena of constant political expression and a battleground for the popularity of ideas, where gamers have the ability to actively create, enact, organise and manipulate situations or even entire contingents of people. Again, few other creative spaces grant this sort of access to tactics. Besides, the entire industry owes a debt of gratitude for the organisational power, cheek and rule-bending tendencies of game communities. File sharing, aka piracy, the free distribution of games organised by communities online and offline, heavily influenced the speed and spread of computer games. People without access to physical stores, or the money to purchase expensive games, got hooked by playing their illegal copy on a floppy disk, then evidently grew into faithful consumers.

The spectrum for these activities could not be wider – the games themselves became merely a palette with which to paint radically different pictures. Little is inherently political about the game *Minecraft* itself – it is designed to be a playground, a space for people's imaginations to take over.[33] However, in 2022, a British teenager was jailed for three and a half years for sending a bomb manual disguised as a *Minecraft* game guide to his fellow players.

He was a member of a Telegram group called 'English Only', where he posted Islamophobic remarks. As part of the trial, the court was shown pictures of the teenager posing with an imitation rifle and doing Nazi salutes, as well as a picture of his dagger, which he had nicknamed 'Jew Smiter'.[34]

The neo-Nazi network on *Minecraft* is much wider than this singular example – for a while, entire structures of forums and systems of influencers existed for making Gestapo buildings out of the blocks, creating miniature Hitler sculptures and luring young kids to explore these spaces. As mentioned, *Minecraft* is the most popular game on YouTube, with an eye-watering trillion views on the platform at the time of writing.[35] Who are the most popular creators of gaming videos? YouTubers like PewDiePie and Ninja have often got into trouble for using racist slurs.[36] Unmoderated hate speech is sadly a regular occurrence on this platform, which still holds enormous power over its teenage demographic.

On the other side of the political gamut of *Minecraft* playership lie inventive political actors who employ the game for egalitarian purposes. In territories where political expression is policed and attempts to speak freely put activists at risk of persecution or worse by the state apparatus, *Minecraft* comes to the rescue. Until his Putin-sanctioned murder, Alexei Navalny was the leader of the opposition in Russia, known for his anti-corruption activism online. Just before his imprisonment in 2021, Navalny released a video exposing President Vladimir Putin's vast undeclared riches, including the so-called Putin's Palace – an enormous, vulgar estate on the shores of the Black Sea. This gold-clad residence of opulence and corruption includes gilded ceilings, baths the size of an average London bedroom, a lap dancing lounge and a videogame arcade room.[37]

Not every youngster finds themselves trawling the internet for anti-corruption videos made by politicians. No, they spend their time on *Minecraft*. Thankfully, some ingenious souls found a way to challenge the homogeneous presentation of the news and recreated Putin's Palace in the game, copying every detail, down to virtual masseuses and crystal chandeliers.[38] Streamers also exist to teach kids how to rebuild the palace in *The Sims* and question the taste and the material sources of this bizarre estate.[39]

In 2021, the non-profit organisation Reporters Without Borders mapped nations that score low on their World Press Freedom Index on those with high usage of *Minecraft*, according to Google data. Based on the results, they constructed a huge building, inspired by the New York Public Library, in *Minecraft*. Inside, players can virtually access books and articles that are banned in countries such as Egypt, Mexico and Russia.[40] It took twenty-four people from sixteen countries and more than 12 million *Minecraft* blocks to create the virtual space, which also includes a plug-in that converts Word documents into books, so that users can add their own. Since it uses blockchain cloud storage, the library cannot be monitored by oppressive governments. Once downloaded, the contents can be uploaded again, allowing the library to grow as it is shared and reshared. Currently, there are over 200,000 copies of the project, making it impossible to shut down, even for the creators.

Videogames as Political Platforms

The actions of communities inside *Minecraft* prove not simply that the entirety of the videogame space is a contested political territory, but also that singular games can accommodate an entire political spectrum of opinions and movements. This array of political expressions inside one game suggests that we view these online multiplayer games less as objects and more as spaces, closer to social media networks than to linear single-player games. Just as social media is utilised to organise protests and to express and exchange ideas, online games are an arena of constant flux. Home to activism during the Arab Spring, and for the #MeToo movement and Black Lives Matter campaigns, these spaces have also nurtured #Gamergate, the election of Donald Trump, the massacres of Muslims in Myanmar and the right-wing riots of 6 January 2021.

Games have the potential to enrich the fight for liberation and social justice, and they can equally be co-opted into tools for spreading hatred towards marginalised populations, trolling innocent people and propagating straight-up fascist conspiracies. This subversion demonstrates that videogames are a politicised sphere, which should have been absolute catnip for the organising left. Sadly, with aesthetics unfamiliar and unattractive to our camp's rigid taste, gaming is dismissed as unattractive or baffling and is ultimately abandoned. This is a grave loss of opportunity and – worse – leaves these spaces wide open to co-option by the extreme right.

As the left still fails to take gaming communities seriously as political subjects, the right is making successful inroads. *Roblox* (2006) is a game creation system whose popularity exploded during the COVID-19 pandemic. The platform features a wide range of user-generated games, referred to as 'experiences'. Some games on the site have millions of active players each month, with around 5,000 different small games receiving over 1 million visits, and a select few surpassing 1 billion visits. The customer base of *Roblox* is almost exclusively tweens and teenagers, which made it even more disturbing when, in 2019, an investigation by NBC News revealed a network of over 100 far-right and neo-Nazi groups affiliated with the game.[41] After the report came out, the Roblox Corporation removed these accounts, but inappropriate radicalising content, including numerous neo-Nazi networks, continues to thrive on this incredibly popular and influential space.[42]

Right-wing influencers engage in grooming and building armies of young, impressionable kids. Innocent role-playing games suddenly carry heavy connotations when they are based on the Confederacy or set on the US–Mexican border. One's identity becomes formed according to prompts by the vigilant carers of these radicalising spaces. This sense of community, of fitting in, may even inspire the desire to help out and become a recruiter oneself. Players may perceive the hate speech as banter at first, but the infrastructures around the game – such as Discord servers or other chat spaces – are gates to deeper exposure and ideological indoctrination. That desire to belong, to feel looked after, causes kids to engage in behaviours that benefit the wider group. Players alter their behaviour to fit the social dynamics and change their language to mimic that of the popular members of the community, however demeaning; they begin to follow the groups that the other members follow, even if it is QAnon.

Gaming companies should bear responsibility for the type of social interactions that take place within their spaces. The tolerance with which the Roblox Corporation, the creators of the game, seem to treat the platform's Nazi problem may suggest a certain curatorial choice. While I'm arguing that games companies provide these vast public squares, loud marketplaces of ideas if you will, with their winners and losers, the developers are not entirely powerless. Their choice of how, or indeed whether, to moderate the interactions in their game, the severity of punishments or the lightness of touch – these dictate which part of the political spectrum gets to express themselves on their servers.

Take the multiplayer first-person-shooter franchise *Overwatch* (2016), for instance, whose developers Blizzard Entertainment enforce a relatively strong code of conduct. While the methods are by no means perfect, and plenty of hate speech still circulates, the level of criticism, accountability and response is also relatively high. It kind of has to be. From the outset, the game was marketed as a non-stereotypical shooter – the cast of playable characters offers a diverse selection of race, gender, age and size options. In order to retain its playership and customers, Blizzard Entertainment is investing seriously in moderation. By contrast, games such as *Call of Duty* or *Counter-Strike*, wise to where their gains are made, may care less if their marginalised players receive frequent abuse. Chances are they are, after all, in the minority.

Game developers provide platforms where amid interaction, cooperation, trolling and competition for social capital or in-game currency, there happens to be play, too. Social media companies operate in a similar way, creating platforms within which a myriad of themes are invented. These are currently under scrutiny for their role in harbouring radicalising movements. At present, websites operating within the United States are shielded from legal responsibility related to user-generated material, thanks to section 230 of the Communications Decency Act. However, momentum is growing within the legislative class to amend this outdated law due to clear manipulations by social media companies to raise engagement, even when the content bringing in the views results in real-life harm.

The condition of the Muslim communities in Myanmar, who have suffered from violence stoked by propaganda mostly circulated on Facebook, demonstrates the dangers of this hands-off approach.[43] Groups looking after young people are also witnessing an epidemic of self-harming and are calling politicians to take action against the social media companies deliberately targeting them with damaging content. We must ask whether game companies are mere platforms or active publishers of harmful content.

Should the rights reserved for free speech and expression really be extended to networking spaces where harmful content is built with the tools provided by the creator of the game? These questions ought to be increasingly brought forward in order to foster more healthy digital spaces, in all their forms.

Yet there are also examples of pioneering gamers communicating progressive politics in videogames. *The Sims* provides an obvious example. In contrast to many other multiplayer games, *The Sims* has always attracted a generally more progressive crowd. The game's early adoption of homosexual relationships as a norm boosted its name as a space welcoming of users who were not stereotypical gamers. The game's potential for concocting strange, surreal scenes and its almost-ironic presentation of commodities (soft furnishings of any kind!) resulted in a community of players who took subversion seriously. So it was no surprise when the imaginary streets of *The Sims* became a territory for protest. As people around the world were turning up in their thousands to the Black Lives Matter demonstrations highlighting police brutality against Black populations, not everyone had the ability to travel to rallies in city centres.

With that in mind, streamers in *The Sims* community organised a virtual Black Lives Matter rally, complete with placards and slogans. It was a beautiful sight – masses of individuals who for one reason or another were unable to attend real-life events, crowding the servers of Electronic Arts with a clear political stance. The Black influencers in *The Sims* community had already taken the battle to the developer by demanding, or sometimes themselves sourcing, more diverse skin tones, fashions and other mods that would fit non-white characters.[44] Now these communities around the world united to stand for an important cause in their own passionate way. 'I was surprised to see players from Brazil and Germany and Korea, as well as the UK and USA, participating and promoting the rally,' said *Sims* modder and streamer Danielle 'EbonixSims' Udogaranya, the organiser of the rally.[45] This and other protests or actions show that gamers with well-formed political ideologies have infiltrated these spaces to widen the reach of their message.

Gamers as Performers of Immaterial Labour

Gamers form themselves into political subjects – sometimes in game, sometimes in the real world. The calculus used by the far right to create spheres of influence within gaming must be studied and contested by progressive forces. Theirs are brittle structures that rule with impunity and offer little material solutions to the problems currently facing players in real life. However, politics in gaming communities begin with the foundational act of becoming a consumer of a product. Any progressive project that scrutinises the games industry and its practices must question and offer mean-ingful improvements to the very act of play itself, while under the current mode of production. So what are the politics of the com-munities booting up a game, even before they form themselves into explicitly political entities within it?

An alternative to the current state of power relations within games could begin with challenging the immaterial labour per-formed by players for the profit of the owners of these platforms. Certain parts of the gaming industry have become deeply depend-ent on fan-created material. Coined by the Marxist philosophers Maurizio Lazzarato and Antonio Negri, the term *immaterial labour* was first used to describe forms of work that produce intangible products, such as knowledge, caring responsibilities and informa-tion, rather than material goods.[46] In the context of the digital age, it also began to encapsulate processes of content creation, such as blogging, posts, videos and other content that may appear stripped of a material relationship, but still ends up generating value, chiefly for the owners of the hosting platforms.

New players of blockbusters such as *World of Warcraft*, *Dark Souls* (2011) or *Planetary Annihilation* (2018) are completely reliant on online forums and videos made by veteran players for learning about the techniques and strategies of playing the game. The majority of these tutorials are created voluntarily (and for free). Workers in the gaming industry, as well as consumers, derive little benefit from this form of bleeding-edge capitalism, where hard and necessary work to support a product is not only unpaid, it is actively marketed as a community-building project that the players are meant to be grateful for.

The relationship between employer and worker is becoming more and more blurred – much of what is currently perceived as leisure in fact produces value, which is paramount for the medium's existence. The consumer is not just a passive terminus, but a complicit and creative relay in the production of profits.

While some single-player, offline, linear videogames still have only a single point of retail engagement for buying the game, the emergence of network technologies and always-online games, which continuously draw data, invites more continuous interaction. An analogy can be drawn with shifts in the world of fine art. Until recently, the relationship between the artwork and the viewer was fairly one-directional. But with the emergence of performance art and, more recently, relational art, the public's interaction with the piece has become imperative; the piece simply cannot exist without it.

Sony's *EverQuest* (1999) perfected this formula. The publishers created a platform, profiting from many post-launch add-ons, but it was the players' creativity and the in-game intrigue that kept people coming back. Activities such as raids and group quests are an integral aspect of *EverQuest*'s gameplay mechanics. Successfully coordinating these endeavours demands a considerable degree of teamwork, diplomacy and various forms of social labour.

Guild leaders, for example, often invest unpaid hours overseeing group dynamics, organising events and ensuring a seamless gaming experience for their members. A multitude of fan sites, guides, and forums for fan art, while often a labour of love, added significant value to the game and its community. Players dedicated extensive hours to farming or 'grinding' for rare items and in-game currency, or enhancing their character's levels and abilities.

In some cases, this enabled individuals to earn virtual wages from engaging in such activities and then selling these assets for real-life money. This practice has now turned into a huge global industry.[47] The margins are covered from so many sides. A relatively thin platform is forged, getting a player to pay for any add-ons and subscriptions. The players themselves spend time to foster the communities that lure more players in. It turns out to be a pretty perfect model for the giant corporation Sony Online Entertainment.

Some did decide to challenge such monopolies, albeit with limited success. In 2000, a class-action suit was initiated by an *Ultima Online* player who claimed that in volunteering as an in-game community leader, answering questions and offering guidance to novices, she had unwittingly been performing a full-time unpaid job. Though her challenge was ultimately unsuccessful, it highlighted the degree to which MMO management depended on the cooperation of its 'playbouring' populations.[48]

Other intellectual property (IP) holders, in opposition to the supposed material interests, treat communities of their games as a mere inconvenience. Nintendo and Capcom are known for imposing IP licensing requirements on community events, such as competitive grassroots tournaments for Capcom's *Street Fighter*.[49] Organisers of all tournaments, regardless of their size, were warned to obtain a community or esports licence from the company.[50] Otherwise, they could be liable for breaching the confines of the IP. Members of a game's community sadly must oblige if they wish to maintain a peaceful relationship with the creators of their favourite pastime.

It's similar to Uber. Someone creates the platform, but what's exercised within it, the main source of attraction, is purely a function of the interaction between the users – the drivers and passengers. Fan fiction, machinima videos, and frag films are all derivative works that were at first prohibited by companies and framed as copyright infringement until the owners realised that, in fact, such activities add value to the brand. Modders forge new creative ideas and players fill these platforms with meaning, joy and activity – often barely curated by the platform holder.

Gamers modify or introduce new content, features or game mechanics, often driven by their enthusiasm for the game and their commitment to its community. They do this without expecting compensation, improving the gaming experience for others while simultaneously extending the game's lifespan and appeal. This unpaid labour adds value to the game and may indirectly benefit game developers and publishers by maintaining the game's relevance and drawing in new players.

Consequently, gaming can be viewed as a form of immaterial labour transforming a computer game into a cultural artefact.

Gaming as Political: A Space for Communal Imagination

In a plethora of instances, gamers have consciously or unconsciously arranged themselves into political formations, perhaps while also expanding the definition of politics. For anyone who wishes to be called progressive, politics must maintain an open-ended and experimental edge, where attempts are made at reimagining the world beyond the current circumstance. Games are uniquely placed to offer this, by requiring interaction and participation and being themselves 'places' where new rules can play out. Let's examine this through two very different phenomena: *Pokémon Go* (2016) and the culture of modding.

Pokémon Go brought gamers into our city squares and broadened expectations of what a videogame might look like. In this mobile game, the player is invited to collect the Pokémon that are situated in various real-life geographical locations. Augmented reality effects on a phone app create the impression of a Venusaur sitting on top of that fountain, or a Rattata lurking in the grass in that park. Is that a cheeky Blastoise behind that grubby trash bin? Finding a Pokémon is followed by a short gameplay sequence for capturing it and adding it to the player's collection.

'Gotta catch 'em all' was the slogan of summer 2016. Many have fond memories of deliriously chasing these strange augmented-reality creatures, phone in hand, exchanging knowing glances and awkward, friendly smiles with strangers on the same hunt. It is difficult to engage with this game without having some sort of social interaction with other people, and pokéflirting was definitely a thing.

The concept of *dérive* (or 'drift') was first introduced as a revolutionary tactic by Guy Debord, a founder of the Situationist International, in his 1958 work, 'Theory of the Dérive'.[51] It involves an impromptu exploration of a landscape, typically in urban settings, where participants abandon their daily routines and allow themselves to be guided by the area's allure and the experiences they encounter. Although not a perfect analogy, *Pokémon Go* shares some similarities, despite its ties to the economic and commodity systems the Situationist International vehemently criticised.

Pokémon Go encourages players to engage with the city in unexpected ways, subverting the intended functions of streets and reimagining the nature of a location and our mental connections to it. As Debord stated, chance plays a smaller role in this activity than it seems; cities possess psychogeographical features, including constant flows, fixed points and vortexes that deter entry or exit from specific areas. Anyone who has played *Pokémon Go* can attest to this experience – the app compels users to re-evaluate their environment and perceive it from an entirely new perspective. A Pokéhunt may create moments where our surroundings are transformed, and we can rediscover elements of our everyday lives, under different names and even in complete, glorious ignorance of the situs.

The Reddit user SlothOfDoom recounted this cheering story about the urban politics of *Pokémon Go*:

Couldn't sleep so I downloaded the game and took a 3 am walk. There is a little park a few blocks from me that had like three pokestops and a gym, so I wandered over there to see what the game could offer. Picked up an Evee outside my house and a couple of trash pokes on the way to the park. So I get there and wander around a little checking out the stops and rustling around in the tall grass, then decide to go a few blocks away to see a couple more stops when I hear from the darkness a 'Yo, my man!' Turning I see two sketchy looking dudes sitting on a bench in the dark. I must have walked right past them without noticing them. Great. One of them waves. 'My man, check over by the blue truck over there we got an Onyx [a valuable Pokémon] earlier.' So I wander over by the truck and sure enough there's a fucking onyx there. Awesome. So I end up chatting with the guys for a bit, told em where I got my Eevee, they convinced me to join red team when I hit level five so we could 'lock shit down' in the neighbourhood. Then the cop shows up. Yeah, so it turns out two twenty-something black dudes and a forty year old white guy chilling in the park at 3 am looks strange. It took a bit of talking to convince the cop we weren't doing a drug deal, and a bit longer to explain the game. Then the cop downloaded the game on his phone and asked us how to get started. Go red team.[52]

The scenarios and commonly agreed scripts as to what can or cannot take place on a street are exposed by a gentle warping of these expectations. In this case, gaming serves as a tool for introducing an astonishing variety of new purposes to our social and urban experiences. Similarly to Situationist writings (minus the corporate angle, of course!), this app does turn a lamppost into a meeting place, or a random car park into a sought-after destination; a straight road can now offer a variety of meaningful stops and the pavement a map of treasures. To many of us who are radically inclined, interested in viewing the world through a historical-materialist lens, the game's commodity form, intertwined in a complex relationship with cellular reception mechanisms and device-making strategies, has little revolutionary potential; but with the current disappearance of poetry from our urban environments, we can sometimes find inspiration in the unlikeliest places.

Perhaps not explicitly political, but disarming, with a divine emotional weight, are the mods created mostly anonymously by members of gaming communities. Mods are alterations and additions to rules or contents of existing games, essentially using commercial games as material for ready-made or home-brewed art. While some are extensions of fan fiction or simple adaptations of a game for a local language or personal taste, others achieve an eerie sense of atmosphere and disjuncture that beats even the offerings of some of the most prestigious contemporary art forms.

Pokémon Go met modding in an accidental manner when it first launched in Russia. Ramblers around the Red Square in Moscow, which neighbours the Kremlin, noticed that the app (coded to correspond to GPS coordinates) was malfunctioning. The signal showed that they were in fact located around the Vnukovo Airport, thirty-two kilometres away.[53] Further research prompted by the players' experiences uncovered a complex GPS spoofing operation utilised by the state's operators. The findings were taken one step further when some players used the misdirections to manipulate the game and catch the rarest of creatures from the comfort of home.[54]

As of the time of this writing, an average of 100,000 people are watching *Grand Theft Auto V* streams on Twitch on any given day, with around 2,000 channels dedicated to a singular game title. One of them, however, is not like the rest. The artist Brent Watanabe modded the game so the human protagonists were replaced by an AI-controlled white deer, which wanders the fictional streets of Los Santos radiating an otherworldly, majestic spirit. Modded to be invincible, the deer couldn't be harmed by bullets, no matter how many hit it. Sometimes the deer appears, looking regal, on the edge of the chaotic city in the evening dusk. Sometimes it moves awkwardly alongside the dirty walls of warehouses, aimlessly falling over steps and bumping into random objects. The deer runs away from police or confidently walks the sunlit downtown streets. At times, it stretches the environment to the limit by diving into the sea.[55]

The trapped nature of this sublime animal, with its apparently self-harming tendencies and its grace, as well as the contrast of its natural elegance to the superficiality and grime of the game's miserable surroundings, have captivated the community. Struck by this subversion of the game, they have left dozens of comments on the stream. The deer is performing a multi-layered *dérive*: challenging structured movement through cities, the human-centrism in both urban and game design and even the norms and practices of streaming culture.

Many mods are not only deeply creative, transcending the medium in their depth and grace, but crucially, they are almost universally free and accessible, a gift from often-anonymous creators who are simply passionate about the community they belong to. Such a refusal to participate in the feast of social and material capital that propels today's cultural-industrial complex is unique and refreshing.

Get in the Game

Gaming is not easy to characterise within the binaries of what is politically wasteful or useful. It holds a spectrum of meanings and functions that need to be called into question. However, when gaming is put under the magnifying glass by those attempting to find civic productivity even within its escapism, it stands up to the challenge. Numerous studies suggest a positive correlation between immersion, gaming, motivation and civic engagement, as well as political participation.[56] As people learn to associate communal cooperation with both communal and individual benefit, they become more willing to work with others in their communities. Having stronger ties to a group encourages people to consider communal needs in addition to their own needs, and this can logically nudge them to participate in their community. When people with a shared interest come together in a multiplayer game, there is the potential for positive, pro-social interaction among them, both in the game and outside it.

Gamers who develop the attitudes and behaviours that are part of belonging to a gaming community are likely to display these attitudes and behaviours in other areas of life. This sense of connectedness to others can lead people to form face-to-face bonds and get involved in their real-world communities. The implication is that there are now multiple pathways for people (especially young people, who are often less engaged in civic life than their elders) to become better citizens.

Those seeking to improve civic engagement would do well to embrace a broad range of media, including online media and videogames, when communicating the importance of participation in civic life. At a time when voter turnout, publicly registered volunteering, charitable giving, political party membership and union membership are in decline, we must look for potential places where that energy is being channelled. The right is equally capable, and more willing in gaming, to spawn such groups. We have a choice: to sneer and ignore, or to at least attempt to create attractive forms of coordinating and formulating the ideas and ideals that bring people into our fold.

When a person's role in the control of their surroundings is diminished, then the allure of role-play becomes very strong. Isolated, alienated by capitalist means of production, reduced as entities to simple consumers, some gamers are desperate to find an identity under a banner where they can claim to be subjects. What kind of politics those banners declare is up for negotiation and contestation. The fight is twofold: existing real-life political communities desire to recreate their allegiances and aesthetics in their hobby spaces, in this case, gaming. Those then get solidified and are given credence and validation. By extension, they fuel or culturally enrich movements.

Unbeknownst to many on the left, enormous numbers of people value their in-game virtual experiences just as much as their real-life ones. The lack of curiosity about and acknowledgement of these populations creates a void in the left's capacity for mass mobilisation and material change. Alienation is not only what we are subjected to by the capitalist classes, but also an energy that we emanate towards members of circles we deem unworthy of our time.

The esoteric belief evinced by many on the left regarding what constitutes a 'correct' political subject can be at times suffocatingly narrow. This attitude causes the left to not only lose ground, but push people away and over to the other side. Sometimes I wonder if we are not doing this on purpose – acting like some political artisans, it feels ever so good to pretend that we hold a secret, as if our knowledge of all the injustices somehow justifies our doing so little about them. As if having more people accepted into our circles would mean relinquishing our sense of being special. It may sound ridiculous, but if anything, it's desperate.

I see a beautiful medium morphing into something quite dark, and if we do not fight to save it, our collective sneering will mark another failure in a long list of lost opportunities, especially when it comes to technology and its relationship to culture. How might gaming be a tool in the fight against our current state of oppression? How might gamers become active agents in the improvement of our material conditions? Many have attempted, with mixed results, but the possibilities remain endless.

Level III: Efficacy

Although gaming communities and the politics brewing in them are under-appreciated subjects, the potential of authored standalone games and their ability to invoke social change is just as great. Such games have the capacity to inform, to subvert, to challenge what is acceptable and round up troops to fight for a better tomorrow. But how?

Unfortunately, the answer is complicated. Many game creators will claim that they are developing socially conscious games. Games concerned with equality, climate change, and other progressive themes are abundant. But apart from being exactly that – socially conscious – are they there to signify certain social attitudes or to change them? Socially aware games are indeed very in vogue. There is no lack of social capital in the field – having a civically concerned theme in your game is catnip for various accolades and overall prestige. 'Games for Impact' and 'Games Beyond Entertainment' have become awards categories in the most reputable gaming competitions. Games for Change is a nonprofit organisation, handing out influential annual awards in a variety of do-gooder categories. Games like *Papers, Please*, dissected in Level I, and numerous other ludic projects imply that our ways should be changed, but never quite push the boundaries beyond the comfort zone. These are beloved by games media as a moral palate cleanser, unlike their usual press release copy-pastes and reports on the more unpleasant news from the industry.

Plenty of self-proclaimed political videogame makers genuinely see the primary mission of their work as an appeal for a fairer, kinder world. Presumably that means planting the seeds of change in players' minds, inspiring them to become agents for progressive values. Since this result is hard to measure, it remains unclear to what extent videogames help achieve that goal. Too many of them end up as PR exercises for the artist – at best. And at worst, their message can be co-opted, merely sharpening the cynicism around art's potential for social good. Can progressive games effect actual positive political transformation? What properties should such endeavours require? And what questions should we confront in the search for efficacy – to create games that truly change somebody's mind? Or to steer them from inaction into action?

That is not to say that all art must do that – change minds. A great deal of exquisite art reaffirms our beliefs through new forms, enhances our horizons or simply offers temporary relief. These works are not self-defined as political, though, and don't sell as such. Political awareness can be a form of currency in the market, but the results of spreading that awareness are much trickier to quantify. Due to its inherent subjectivity, it is not easy to determine what exactly changes an individual's mind. At what point does someone encounter a piece of art and change camps politically? While much discussion of videogames in the media is around their perceived role in turning players into reactionary violence machines, the potential for games to introduce more egalitarian ideals is ignored. What type of social relations are being produced by explicitly progressive games? Who are these games made for, and why? What would it mean to, instead of making political games, make games politically? This level explores examples of political art in the wider culture, as well as offering a rich theoretical grounding.

The Punchline Is Gonna Be Real Good: Social Capital and the Arts

The concept of social capital is important to this level. The extent to which a videogame has the potential to truly effect social change is not necessarily proportionate to the level of social capital the game's creators are set to gain. The games industry is market-led, after all, and what becomes popular within this sphere can often complement trends which tend to reproduce current conditions rather than truly challenge them. A political videogame preaching to the converted is likely to receive more praise than one that catches the player off guard. When the French sociologist Pierre Bourdieu defined the term *social capital*, he was interested in exactly these dynamics – it is seemingly much easier for people to gain material capital if they are, essentially, liked. Social capital is a property of the individual, rather than of the collective, and is derived primarily from one's social position and status. It is an accrued actual or virtual resource, linking social connections and one's ability to then use them for advancement.[1] In other words, someone who enjoys prestige and social popularity also tends to achieve economic advancement. People who are affable and talk in a language already familiar to their audience are generally deemed more likeable.

In gaming, as in any cultural industry, such connections are also evident and in constant play. In the absence of actual material arte-facts resulting from cultural signifiers, the drive touching on those narratives is incredibly strong. Instead of getting involved in the boring, unpredictable and unrewarding world of policy-making or grassroots movement building, game developers are much more likely to receive social capital by simply tackling a troublesome theme. The games industry's arbiters, tainted by their own, often nefarious procedures, can conveniently absolve themselves by granting prestige to games that signal values antithetical to the industry's own modus operandi, so long as this signalling is safe and contained, of course. This set of conditions nurtures a progressive videogames climate where the material celebrated is acceptable, palatable, familiar and obvious to those in the know. A bit of representation here and a touch of a political story there (usually without an actual twist) – games comfortably confirm the player's politics rather than subverting their existing set of beliefs.

A powerful collection of essays called *Art, Activism and Recuperation* raises tough questions about the insular, multi-beneficial and vitally important relationships and power play between art, activists and cultural institutions.[2] What are effective strategies against recuperation – the process by which subversive ideas, oppositional to the status quo, are co-opted or appropriated by the dominant market-led culture, effectively voiding their original disruptive potential. Could recuperation, the filtering of the challenging to the palatable, sometimes be the goal, not just an unintended consequence? In the collection, the curator Nav Haq discusses the 2004 book by his Swedish colleague Maria Lind, *This Is Going to Be Really Funny: Notes on Art, Its Institutions and Their Presumed Criticality.* Here Lind neatly exposes the futility of many contemporary socially aware cultural practices.[3] She crafts a simple yet effective analogy between the act of telling a joke and the declarations inherent in much political art. If, before telling a joke, you say, 'This is going to be really funny!' then the listener will most probably not find it funny at all. Something about the initial declaration defuses the humour. The surprise factor is removed, and the listener can prepare in advance for the punch-line.[4] This analogy extends to critical or political games: proclaiming that one's work is profoundly critical can instantly strip away that intended effect. In fact, a certain ambiguity about the artist's intentions empowers a more potent critique – as with funnier jokes.

Should we engage with and judge political art in the same way? What is our mission here? If the aim is to inform, then explicit declarations stand a chance of succeeding. The emphasis will be placed on the new information learnt. But if the objective is to explicitly change the thinking of people who are not already invested in the cause, artists are likely to fail with this technique. Too often, in arts, games and other cultural realms, the goal remains within the reassuring boundaries of our existing beliefs. Staying inside the bubble is safer and, crucially, more profitable.

Playing with Politics – Who Wins?

As a creative medium with similar aesthetics and a possibility for interaction, games can learn from the fine arts, which have been challenged and tested in all kinds of ways. Despite their different methods of production, both media are made by creatively ambitious people who probe, promote and occasionally fall short in somewhat similar ways.

What can games developers learn from the fine arts about the difficulties of cultural production? Consider *Wheatfield* (1982), a six-month installation by the American artist Agnes Denes. With the support of the Public Art Fund, she planted a field of golden wheat on two acres of a rubble-strewn landfill near Wall Street and the World Trade Center in lower Manhattan. The field was open to the public, and the harvested grain was distributed across the globe. Beautiful, certainly. And if the piece did little to

reduce world hunger, it undoubtedly helped to gentrify the neighbourhood and increase the artist's social and material capital.

In *Idol Worship* (2007), Laura Keeble replaced the normal tomb-
stones in a British cemetery with stone sculptures of brand logos
such as McDonald's, and the local church gained a stained-glass
window with the Chanel fashion house logo. Beyond the brazen
gesture, it is unclear what the intentions of this 'brandalism' were.
Mark Coreth created a life-sized sculpture of a polar bear at the
COP 15 climate summit in 2009. Just how much energy was
required to freeze nine tonnes of ice or to create the 500-kilogram
bronze cast of the skeleton is unknown, but the World Wildlife
Fund, which funded the sculpture (along with consumer electronics manufacturers Panasonic and Nokia), still advertised it as 'art
in service of the environment'.[5] Similarly, in 2019 the beloved and
self-congratulatory eco-artist Olafur Eliasson ripped up and transported tens of kilogrammes of moss from his native Iceland for
his exhibit at the Tate Modern in London. He also presented huge
ice cubes at the entrance to the gallery. This was a baffling waste
of resources that made little to no point other than that the artist
cared about the issues of the environment, and he benefitted from
major production budgets as a reward.

In 2022, the Finnish pavilion at the Venice Biennale hosted
Pilvi Takala's work *Close Watch*. It follows Takala's journey to be
part of the common people by working as a security person at a
shopping mall. She then sides with the management when one of
the workers is reprimanded for making a sexist remark. She
observes the workers with scant empathy, but rather passes judgement. The other security staff presumably received no material
reward for their involvement, but the piece brought maximum
exposure to the artist. Crucially, the power and the audience's
sympathy lie with the artist and the management, not with the
workers. Viewers are asked to side with the white middle-class

Finnish artist rather than with a poor migrant worker, whose politics may be slightly less refined. They are invited to appreciate the profound artist, who took an actual job for a few months, and to shake their head at the moral failings of working-class mall security guards.

Crudely speaking, this is art for the sake of its own spectacle and the artist's material gain, rather than for a change of heart. Equivalents in the gaming world are regrettably numerous. To support their efforts in raising awareness about our planet's dwindling natural resources, the band Linkin Park, in combination with Kuuluu Interactive Entertainment, created *LP Recharge* (2013) – a game where humans and robots battle for the earth's remaining ores and minerals. Players are tasked with fending off the androids while creating new and sustainable energy sources. The extent to which *LP Recharge* 'brings attention to energy poverty and clean energy solutions', as its PR campaign suggests, remains a mystery, but the game was certainly an original way to introduce a new single for the band – even *National Geographic* covered it.[6]

Another game, called *Get Water!* (2013), puts the player in the role of an Indian girl who wants to study but keeps getting interrupted by the need to go and fetch water. Developed by a Montreal-based start-up, the game launched on World Water Day and drew accolades from the United Nations Alliance of Civilizations. *Alba: A Wildlife Adventure* (2020) by UsTwo Games invites the player to traverse a Mediterranean island, documenting wildlife, solving challenges and rallying the community to preserve nature against a harmful construction project. Themes of ecology, climate change and the preciousness of nature are woven into a moving story of perseverance. While the ecological themes of the game were undoubtedly a profitable selling point, the studio also committed to planting real-life trees for every sale of the game. To date, reportedly over 1 million trees have been planted on behalf of the studio – a fine result which no doubt also assisted the title in receiving the Apple Design Award for Social Impact in 2021.[7]

Darfur is Dying (2006) was a flash-based browser game about the crisis in Darfur, western Sudan. Made by American designer Susana Ruiz as an undergraduate project at the University of Southern California, it was partially sponsored by the popular channel MTV. The game puts the player in the role of a displaced Darfurian living in a refugee camp. The objective is to navigate through the challenges faced by refugees, including finding water, avoiding militia attacks and maintaining the camp's well-being. Some critics, such as Ian Bogost, brought up the fact that sometimes, self-described activist videogames have a greater impact on the game maker's career than on the cause being championed. Although more than 1 million people had played the game by April 2007, Bogost found little evidence that the game engaged with the issues it was raising in a particularly productive, effective or innovative way. He wondered if MTV's involvement was anything more than a marketing ploy, and whether the funds could have been spent on a more useful cause.[8]

Art critic Claire Bishop's seminal work *Artificial Hells: Participatory Art and the Politics of Spectatorship* is an astute, empathetic critique of participatory fine art. In it, Bishop carefully dissects the victories and failures of recently fashionable contemporary art in 'involving the community', 'creating dialogue' and 'inviting to participate'. A few lines perfectly illustrate the necessity for art and games to grow beyond the attitudes criticised here:

> The urgency of this social task has led to a situation in which socially collaborative practices are all perceived to be equally important artistic gestures of resistance: there can be no failed, unsuccessful, unresolved, or boring works of participatory art, because all are equally essential to the task of repairing the social bond. While

sympathetic to the latter ambition, I would argue that it is also crucial to discuss, analyse and compare this work critically as art, since this is the institutional field in which it is endorsed and disseminated, even while the category of art remains a persistent exclusion in debates about such projects.[9]

Similar framing can and ought to be applied to games. Art is at risk of being segregated into the liminal space of perpetual commissions, interpretations and a loop of projections and normalisations of conditions.

Though they may have the best of intentions, these kinds of artistic practices fall into the category of mundane preaching, leaving the audience feeling talked down to rather than empowered. Or, in the worst-case scenario, used purely as a tool in promoting equally oppressive structures. Surely, that kind of artistic creation does not possess the charge the artist wanted for it. My aim isn't to determine definitively that these projects have failed, but to question why failure never seems to be an option in the defensive and linguistically confined spaces of videogame reviewing.

Still, even less consistent are the practices of games developer and author Jane McGonigal. She has become known as a proponent and creator of games with a so-called higher purpose, but in the introduction to her best-seller *Reality Is Broken: Why Games Make Us Better and How They Can Change the World*, she demonstrates a discomforting hypocrisy.

Eventually, as a result of my research, I published several academic papers proposing how we could leverage the power of games to reinvent everything from government, healthcare, and education to traditional media, marketing, and entrepreneurship – even world peace. And increasingly, I found myself called on to help large companies and organizations adopt game design as an innovation strategy – from the World Bank, the American Heart Association, the National Academy of Sciences, and the US Department of Defense to McDonald's, Intel, the Corporation for Public Broadcasting, and the International Olympic Committee. You'll read about many of the games I created with these organizations in this book – and for the first time, I'll be sharing my design motivations and strategies.[10]

Collaborations with institutions such as the World Bank, McDonald's and the US Department of Defense for the purpose of 'change for good' must be viewed with suspicion. McGonigal then becomes an agent for regressive forces. She speaks the language of kindness and goodness, with no other purpose surely than whitewashing some shady business practices.

Consider this quote from art curator Nicolas Bourriaud:

One should never mistake good intentions for strong art. Political commitment is a beginning, not an end, as generous ideas can sometimes lead to a reactionary artwork, contradicting those original intentions. Art has to start changing the world through questioning its own conditions of production and diffusion.[11]

Bourriaud, best known for coining the term *relational aesthetics*, has observed that many contemporary fine artists choose to incorporate interpersonal interaction as part of their pieces. Beyond performance art, a variety of happenings, events, social actions and spaces for meeting are now a common artistic offering.[12] This exposes another space for potential convergence between arts and games, with the latter providing ample settings for interpersonal participation, communication and interaction.

Artists working within the constraints of a gallery, but who approach their practice critically, often acknowledge the limitations of such engagement. Should we expect the same of game developers?

Only by vocalising those boundaries can we challenge them and nurture more ambitious processes. We should try to avoid the mistakes of the art world, such as street art transforming graffiti into capital without addressing the demands of the social classes who birthed the movement. Likewise, in relational aesthetics, social relations are folded into a look, rather than galvanised into a productive exchange.[13]

Perhaps the words *play* or *games* are holding the medium back, infinitely dictating that videogames ought to be about fun, joy and gratifying rewards, even if the aesthetics are gruesome. Feelings of discomfort and disgust, of being challenged, confused or called upon to take action, are much more cumbersome investments. Demanding the efficacy of games is a tall order, but unless they are interrogated in this light, they risk getting stuck in the realm of social – and, by extension, material – capital.

Political Art Politically Made

One redeeming feature of a game like *Papers, Please* is its ability to interrogate our sense of guilt. The player is confronted with moral dilemmas as the game progresses. For example, players must decide whether to allow the supposed spouse of an immigrant through, even though they lack the correct papers, at the risk of accepting a 'terrorist' into the country. As guards, players occasionally take bribes in order to feed their own family. The game not only creates simplistic, symptomatic social commentary, but also forces players to admit that they are part of the problem, making them feel actively responsible.

Brenda Romero, the spouse of the id Software *Doom* legend John Romero, and a hugely successful and influential game designer and educator in her own right, created a similar piece in the form of a board game called *Train* (2009). In it, the players transport passengers along a railway. Ultimately – spoiler – it is revealed that the final destination is a Nazi concentration camp and that the player has been unknowingly complicit in the atrocities of the Holocaust by moving the train in that direction. The previous examples may awaken the players' feelings of complicity, especially if used as educational tools for younger players, but it is questionable whether they would be effective for adults with diverse opinions. After all, presumably the consumer's choice of the product signals that they already have a certain level of empathy for the subjects of these games.

So, the problem besetting the progressive games scene – beyond the cursed modes of production, which are discussed further in Level IV – is a misalignment between its stated mission and the results. Games for good is a great ambition, but often the execution falls into the most obvious trappings of the spectacle, and the information provided simply does not add up to efficacy. Though the art world certainly suffers from the same issue, a few contemporary examples that use innovative angles stand out as ambitious attempts at finding ways to inform a viewer of a new perspective. Examining the practices of these artists could hopefully provide new conceptual frameworks for how gaming – already an influential and potent medium – can deepen its impact.

Papers, Please and *Train* are somewhat reminiscent of how the Spanish artist Santiago Sierra uses complicity to explore the intricacies of migration, class and guilt. For instance, he presented a performance in 2008 at the Tate Modern in London where he paid homeless women the price of a one-night stay in a hostel to stand facing the wall of the gallery for an hour at a time. In other performances, he paid migrants minimum wage to sit inside wooden boxes, get tattooed, or dig and fill holes in the ground. Although these performances have been publicly denounced as exploitative or otherwise problematic, viewers quickly understand that the real injustice lies not in how these subjects are treated within the exhibition walls, but in the fact that they are treated much more harshly in the outside world and mostly ignored by the general public.

During his artistic career, Sierra has received frequent criticism for 'unethical treatment of his subjects' and for presenting what some ungenerously see as 'poverty porn'. Some viewers were concerned that he used the individuals involved in his art as props. Ironically, this line of reproach enhanced the social capital of these viewers who had fundamentally misunderstood Sierra's project. He explains:

> At the Kunstwerke in Berlin they criticised me because I had people sitting for four hours a day, but they didn't realise that a little further up the hallway the guard spends eight hours a day on his feet . . . if they think it's a horror to sit hidden in a cardboard box for four hours, they don't know what work is . . . The museum watchman I paid to live for three hundred sixty-five hours behind a wall at a gallery in New York told me that no one had ever been so interested in him and that he had never met so many people. I realised that hiding something is a very effective working technique.[14]

The type of experience Sierra curates reveals the hypocrisy of the exhibition-visiting population. I linger on this because this type of discomfort is even less appreciated within the games realm. Comfort, safety, a transaction of convenience and resistance to arduous experiences – those are the favoured parameters of my beloved playful medium. In other words, Sierra does not preach and say, 'Oh, *you* should know better'; he says, 'We should *all*, as a society, know better.' He leaves himself vulnerable to a very particular and painful critique, just to return to the point of the issue. In contrast to Pilvi Takala, who also uses working-class figures in her art, Sierra creates an environment in which the viewer becomes part of the problem of the current conditions. Takala presents herself as an archiver, a saviour, an unbiased martyr, a hero. The workers are subjects, some more deserving than others, and the viewer is a silent witness to the artist's genius and sacrifice. Sierra's themes are, in contrast, unambiguous about art's relationship to wage labour, the monetisation of the art world and the displacing of value and exploitation within it.

In one of Sierra's more controversial pieces, only individuals carrying a Spanish passport were allowed to enter his pavilion at the 2003 Venice Biennale, effectively highlighting the plight of millions who have lost out on the passport lottery from birth and find it difficult to cross borders. Once again, Sierra created a space for friction and self-evaluation.

What Sierra does so effectively is to confront the viewer in an unexpected manner. In a videogame, the barrier to being actually surprised is incredibly high. Consumers must seek out a particular videogame with its own set of files and install it onto their machine before playing. Artists working in the public realm have many more opportunities to surprise the viewer, and they do so in ways that could inspire socially conscious games developers.

Now I wish to present a tapestry of contemporary fine art works that, in parallel, are going through exactly the same journey – attempting to find efficacy. The following examples present pieces that are succeeding in terms that have the potential to inform games.

Hank Willis Thomas and Dr Baz Dreisinger explore the notion of catching their viewer off guard with their ongoing study titled *Writing on the Wall* (2019). This travelling installation is composed of essays, poems, letters, stories, diagrams and notes written by prisoners around the world. The installation has appeared on the streets of various cities – New York's

High Line was the most prolific and centrally located thus far. In contrast to Lucas Pope (author of *Papers, Please*), Thomas made sure that representatives of various criminal justice reform organisations were invited to be part of the public events programme supporting the exhibition. A subtler project in the same vein is the restaurant and art project in Pittsburgh called *Conflict Kitchen* (2010), which served traditional meals from countries the United States was then at war with. What would be an equivalent attempt in games to highlight such an issue? Perhaps a game that is only available for play in countries that the US is currently at war with? We must attempt these kinds of audacious changes to how we offer and deliver games if we are to spur the medium to maturity.

Videogames are often hailed as a successful tool for presenting information and data to new audiences in an unexpected way, but the effect and quality of that encounter in an open games market are rarely studied. Is anyone particularly surprised when they learn more about a certain theme, however sensitive, given the amount of store blurbs and reviews we read before even loading the game? On the other hand, few were ready for what was about to transpire when they accepted the invitation to visit one of Hans Haacke's art show openings. For his seminal piece *Shapolsky et al. Manhattan Real Estate Holdings, A Real Time Social System, as of May 1, 1971* (1971), Haacke collected the documented evidence of corruption and insider dealings of New York City's slum landlords. Photographs and a meticulously curated paper trail were to be arranged on the walls, confronting the viewer with evidence of bribery, money laundering and fraud committed by the real-estate magnate Harry Shapolsky. The piece was due to be shown at the Solomon R. Guggenheim Museum in New York, but the exhibition was cancelled six weeks before opening.[15] The museum's trustees, many of whom had connections to the New York property market, protested the work and even had the curator, Edward Fry, fired for supporting it. In his subsequent pieces and exhibition openings, Haacke often returned to the investigative format and surprised the viewers with the results of that research. Visitors were often unaware of the information they would encounter.

Mark Wallinger also used his platform – in this case, a 2007 exhibition slot at Tate Britain – to raise uncomfortable awareness of the case of Brian Haw's camp, which once sat outside of Westminster Yard. The UK's draconian anti-protest laws include the Serious Organised Crime and Police Act (SOCPA), which prevents any protest from being held within a kilometre of the Houses of Parliament. A special injunction was granted to peace activist Brian Haw, who built a ramshackle tent city and protest camp on the lawn opposite Parliament. He snagged passers-by with posters of the numerous human rights violations committed by the British soldiers and government against the Iraqi people during the 2003 invasion. Haw finally passed away in 2011, after years of residing in the camp, and the police dismantled and destroyed it.

Partially located within the designated SOCPA circle, Tate Britain was a perfect place to reinstate this important piece of British protest history. An immaculate reproduction of Brian's camp was built inside the neo-baroque halls of this pompous gallery, with the addition of graphic images of deformed babies representing the threatened and terminated pregnancies that have resulted from the war's atrocities. Some visitors to this conservative art institution may have been confused to see a meticulous reproduction of a camp they'd been used to looking away from in the street, or stepping over on their way to an exhibit. Something that had been repellent to most passers-by was now confronting the gallery viewers. Haw, with little to no social capital, could not bring in the crowds that Wallinger was able to attract. But it was the displacement of this crucial information, from the space of the ordinary to a fetishised space of the extraordinary – crucially, to a space that is more known for its sixteenth-century paintings of royalty than for contemporary political protest – that was most perfect.

Comedian Mark Thomas put himself even closer to action when he organised the Mass Lone Demos campaign in 2006. During the campaign, Thomas encouraged members of the public to apply for their own individual permits to hold a demonstration within the SOCPA zone all at the same time, causing a logistical nightmare for the police and, in the process, highlighting the ridiculousness of the law. Nearly 2,500 people turned up to Parliament Square at an agreed time one day, possibly breaking the world record for the highest number of demonstrations in a limited space within a day. This work is an excellent example of performance artist Tania Bruguera's observation that political art should be 'made when it is unfashionable and when it is uncomfortable – legally uncomfortable, civically uncomfortable, humanly uncomfortable'.[16]

Another question often haunts me, even before political videogames that are executed in an original manner: aren't games a terribly inefficient way to make a point? Consider the dozens of people who work on a game for hundreds of hours and all the hardware and the stores necessary for its production and distribution. Fine art has a certain agility that is often unattainable for videogames.

While Wallinger created an anti-war message in an optimised manner, Chris Burden's 1971 piece of performance art reduced the amount of time needed to make a point to one second. In a crowded white cube gallery in California, Burden instructed a friend to shoot him. Burden stood against a white wall in a white T-shirt and jeans and barely flinched upon receiving a .22-calibre rifle bullet to his left shoulder from four metres away. Some photographs were taken and initial wound dressing applied. Burden chatted calmly with the show participants before being taken to a hospital for medical assistance. This was a well-done anti-war statement, but it was even more effective as a seething critique of police brutality, racism and gun violence. The fact that the shot took place inside the pristine walls of a chic art gallery shielded the subjects from intervention by the police and the state. The same act committed outside of this setting would have had completely different consequences, especially if Burden hadn't been a privileged, hip white man.

Such graphic and wonderfully minimal performance pieces exude an ease that games cannot. The hardware, lengthy planning stages, production and distribution of the game are all burdensome processes that sometimes take years and cost millions. Similarly, Tehching Hsieh dedicates himself to fine art that is much more involved and could hardly be called efficient. In his performances, Hsieh commits to spending exactly a year in extreme circumstances. In one instance, he spent a year in New York City without entering any space that had a roof. In his artistic collaboration with fellow artist Linda Montano, they spent a year connected to each other by a two-and-a-half-metre piece of rope – after which the two never spoke again. In his most pivotal and extreme performance to date, Hsieh photographed himself putting a card into a punch clock every hour for a year. That meant he could never sleep longer than fifty-nine minutes at a stretch or go any distance beyond an approximate thirty-minute radius of the punch clock.

This dedication can be compared to the months and years game developers spend crafting their creations, sometimes for themselves in the case of an independent career, sometimes crunching unbearable hours for a boss. Perhaps the lack of a romanticised tortured artist is just one more barrier for members of the game industry to being taken seriously, not just for the hours worked, but also for their creative process – think of van Gogh or Pollock.

Finally, games are not an industry that has ever been interested in creating work referencing its own failures. The compulsion to create the next big thing, inspired by Silicon Valley, stifles any tendency to look inwards and assess whether our work is useful or legitimate. A healthier industry might embrace such self-critique and have a market for it. Game creators who do question the limits of how the medium is framed remain at the margins, and the more deeply they critique the methods of production necessary for enjoying games, the more they are sidelined.

A confident medium that did not perceive itself as being particularly harmful would not feel the need to justify its own merits. For all gaming's faults, it is at least free of some of the ailments of the art world! For instance, gaming does not suffer from the preciousness and the inequalities that come with the fetishism of the aura of an art piece, that is, the insistence that it evokes a unique and distinctive feeling or atmosphere simply by existing in a particular time and space that are exclusive and unrepeatable. This in turn results in a market of scarcity – the more uncommon a piece is (or is praised as such by various fine art PR agencies), the more expensive it is, and in need of security, of course. Such commodified protection of the aura culminates in masterpieces being locked up in temperature-controlled safes, utilised for tax dodging and money laundering, and rarely shown in public.[17] Games are much more democratic on that score: accessible to many and increasingly to most, easily pirated, and free of the grandeur, or the speculative scarcity, of the arts.

Yet the art world, for all its complacency, excels in institutional critique, a subgenre concerned with assessing and judging the arts industry itself. For instance, Andrea Fraser's performance pieces shedding light on the hypocrisy of the very structures that will inevitably uplift her – something rarely seen in videogames, even in the more radical designs. For *Museum Highlights: A Gallery Talk* (1989), Fraser played a museum docent giving a tour of the Philadelphia Museum of Art's collection. But instead of discussing the art, she talked about the museum's budget, the salaries of its staff and the role of corporate sponsorship in funding exhibitions.

In *Official Welcome* (2001), Fraser, at the opening of her own exhibition in Hamburg, parodied the inflated language used to describe contemporary art and the absurd prices that collectors pay for it. During the performance, she was charismatic; her humour and jibes at the contemporary art industry were canny and self-aware. She stripped her clothes off and put them back on, and she was visibly moved to tears by the end of the performance – exposed, powerful, stuck in a wonderful dialectic of adoration and disgust.

In 2003, she took the art world by storm by holding a mirror up to it with her *Untitled* performance. Arranged by the Friedrich Petzel Gallery, Fraser entered into an agreement with an anonymous art collector and got paid $20,000 for a sexual encounter with him in a hotel room. The liaison was filmed. Five copies of the sixty-minute DVD were produced, three of which are in private collections, including that of the collector she had the fling with. The piece caused a furore within the art scene for her radical methods, although *Untitled* simply put many of the transactions and relationships of the art world into another form.

But Will They Get You Banned?

This sort of urgent self-examination rarely happens, or is encouraged, in the games industry. While many games reference themselves and the medium, very few dare to truly challenge the games industry as an institution in any meaningful way. The ones that do, however, are frostily received by industry insiders. For example, Italian game developer Molleindustria's practice has been one of the longest running projects of explicitly counter-cultural, leftist game making. The artist behind the project, Paolo Pedercini, created numerous pieces critiquing various aspects of capitalism, like *Tamatipico* (2003), based on the life of a worker, produced in support of the 2003 Italian referendum on workers' rights, or *McDonald's Video Game* (2005), which portrays the inner workings of the fast-food industry.

But it's Pedercini's *Phone Story* (2011) that provides the most impressive and lacerating example of a game confronting its modes of production and distribution head-on. This mobile game is composed of four distinct mini-games, each tasking the player with a different activity related to the exploitative process of producing the mobile devices on which videogames are played. They include forcing children in developing nations to extract coltan, and preventing suicides at a Foxconn manufacturing facility. The *Phone Story* website contains extensive information about the issues portrayed in the game, and all profits from the sale of the app go to labour charities, including a donation of over $6,000 to a girl injured in a suicide attempt at a Foxconn factory. Within days of *Phone Story*'s release, Apple banned the game from its digital shopfront. The game still exists on the larger Android stores, which do little to alleviate the brutal work conditions that the game critiques. This game correctly cuts close to the bone of these insecure institutions, which do everything in their power to hide their vicious methods of operation.

It is not easy for such subversive videogames to reach their audience. In 2018, Valve Corporation announced that they would remove games that were deemed 'offensive, illegal, or straight-up trolling' from Steam, the world's largest online store for PC

gaming, which they own and operate. While this rule is somewhat understandable in online spaces that carry so much obscene,
unregulated content, especially on social media, it is less relevant
to a curated store. A platform showcasing the best of gaming
should not be afraid to accommodate content that could be termed
illegal – just look at the practices of street artist Banksy or performance artist Tania Bruguera. In 2009, Bruguera invited
famous art critics to her exhibition and presented them with lines
of pure cocaine – all to highlight the terrible plight of those
involved in the making of the drug, which members of the art
scene so frequently indulge in. Technically, doing graffiti and
giving out class A drugs are illegal acts, but in the right context,
they provide an excellent and necessary reflection of the society
we live in. Granted, public areas and institutions are spaces much
more open for negotiation than private digital storefronts. But if
game makers are serious about their ambitions to push cultural
boundaries and create groundbreaking art with their games,
they must engage in a critical conversation about where those
games are hosted.

The habit of banning games from storefronts applies not just
to illegal materials, but also to controversial games or games that
engage in mocking critiques – what Valve called 'trolling' – a very
broad parameter which covers much art (and most trash, for sure).
What is deemed 'offensive' can be interpreted differently by marginalised communities and by the elites, and critique of the latter
can be neatly disallowed under such rules. Unless new definitions
are drawn up, game shops can systematically erase dissent and the
work of creators thinking outside the box. For instance, there was
an understandable outcry when Apple's App Store banned Danish
game studio Lovable Hat Cult's creation *La Petite Mort* (2016),
which invites the player to simulate sex on a series of abstract
vulvas in order to bring about an orgasm. What should have been

an educational game exploring the physical satisfaction, sensation and performance of people with vulvas became a detonator of moral panic for the conservative storefronts seeking to curate the safest collections possible.

Among other apps swiftly removed from the App Store is *I Am Rich* (2008), which had little to no function, but was priced at a plum $999.99 (equivalent to more than $1,400 at the time of this writing). The game simply acted as a sort of status symbol, a grotesque extension of the iPhone's status itself. Eight copies of the app were sold before being pulled from the store. This reflects in some way the work of the artist Carl Andre, who also played around with the concept of price and on one occasion, decided to sell his works for 10 per cent of the buyer's income. 'I'm disappointed that artists do not try to play with the market that way. Everybody is letting the dealer set the price. In that respect, I think the artists have given up a role they might play,' commented curator Ralph Rugoff on Andre's work.[18] Due to their proximity to their clients, enabled by digital storefronts that let creators control pricing, independent game creators have been creative in this sphere.

LAZA KNITEZ!! (2014) is a fast-paced jousting death-match game for up to four players. At eleven megabytes, it is tiny, but makes a grand statement with its purchasing model. The team had been discussing the labour and other sacrifices involved in making games and decided to price it at $100, marked down with a 98 per cent discount for the first five years. In 2019, the game that used to cost $2 went up to the originally intended price of $100, making a satirical comment on the state of game longevity, or lack thereof, pricing and sales practice.[19] The labour, the hours and the emotion invested in crafting a game are rarely reflected in its price or in the profits gained – the realities of the market are such that the vast majority of released games flop, and the successful ones have their profits pocketed by the few who hold the rights to them. *LAZA KNITEZ!!*, then, simply gambles with the state the industry is in.

Like Carl Andre, the authors of *Oikospiel Book I* (2017), a game about 'fevered landscapes, classic literature, operating systems, opera and the need for dog-based unions', also had a self-aware, clever pricing system.[20] Players had to fill in a form revealing their income and the number of members in their household in order to generate the price they would pay for the game. Potential customers were then invited to spin a seemingly pointless two-dimensional wind turbine, using their cursor, to reduce the suggested price by pennies. Both *LAZA KNITEZ!!* and *Oikospiel Book I* were feted by the gaming press, unlike the minimal and more vulgar-presenting *I Am Rich*. The latter was covered more by the mainstream press, but only in terms of its attempt to adjudicate the bizarre digital app economy.

The history of modern art is punctuated by a constant tension between the artists who pushed boundaries and were considered immoral or uncomfortable, and the gatekeepers of cultural morality and dominant ideology. In games, that sentiment thrived in the early days of the internet, and is now more institutionally enabled by smaller indie online retailers such as itch.io. Introducing and widening this selection into the mainstream will be beneficial for games in the long term.

Still, it is worth underlining that critical practices like Sierra's and Fraser's are nowadays not just tolerated, they are specifically invited to be part of the elite art scenes, international biennales and global high-end gallery circuits. The critique they level is almost entirely contained within the medium, nurtured and celebrated, posing little danger to the art world that coddles these exhibits. Most such practices are part of lofty art collections and are coveted by most reputable curators. Self-critical, self-referential and critical in an aesthetically pleasing manner – these practices are folded into the art world and increase the prestige of the arts industry.

Games like *Phone Story*, on the other hand, are actively shooed away from the market-facing fronts of the medium. They remain unpromoted, seen as an abomination rather than a clever invention. Very few in the games media or distributors would rate such work as anything more than a token novelty or a nuisance, rather than as valuable staples of institutional critique. And therein lies the kind of subversive potential that seems to have been neutralised by the all-accepting art world.

One game that effectively questions the form necessary for playing it is *Send Me to Heaven* (2013). The game uses the accelerometer of the device (usually a mobile phone) that the audience is playing the game on to measure a score, calculated by how high the player throws it into the air. People with this app compete against each other by seeking to throw their phones up higher than anyone else, at the risk of damaging or even destroying their devices. Apple once again demonstrated its thin skin by banning the app from the App Store. It is currently still available to download on Google Play, where it has garnered a devoted fan base.

In a similar vein, *Lose/Lose* (2009), a shoot-em-up art videogame released for Mac OS by the American designer Zach Gage, invites the player to control a spaceship and shoot an alien in their path, with little to no difficulty. However, with every felled alien, the game permanently deletes a random file on the player's actual Mac machine, resulting in a potentially corrupted operating system. The game became notorious for its Russian-roulette-type mechanic and the coveted leaderboard: how long could players last before their computers were permanently disabled?

These examples represent art at its most intriguing – subversive, dangerous, risky, generous with varying interpretations and outcomes. But such extreme or abstract experiments are not all that could be interesting about the intersection of games and politics. *Untitled Goose Game* (2019) stars a pesky goose that wreaks havoc in a traditional conservative English village. The game lures the player in with relatively safe and cute aesthetics and an unassuming protagonist. Its sudden turn into subversive mischief may intrigue players, who perhaps were not prepared for anarchist scheming and the cheeky inducement of chaos. A percentage of the game's profits have funded indigenous resistance campaigns in Canada. The goose quickly became a leftist meme, most notably around the Brexit issue.

The Estonian-British studio ZA/UM's 2019 megahit *Disco Elysium* is cited as one of the most powerful and successful current political videogames. With a reportedly gruesome years-long development process involving no fewer than nine writers, this indie endeavour embraced dialogue and role-playing mechanics in order to tell a story defined by its breadth and nuances. While controlling the protagonist, Detective Harrier 'Harry' Du Bois, the game invites players to empathise with non-playable game characters from all walks of life and with a variety of political leanings. Players from both political extremes were able to find something in this game and to meet their opponents in the process. The creators drip-feed deep revolutionary communist politics throughout the various plot and subplot lines, but this is never done heavy-handedly or with an intention to only talk to their own camp. This game deals primarily with the player's own political and spiritual discovery, so the sense of being capable of making a choice steers the narrative here, rather than a projection of the creators' own values. The game design and narrative tricks make space for a fluid, noncommittal and steady persuasiveness.

As one player describes it: '*Disco Elysium* deals with fascism by showing not why it's wrong, but why it's appealing. It shows it from its strongest, not the weakest side. This makes for a much more honest antifascist game.'[21] It also includes a glimpse of the institutional critique sorely lacking in games – at one point, the protagonist is confronted with the failures of a fictional indie games studio, partially referencing the early days of the real studio, but also foreshadowing the infighting between, and ultimate dramatic exit of, some of the real-life creators of the game.[22]

Culture as Tools, Not Just Signifiers

Presenting information in innovative ways is one of the key methods political games use to justify their existence. *A Hand with Many Fingers* (2020) attempts to do that in a manner not dissimilar from Hans Haacke's aforementioned practice. Here, the player is invited to delve into an intricate plot involving real-world CIA conspiracy and corruption, advancing the narrative by sifting through real documents, pinning notes and revealing buried secrets. The game provides a stimulating journey through themes of authority, secrecy and institutional involvement. Again, one might question the efficiency of such presentation, but having the players go through the material by themselves and uncover the secrets does make them more invested in the information discovered. In 2018, *Vice* and other outlets covered a little text adventure gem by Kris Ligman titled *You Are Jeff Bezos*, where the player receives a variety of virtual purchase choices, such as the latest iPhone, jewellery, lifetime subscriptions to various covetable, cars, and mansions. It rapidly becomes apparent just how much of a chore it is to spend all this money. Many clicks later, barely a dent has been made in the billionaire's wealth.

Ever since I first saw coverage of the game, the most intriguing example of a political videogame for me has been *The Uber Game*

(2017). The plot is essentially that of an Uber simulator: the player is put in the shoes of a freelance driver, who spends their day taking sometimes difficult passengers around town, making money on the Uber app. Clever writing tricks allow players to form an emotional relationship with the main character, all in the space of a quick ten-minute game. The numbers look relatively healthy until after a few days – spoiler – it's time to address fees for car maintenance, petrol, insurance, repairs and Uber's cut. A tiny fraction of the total take, representing only half of the minimum wage, remains in the driver's pocket

Albeit well-made, the game's content is no more fascinating than that of the games I usually critique – these are hardly revolutionary gameplay mechanics, right? The kicker is the location of the game: it was commissioned by, and is playable for free on, the website of the *Financial Times* – a prominent centre-right publication. By fostering a sentimental bond between the player and the character, then sneaking in a progressive message through that bombshell ending, the game holds a substantially larger chance of actually effecting a change of heart. Crucially, it targets players who might not naturally feel solidarity with an Uber driver. In other words, the developers skipped the 'this is going to be really funny!' moment. The average *FT* reader was probably unprepared for the punchline, which is precisely why it's so powerful.

The Uber Game and *Phone Story* spotlight the question about whether it is really the design, aesthetic and mechanics of a game that create a persuasive political argument, or could the method of distribution be key here? *The Uber Game* would be way less effective if it had been presented to already centre-left *Guardian* readers or simply left on a neutral game store, where it would be picked up mainly by progressive gamers who need no convincing that Uber drivers deserve a better deal. Could it be, perhaps, that among the many other techniques outlined here, the modes of dissemination and the sophistication of marketing are among the strongest factors in actually changing minds?

Alternatively, how can games become tools for social change, rather than mere statements or pieces of propaganda? Again, I am reminded of a fine art practice. The Polish artist Krzysztof Wodiczko turned ordinary shopping carts into storage spaces that unfolded into beds. He then distributed them to the unhoused residents of New York City. In 2005, Argentinian artist Judi Werthein set up Brinco, a brand of trainers, and gave them away free to people attempting to cross the border illegally in Tijuana, Mexico. The shoes featured a torch, a compass and pockets to hide money and medicine. Printed on a removable insole was a map of the border area around Tijuana. At the same time, just over the border in California, she sold the shoes as limited-edition art objects for $200 a pair. Part of the money generated went to a Tijuana shelter helping migrants in need. The shoe is part of the permanent collection at the Tate Modern. Such pieces provide real-life means for solidarity and the implementation of moral values. Rather than being mere signifiers, they become objects devised and effectively mobilised for change.

In principle, nothing prevents games from doing the same thing, especially given their deep digital footprint and capacity for original presentation. But somehow, little to no effort is genuinely invested here. Yes, the computerised aspect can be seen as a limitation, but there is no lack of space for innovation, or perhaps the digital facet can prove to be more powerful in some ways. Instead of mining money-laundering cryptocurrencies, could cleaner computer power be utilised for the automation of some digital activism? Time and levels of creativity in this area will tell. The axis for efficacy should be examined also, not just the political affiliation, to assess the scope for drawing action from inaction.

To be clear, other media also often fail to be very useful or practical. Claire Bishop notes as much about parts of the art world. She detects that the perceived social achievements of a piece of political art are never compared with those of real-life social projects. Instead, they derive their critical value in opposition to more traditional or abstract art, which is not concerned with saving the world. Socially aware art validates its own existence precisely because it doesn't present as 'artistic'. The aspiration is always to move beyond art, but never to the point of comparison with similar projects in the social domain.[23] Instead of inquiring about efficacy, the tendency is to compare artists' projects with those of other artists on the basis of ethical one-upmanship. Contemporary art, as outlined at the beginning of this chapter, can absolutely ooze mediocrity, too. However, the capacity for experimentation and inquiry, rather than just product-crafting, is still much more extensive in the art sector.

Few examples are needed to expose the corruption and intricate hypocrisies that taint socially conscious fine artists and the galleries and biennales exhibiting them, funded by money from the darkest parts of the contemporary economy. The Tate galleries and the British Museum run large-scale public relations campaigns around their work in diversifying the cast of artists they exhibit, while simultaneously taking money from the oligarchs who immiserate the oppressed classes of the world.

Even so, there exist enclaves of artists who forfeit social and material capital in the pursuit of sustainability or purity, in some sense. Although the anthropologist David Graeber dedicated most of his career to examining forms of economy and history, his thoughts on the sovereignty of the artist also ring true:

Artists and those drawn to them have created enclaves where it has been possible to experiment with forms of work, exchange, and production radically different from those promoted by capital. While they are not always self-consciously revolutionary, artistic circles have had a persistent tendency to overlap with revolutionary circles; presumably, precisely because these have been spaces where people can experiment with radically different, less alienated forms of life . . . Many artists are deeply cynical about what they do. But even those who are the most idealistic can only feel they are pulling something off when they are able to create enclaves, however small, where they can experiment with forms of life, exchange, and production which are − if not downright communistic (which they often are), then at any rate, about as far from the forms ordinarily promoted by capital as anyone can get to experience.[24]

What Would Adorno Say?

Surveying the pitfalls and successes of the art world's political efficacy may be a useful exercise, but games hold some unique challenges, too. Something about games and many of their designs points to more fundamental flaws. My conflicting feelings about the medium continue when I observe that their design is so often fundamentally tied up with competition and accumulation, justifying and validating many experiences under capitalist systems. Always chasing, panting to get ahead, needing to grind to succeed, to win or simply to survive. Even the more wholesome games, stripped of all such mechanics, tend to subdue us into inaction. The theorist Theodor Adorno would remind us here that much of entertainment is a ritual in which the subjugated celebrate their subjection.

As a leisure activity, the Frankfurt School philosopher Adorno would no doubt insist, gaming merely underpins and highlights our own position as permanent commodities in the labour market. It offers a few hours given over to relaxing on purchased products, with money given to us, so we have less time to actually express ourselves and play. Free time is nothing but a shadowy continuation of labour.[25] Screenwork and leisure bleed into each other. We complete tasks on pieces of hardware that fundamentally create more work for us, and every second of our engagement with it boosts the profits which will be used to make our lives even more miserable.

Adorno is not alone here. Modern thinkers offer a similar critique:

> Games may offer a sense of order and control, a moment of recuperation and a sense of escape from the insecurity, inequality, and tension caused by capitalist systems, but these very same qualities also have a potential to trap the player within game spaces that are less about the creative powers of play and more about soothing citizens' anxieties within sanctioned commercial leisure spaces.[26]

Workers with discretionary leisure income pay to be entertained, to be compensated for the boredom of their working lives. Collectively hallucinating and preoccupied with survival instead of overthrowing the structures that engender our suffering, we are stuck in pockets of culture as the only space we have any chance of controlling. In the absence of material autonomy, enclaves of entertainment and popular culture stand in as arenas where irrelevant people can get at each other or command the admiration so often lacking in our everyday alienated experiences.

Even the once relatively private activity of play has been commodified beyond recognition. Every sort of image imaginable – still, moving, and capable of being played with – are now commercialised, consumed and sold for the benefit of the owner, by third parties that make a cut on the deal.[27] With the rise of market-driven artificial intelligence apps, one does not even need to own the image in order to control, manipulate and benefit from it. Images have taken precedence over the real, creating a pseudo-world that obscures the real one. Games are a collection of images to be interacted with, morphing an individual into at once a passive spectator and a consumer.

In such a surface culture culture, the representation of an artist or an artwork is often more significant than the work or the artist themselves. An artist with more social capital might have a larger, more influential public profile. And again, leading to more success. This type of image supremacy means that gaming marketing campaigns, public relations efforts and even the social capital of developers or studios play a major role in shaping consumer expectations and reactions. Progressive videogames are not excepted from this spectacle machine, with their efficacy measured more by how many people downloaded the product and what awards the author wins than by the real-world changes they inspire.

The cultural theorist Walter Benjamin warned that it is not enough to pass something off as having 'revolutionary content' while still utilising contemporary relations to production. In his seminal work 'The Author as Producer' (1934), he argued that it is essential for the author, artist or activist to become a conscious producer, one who considers and evaluates their own work, and their relation to the formal means of production, in a 'truly revolutionary way'.[28] This becomes critical when taking seriously the methods involved in making games (that will be the battle of Level IV). Any product with ethics as its selling point can never truly be valid if said ethics negate the conditions necessary for that product to exist. Furthermore, the game risks appearing sinister if it insists on its own value.

This should not be a controversial take – if an artist or a game developer is serious about the efficacy of their work, and is selling it on this merit, they must be equally invested in demonstrating a level of awareness towards the methods by which it has come to exist. I personally have been reproached for suggesting that collaborations with institutions or products that promote inequality and destruction, while attempting to sell their own progressive cause, are wrong.[29] A necessity for social capital, rather than systematic and institutional solving of injustices, still rules too much of this industry. The hope is that this is a temporary tussle as we work to find new and reliable methods of restructuring how we make games and signal politics in them. In the meantime, however, it can certainly be a dispiriting and exhausting path.

Even within the high-end art milieu, very few practitioners are driven to cohere with much of Benjamin's guidance. Hito Steyerl comes to mind – the filmmaker and moving image artist is keen on producing carbon-neutral work and shows, as well as limiting the buyer pool of her works according to their ethics.[30] Steyerl often cites historically materialist literature as a frame of integrity for her that provides a challenge and a sense of security. While she does not pretend to work to reach audiences outside of the sophisticated art scene, Steyerl attaches importance to nurturing an ethics in the actual processes of her artistic expressions.

Videogames are a classic expression of the capitalist modus operandi: seizing play, a part of a human's cognitive growth and basic interaction, and appropriating it for speculation, exploitation and all that an obsessive lunge for profits results in. An activity that in and of itself should not be moralised – playing on digital displays – currently relies on exploitative routes to make those products, almost automatically rendering them tainted. With little to no choice, we are locked into a relationship of passive consumption, entertained in a circus not only while the world burns, but as we – with every push of the button – burn it ourselves. 'Humanity's self-alienation has reached such a degree that it can experience its own destruction as an aesthetic pleasure of the first order,' Benjamin wrote.[31] Videogames are extremely good at this. Are there alternatives for the medium beyond that?

Level IV: Modes of Production

After reading Level III, my partner turned to me and made a grimly spot-on remark: 'You do know that all of the games you're dissecting in this Level, plus all of the games like them, put together, are probably bringing in just a percentile of the revenue of a single high-end waifu game?' He is devastatingly right. The kind of circles I move in as part of the Western indie, arty, politically aware games scene make up a tiny speck in the global videogames industry.

A *waifu* is a fictional character, especially popular in anime and manga, whom a player regards as a romantic partner. It is typically a non-playable character of a given game whom the player can interact with; waifus have oversexualised features and their attraction to you, the player, is directly linked to how good you are at a game. How good you are, however, in games centring this type of interaction is usually determined by the amount of real-life money you have invested into loot boxes, an in-game gambling mechanic where items and improvements are given (or not given) at random. So the impact of a gambling mechanic that uses waifus or *husbandos* (yes, this is a real term) in a mobile game like *Genshin Impact* (2020), which has garnered more than 50 million monthly players and a \$4 billion revenue in its four years of existence, is most definitely larger than the entire serious or artsy games milieu.[1]

The top ten mobile games, clogged with microtransactions around purposefully unchallenging themes, are substantially more profitable (\$12 billion revenue in 2022) than the narrative-driven releases for PC and console. *Dungeon Fighter Online* (2005), a game with unexceptional graphics, scantily clad characters and seriously addictive mechanics, has had more unique players than the entire population of Europe.[2] The vast majority of digital gaming is currently preoccupied with profiteering gacha mechanics,[*] rather than with aspects of culture that resist domination and extractivism.

Level IV presents the toughest challenge yet. In order to encourage the brilliant parts of this fascinating field – digital gaming – and to begin to eliminate other parts, we must understand how games themselves are made. Not only the assembly line behind them, but the complex finance and income models that shape the videogame culture. Only by dissecting the layers of production and inspecting the various cogs in this massive global machine can we hope to steer it in another direction. As this chapter demonstrates, there are many parts to the creation, storing and selling of a videogame; a range of pressure points can and should be adjusted, and the industry should be completely reimagined. The single item of a videogame – depending on its size and scale – can reach like an octopus far and wide into many adjacent industries. One solid product has various levels of questionable politics and points of

---

[*] Gachapons are capsules sold in vending machines that contain random toys. A gacha game, then, is a videogame that implements the gacha (toy vending machine) mechanic. Similar to loot boxes, gacha games entice players to spend in-game currency to receive a random in-game item.

resistance. How are games made? Which parts of this global machine can be justified and which must be bravely and immediately brought to game over?

Creation

From the very first moment of opening of a New Game Project file on a computer, game developers are already part of the process of profit extraction and cost-benefit relations with other products. Most games are crafted on pieces of software called *game engines*, computer applications that a game creator (or a team) can use, layer by layer, to build graphics, code, design and audio systems that will bring a videogame into existence. The ways these engines are sold varies. The most advanced engines are available through hefty licensing deals, complicated crediting and profit-sharing mechanisms. Those utilised by independent game creators can have a less involved pricing system, but, by the same token, a more basic tool set. Large game engines such as Unreal and Unity are not only major pieces of commercial software in themselves; entire large-scale independent companies now base their business on crafting *middleware*, the numerous plug-ins that tie into these engines, creating mini-industries that orbit the big hitters.

Huge productions like CD Projekt's *Witcher* series (2007 onwards) and, until recently, *Cyberpunk 2077* (2020) work on their own custom-made proprietary game engines, and some independent game creators craft them, too.[3] However, the majority of games are built with commercially available tools whose influence is growing ever greater. Unreal, for example, is one of the largest commercial game engines (developed by Epic Games, the creators of the mega-hit *Fortnite*) and is now being used to build many of the visuals around us in more than just games. Game engines have become the backbone of production in movies, television, advertising, construction and architecture. Prized not only for their visual aspect, but also for simulations of physics, they play an intrinsic role in modelling many real-life cultural, engineering and infrastructure projects.[4]

Game engines are also the base of the software which holds considerable information about players and their habits. This includes session time, at which point during the game they decide to stop, behavioural patterns, length of play and other game-related data. Depending on the game, some engines may also hold much of the player's private information, such as their bank details and social contacts.[5] Much of this data is used by the engine companies themselves or by third-party contractors, who package it into an interface for those who'll pay to access it. Such practices have caused international outrage. For example, Western players distrust products from Epic (owners of Unreal Engine), as 40 per cent of the company is owned by the Chinese conglomerate Tencent. In 2019, the CEO of Epic, Tim Sweeney, did his best to refute the accusations that Epic Games Store was spyware for the Chinese government.[6] European and American regulators nonetheless demand that game studios operating in subsequent territories box their databases so that no one from Tencent is able to access them. Game makers are therefore mired in global geopolitical tensions and are in relationship with major influential software corporations at the point of booting up the tools they use to craft their art.

And yet, the prominence and relatively easy access of these engines have had some democratising effects, too. By the late 2000s, teams as small as one or two were able to deploy these tools on simple computing machines to build impressive and deep game worlds, birthing the indie games movement. Game engines – the access, the variety, ownership and implementation –are often cited as a shorthand for indicating how games are made, sold and even perceived. Built on Unreal? Probably large, AAA, big-budget and spectacular, with detailed graphics (for example, the *BioShock* series). Unity? More economic graphics, great for mobile games, used for building cherished indies as *Firewatch* (2016) and mega-hits such as *Genshin Impact*. Disparate approaches to drawing up a game emerge at the software level. Capital inserts its profit-seeking tentacle already at this nascent stage.

What type of people make games and how do they assemble together?

Work conditions in the AAA (large) studios were brought into the sunlight with the aforementioned 'EA Spouse Letter', describing the gruelling conditions at one of the biggest and most profitable game companies in the world:

> The current mandatory hours are 9 am to 10 pm – seven days a week – with the occasional Saturday evening off for good behavior (at 6:30 pm). This averages out to an eighty-five hour work week . . . And the kicker: for the honor of this treatment EA salaried employees receive a) no overtime; b) no compensation time! ('comp' time is the equalization of time off for overtime – any hours spent during a crunch accrue into days off after the product has shipped); c) no additional sick or vacation leave.[7]

In the period since 2004, when this pervasive industry-wide problem was publicised, matters have barely improved. In 2010, the industry was again presented with an open letter, this time from 'Rockstar Spouses'.[8] Workers at Rockstar Games, the creators behind *Red Dead Redemption* (2010), *LA Noire* (2011) and *Max Payne 3* (2012), all reported engaging in crunch at their San Diego studio. Anonymous employees of Epic Games later described work weeks that stretched between eighty and 100 hours in the run-up to the release of *Fortnite Battle Royale* (2017).[9]

According to a 2019 survey, 40 per cent of game developers experienced crunch at least once that year. Only 8 per cent reported receiving extra pay for their additional hours. The survey was conducted by the International Game Developers Association, which mainly represents Global North workers.[10] One can assume that matters are even worse in the regions such surveys don't reach. Studio workers say that crunch is increasingly factored into production schedules: it is becoming the rule, rather than an exception. Developers rarely complain – their passion for games and game making is taken for granted. The presence of table tennis, foosball tables and beer fridges in the offices, as well as occasional free merch for the title they worked on, are meant to keep the workers feeling special and in no need of protection from the darker parts of the industry.

Crunch is probably the most intensely discussed problem, but it is not the only one affecting games studio workers. Sexism and other forms of discrimination are sadly still a persistent issue in this male-dominated field. To give just one well-reported example, Jessica Price was unceremoniously fired from her position as the narrative designer for ArenaNet, the creators of the *Guild Wars* series (2005 onw.), upon challenging a sexist fan on Twitter.[11] Sexual harassment at industry events, or male bosses abusing their position and dating their subordinates at work, is a common and mostly tolerated occurrence. The dark cloud of misogyny that was made cool by Atari back in the 1970s still casts a shadow.

In 2022, Riot Games – the team behind huge titles such as the *League of Legends* franchise – agreed to pay out a whopping $100 million to settle a class-action lawsuit brought by its women employees. Unwanted sexual advances by male colleagues, pay disparity and lost promotions due to their gender were just some of the alleged offences.[12] The payout presumably barely made a dent in the corporation's coffers, as its main performer's *League of Legends* revenue reached $1.6 billion in 2015.[13] Also in 2022, Activision Blizzard settled a lawsuit, paying $18 million to its women employees, and 'agreed to take steps to prevent and address discrimination and harassment.' In one of the most notorious and bizarre breaches of conduct at the studio, men employees allegedly stole breast milk from the office fridge.[14]

Sudden and mass layoffs are also commonplace in the industry. The following are just a few examples. In 2018, Telltale Games, the studio that crafted *The Walking Dead* (2012), abruptly fired 250 employees without any severance. That same year, Capcom shut down its Vancouver subsidiary, leaving 158 people jobless. In February 2019, Activision Blizzard cut nearly 1,000 workers' jobs.[15] In 2023, EA fired 800 people weeks after reporting a $7 billion revenue. And 600 people working on the Unity game engine were fired in 2023, heightening fears that Unreal Engine, owned by Epic Games, would soon become a monopoly. Embracer Group, which spent billions buying up game companies, most actively in Scandinavia, proceeded to then shut down numerous studios, leaving thousands of employees without work and unfinished games that will never see the light of day.[16]

Job insecurity is an everyday reality for the majority of people working in the videogames industry. Severance pay is a rarity, and fighting to get it can be hard. Crucially, though, game makers are often working under strict NDAs (non-disclosure agreements) that prohibit any discussion about unannounced projects. If a project is halted mid-production, game developers are not credited and cannot show their own work to potential future employers, regardless of the number of years they spent on that project. I personally know many unlucky game developers who have worked in the industry for more than a decade, but struggle to find new employment, since their projects have been randomly cancelled – experience is measured by the number of releases worked on, rather than years in the job.

Quality assurance (QA) workers, who bear the brunt of strenuous, repetitive and undervalued work in videogames – making sure they actually run – usually endure the most intense crunch and enjoy few rights and little appreciation. Playing a game hundreds of times and discovering and filing bugs before the release of the game can, unless managed properly and ethically, lock workers to a desk for days. QA is the most frequently outsourced part of game making, often passed on to invisible workers in the Global South and Eastern Europe. Working in QA is often the most accessible path into the games industry for people who were unable to study it at university or find another way in.

Writer Ian Williams describes it this way:

> When we see a presentation given by a game CEO at PAX (a prestigious games industry summit), we look past that lone figure and see the toil and love of the dozens who made the platform he or she stands on.[17]

A general class disparity exists within the industry. In the UK, for instance, game developers are twice as likely as the population at large to have parents in managerial positions. Similarly, British game devs are twice as likely to have received a private-school education.[18] Certainly, individuals who are a minority in the industry – be they women, migrants, or people of colour or from poorer backgrounds – can be tokenised and made to feel unwelcome within a dominant group that has never worried about security.

In contrast with the perceived glamour and growth of an industry full of Twitter celebrity game developers and successful boutique studios, the workers who truly hold this industry together are underpaid, outsourced, alienated and constantly overlooked. The inability in the gaming industry to understand poverty is a problem not only within corporate board meetings, but also among its core workforce. Romanticised though they are, indie companies can be even more culpable in this regard. Structured as an opposition to the major company structures creating AAA games, with hundreds of people in dozens of teams building one major release, indie teams were supposed to have a more horizontal structure and offer developers more choice as to how and when they wanted (or didn't want) to work. They operate with a smaller gap between the creation of the game and its release. Employee salaries in indie set-ups are usually lower than the industry standard; moreover, the insecurity is greater, so that people working in indie studios are perhaps already more materially stable. Working for an independent company may require employees to practise more than just their craft; since indie employees often need entrepreneurial skills, the positions are more accessible to those who have been to business or private school.

Although the ethos of indie studios is meant to be the antithesis of big game company cultures, sadly they too are mired in issues that only underline the need for a more universal safeguard. Any for-profit company structure, no matter how small and cosy, has its problems. A more institutional solution was needed. In 2017, game workers began looking into establishing trade unions. These historically tested structures ought to assist studios, both large and small, in bringing ethical considerations into this largely unregulated field.

The dozens of local unions which have sprung up in numerous countries under the Game Workers Unite umbrella movement since 2018 offer a hint of optimism. They have their work cut out for them – still, numerous victories have already been achieved. Of course, this didn't happen without a fight. Company bosses sang the same tune previously heard from Silicon Valley tech bosses: we're special, we're different, we need bespoke solutions. The self-narrative of those in positions of power in the games industry is one of uniqueness; it claims that the usual structures for holding employers accountable are unsuitable for the world of technology. Gaming is different from an assembly line and the old ways of organising a workforce. This shroud of tech mystique cannot be pulled away without trade-union support.

Not all unions are the same, and it is worth noting that their effectiveness, as well as their political affiliations, form a broad spectrum. Some, like STJV in France, are horizontally run, radical unions that fight for their workers tooth and nail. Some sense a financial opportunity, with those game dev salaries filling up the coffers of union dues so they gather game workers into unions with scant care for their specific needs. Some are more interested in retaining a clean social media profile among upper-class games industry influencers, and even bosses, than in protecting their vulnerable members. They are keen to appear mature and non-confrontational, so as to fit in with the comfort-seeking parts of the industry, instead of embracing class antagonism, which is likely to lose them friends in high places.

On the other hand, publicly facing unions are more exposed than ever. They are often seen by game workers as a service rather than a space for solidarity or for building a movement. So when something bad happens within the union space, the urge among many in an industry attuned to neoliberal values is to call the manager rather than work together to shape a better tomorrow. The activist Alex Fernandes describes the dynamic as follows:

> Every time a union does a perceived Good Thing or Bad Thing there's a flurry of people joining or leaving as with BFAWU/

UNISON at the moment and I can't stress enough how that's not how any of this works. Stop treating trade unions like they're clubs, please, for fuck's sake.[19]

The games industry union movement is young and at times clumsy; it should be allowed to make mistakes and grow. A rising number of gaming employees are now part of solid, tried-and-tested union movements that consistently deliver for ordinary workers. New generations of potential union organisers are getting involved in the movement, and, overall, it is truly astonishing. I had the privilege to witness this burgeoning movement from up-close and, although my personal story in the movement ended in burnout and sadness, I am still in awe of the incredible people around the world pushing this crucial, hopeful part of the industry forward.

Unionisation is an essential tool in resisting what's to come: an ever-aggressive, powerful and consolidating industry with little restraint or supervision. The top five games companies in the world made a whopping $90 billion in revenue in 2021.[20] In 2023, Microsoft bought Activision Blizzard for nearly $70 billion, successfully adding huge catalogues of games onto their Xbox – a subscription-based game sales platform driving gamers to a single closed system.[21] The largest company in the world, with a $30 billion revenue – the Chinese giant Tencent – has been buying up studios, and studios that own many other studios, all over the world. The monopolisation of the industry is ongoing and, with tens of billions sloshing around in consolidation deals big and small, it is increasingly difficult to exert any influence over power of such magnitude. The future of games is decided in pristine board rooms, with little to no input from those who actually craft the games or from the masses of those who play them.

And while people from ever more diverse demographics are developing more varied games, this centralisation is still likely to shrink the choice of games overall. Bigger and bigger companies are busy working on a smaller catalogue of old intellectual property assets, or even on a single, financially evergreen game. At the same time, most app stores are steadily removing old games from their digital shelves. Other IP never sees the light of day – projects are discontinued mid-production, and the IP is bought so that another company cannot profit from it. This echoes the wastefulness currently rampant in the film industry, where big-budget projects are scrapped before release. For example, the *Batgirl* film cost $90 million to make yet will never be screened or streamed.[22] In 2023, Disney Plus completed production of the *Nautilus* series in Australia, involving hundreds of cast and crew members, only to axe the show before its release.[23] With marketing budgets now rivalling actual production costs, merely completing the shoot meant that half of the budget remained to be spent, not to mention the savings on reshoots and royalty payments.

The small number of conglomerates, which own vast amounts of IP, stifles creativity, too. The decision as to what to do or not to do with frozen projects, which is made by fewer and fewer people, creates a morphed picture of what's on offer. Some projects are propelled, and versions of them are released and re-released. Others are stuck in limbo. For example, the beloved manga legend *Sailor Moon*, involving a cast of Tokyo-based students with superpowers (adored by this author!), only had a handful of gaming adaptations in the early 1990s and nothing since. The much-anticipated *Disco Elysium* sequel is looking to be canned due to corporate IP disagreements. Huge IP projects are bought up and teams moved to other projects, but without advocates to root for them (apart from the players, of course), quality games IP can die a slow death.

Yet similarly to the Marvelisation of Hollywood, some gaming IP is being made into every form possible, for every device that will hold a videogame. *Super Mario* has been spun into the *Mario Kart* series, *Super Smash Bros*, the *Yoshi* series and so on, which are available in every format imaginable. The *Pokémon*, *Metal Gear* and *Warhammer* series have been similarly franchised. As a result, it is much harder for new ideas to break through; if they do, they must have a sequelisation or prequelisation plan lined up. Centralisation results in larger budgets – the only way big machines operate – which result in higher risk factors.

Seeking to lower the risk, conglomerates avoid new ideas and lean on their existing fanbase. Again in contrast to the arts, where pieces are relished for their singularity and where intellectual property is less protected, with a clearer history of 'inspiration', in games, creativity is framed in terms of profitability and re-envisioning previous products with small differences, rather than true trailblazing. At the same time, smaller studios, which do not own established IPs, may struggle to compete with the financial and marketing resources of larger companies, leading to fewer opportunities for the emergence of new and innovative game concepts.

A complete market dominance by very few actors will obviously affect the workforce, too. Similar to what was cited by film industry workers during the 2023 writers' strike, owners of these organisations will be able to claim content overload when the workers actually making these products demand better conditions. Not only are potentially interesting releases being ditched, but strikes also impact on the teams that were perhaps working on projects that were about to go into production. Overcommitment and the sudden shocks dictated by the monopolisation of the industry result in mass layoffs and devastating life changes for the employees.

While much of the prevalent moral discourse around videogames is stuck in banal anxieties about their potential to turn people violent, a much more urgent and consequential movement is taking place. The consolidation of game companies into a few mega conglomerates will affect consumers and creators alike, but – most importantly – it will fuel all of the dodgiest practices already cultivated by this industry. The PR and lobbying campaigns behind the 2023 Activision Blizzard buyout by Microsoft have been effective in convincing regulators to accept this move. The European Commission in charge of competition policy actually stated that Microsoft's ability to enhance the cloud gaming services economy was the main reason why the deal was allowed to go through.[24]

Curation

Publishing a game is also steeped in politics. Historically, the industry was similar to book publishing: game creators approached publishers with a proposal or a semi-finished product, looking for funding for the rest of the project and negotiating profit sharing. Publishers then arranged the logistics of the game, identifying its audience and reaching the consumer.

With notable exceptions – studios that are too big or too small – most videogames currently on the market result from a deal between a studio and a publisher. Most often, game companies receive regular payments from publishers in order to complete their game, and a revenue split is set up. Usually this is meant to support game creators who lack the resources or knowledge to deal with marketing and distribution of games, and are unable to fund the entire production upfront.

Depending on the agreement, this can result in majority or absolute control by the publisher to dictate the schedule and even the content of the game. Under this pressure, crunch and creative corner-cutting are common. Publishers often retain ownership over the IP; if they don't do a good enough job promoting the product, creators may find themselves limited in how much they can do for the marketing of the game, as the rights to their own game simply don't belong to them anymore. Layers of NDAs and legal tie-ins may bar them from mentioning the product altogether.

And while that is still overall the standard relationship, the monopolisation of the games industry has allowed for large studios to look into self-publishing, thus getting rid of the middleman and consolidating even more power. Companies such as Sony or Microsoft, possessing the holy trifecta of necessary tools for game releasing and consumption – hardware, game development and game publishing – are almost invincible. They can print money within the closed ecosystem, then grant themselves obviously beneficial deals to conjure up the product on the said hardware. Given the internal emails within Microsoft musing about buying out a giant like Nintendo, it seems like the consolidation game has only just begun.[25]

Unlike the game makers, who are more often driven by creative ambitions, publishing is mostly a numbers business. Here again, the analogy with the film industry fits – churning out yet another *Call of Duty* game is more profitable than investing in smaller, more experimental titles. That lean into the familiar is what drives the bulk of publishing deals, too. Most game pitching decks now contain selling points such as 'X Familiar Game meets Y Familiar Game', or 'X Familiar Game Mechanic meets Y Familiar Game Mechanic'; the familiarity is often seen as a plus. '*Dark Souls* meets *Star Wars*', '*Grand Theft Auto* meets *The Walking Dead*' or '*Street Fighter* meets *Slay the Spire*' are examples of pitches that are likely to secure funding. Reduced consumer choice is justified as simply presenting players with what they want. This limited view of what gaming can or should be is baked into the financial modelling, and certainly affects how the industry is shaped.

More broadly, publishers are also at the mercy of the online app stores. Steam – the largest distributor of PC videogames – has more than 400 million sales annually.[26] That's hundreds of millions of sales of games, with prices ranging from a few pence to thousands of dollars for collector's editions. For each game, Steam charges the publisher or studio a commission of 30 per cent from the first $10 million in sales. For all sales between $10 million and $50 million, the commission is 25 per cent. For every sale after the initial $50 million, Steam takes a 20 per cent cut. Additionally, Steam charges $100 for any game that is put on the platform. So, just being a digital storefront with few expenses apart from some server space is incredibly profitable – in 2021, for example, the platform generated $10 billion in revenue.[27]

Steam's revenues are only a tad bit smaller than those of Ticketmaster (part of Live Nation), say, who own nearly 80 per cent of the online ticket purchasing business for live events.[28] Ticketmaster is close to a monopoly for analogue events, at least in the US. Steam, however, shares business with other huge stores selling games to other platforms – consoles and mobile games. Sony owns PlayStation console and Microsoft owns Xbox console; both have their own stores and report revenues in the many billions.

The field where gaming is dominant, however, and is forecast to grow even more substantially, is mobile gaming. It is set to completely eclipse PC and console gaming in number – the revenue of mobile gaming reached $98 billion in 2021; dwarfing the revenue from PC and consoles at $37 billion and $43 billion, respectively. Google Play's revenues stood at around $40 billion in 2022.[29] One mobile game – *Candy Crush Saga* – brought in $660 million in revenue in the United States alone, placing it between giants like YouTube ($770 million) and Max (formerly HBO Max; $580 million).[30] Mobile games made up $110 billion of Apple App Store's

$167 billion revenue throughout 2022, proving that mobile is king now, and will continue to be so.[31] Again, these are not people making or publishing games. These are simply digital storefronts.

Currently hosting tens of thousands of games, it would be a mess of a platform without the all-important shopfront curation. Similarly to Google, which puts favourable (mostly paid-for) websites at the top of its page, Steam also utilises a sophisticated algorithm and personal preference models that shape which games appear at the forefront of the store when it loads up. With this digital real estate making multimillion-dollar swings in either direction for game publishers and game makers, the task of getting the attention of game store owners is a make-or-break moment for any game. A similar thing is happening in other digital storefronts, like the Apple App Store, Epic Store, GOG, Xbox Store and others; a slight bump of any title to their front pages can have a huge influence on sales, as well as on which parts of the industry receive recognition. Naturally, then, entire side teams and mini industries exist to game the algorithms, as well as to shmooze the executives curating these stores.

Of course, curation is not just a matter of store shelves, but is also driven by influencers and journalists. In this case, the sometimes curious relationship between game reviewers and game makers also contributes to the sense of fakeness in the industry. The common phenomenon of game critics donning branded clothing and merchandise for the game they are reviewing and openly declaring their love of a certain game brand, a studio or its creatives, exposes the imbalance between criticism or even honest consumer reviews and blatant fandom. Reviews are aggregated in websites like Metacritic, whose unwavering power dictates which games receive the hype.

What this entire process exposes (and we're nowhere close to seeing the end of it) is the layers of compromise, alienation and loss of control that most creators experience when working within this medium. It's not some grand conspiracy; it's just the repetition of a familiar process. An activity that does not by itself have to be politicised – digital gaming – can still propagate high ambitions for innovation and artistic, cultural and political integrity, but these are diminished or killed by a thousand cuts of commercial interests. The act of playing football is very different to the global football industry. Gaming is similar in that sense, but that moral distinction is barely ever made by the mainstream media, and most certainly not by dedicated progressives.

Reach

Gaming has its tentacles everywhere. Sports? Electronic sports are a multibillion-dollar industry, with major leagues of players competing for multimillion-dollar prizes. Some competitive games have been part of the digital realm for decades, such as the *Tekken* series (1994 onward) or my beloved *Quake III Arena* (1999). Some, like FIFAe World Cup, are offshoots of existing sports, repurposed in digital format.

The size of the competitive gaming scene is fluctuating – sometimes overpitched due to large injections of venture capital, inflating its size artificially. In 2021, the largest esports gaming event for *Dota 2* – a multiplayer online battle arena game – had a prize pool that reached an eye-watering $40 million. This plummeted to $19 million in 2022, exposing the shakiness of this strange periphery of the gaming world.[32] Still, with tens of millions on the line across many different titles, esports academies and boot camps have flourished across the world. The first Olympic Esports Games were held in 2023, so despite the slump, it is possible that the heyday of this peculiar, fascinating competitive space is yet to come. Professional esports by themselves are a wonderful pursuit.

Sadly, as with many good things in life, this field is also mired in corruption.

Match fixing, nepotism and doping are the other obvious issues. Team ownership can sometimes be opaque, with the same invisible conglomerate owning several teams, which will then compete against each other – guaranteeing that the prize money pot goes back to the owner regardless. The Overwatch League's competitive teams have become notorious for recruiting professional players into their mix using fake identities.[33]

Esports players are pumped with energy drinks, and use of stimulant drugs is barely ever tested – unfair disadvantages are seldom controlled. With multimillion-dollar prize funds, the willingness to risk a competitor's health to get that money is on the rise. Gamers allegedly regularly use drugs like Adderall, Vyvanse, Ritalin and other medications to stay locked in during a long day of training.[34] Increasingly, though, players taking performance-enhancing amphetamines are caught during the actual competitions with money at stake. While fines and bans are then issued, testing is still very rare.

Major banks such as Barclays are investing heavily into esports and other gaming initiatives. They will fund LGBTQ+ initiatives within the influential Western gaming milieu with one hand and with the other collaborate with brutal dictators in the Global South who legislate oppressive laws for the same community. Depressingly, money talks and suggestions of pinkwashing and greenwashing are met with derision by people dependent on the corrupt organisations.

Consciously espousing a particular look, the professional esports aesthetic is both poignantly masculine and exclusionary, seemingly oblivious to the potential for broadening its reach and diversity. While the in-game characters and players themselves are increasingly diverse, the way competitions are presented continues to be incredibly homogeneous. From uniforms to stage design, stream editorial choices, music, sponsors and casters (commentators),[*] the ruling aesthetic mimics those of non-digital sports, with an added layer of pubescent imitation of a man-cave, adorned with plastic and neon lights. Almost without fail, professional tournaments feature individuals wearing highly synthetic 'uniforms' – clothing that is not there for reasons of enhanced movement, but more of a loose-fitting space for sponsors to place their ads. Tournaments are held indoors, where cabling of various computers will be served best. For some reason, players are surrounded with hardcore dubstep remixes and given high-density caffeinated beverages.

For an entertainment strand so varied and so full of distinctive personalities and traditions, it is regrettable to see it reduced to a hyper-capitalist image of heavy electronic music, energy drinks, booth babes and adverts, adverts, adverts.[35]

Esports tournament organisers might believe that the artistic choices in their events will attract maximum popularity with their 'neutral' or 'universal' aesthetic, but these events simply maintain the status quo, rather than provide a well-researched, nuanced approach on how best to showcase skill, speed and grace. There is a particular joy in spectating an athletic event – the participatory thrill, the communal experience – but the styling of such events is often exclusionary and directed at a very limited audience.

Certainly, promotion and generation of income for multinational corporations such as Blizzard, Riot and Valve has become the primary function of esports, but the grassroots esports communities have always bent the expectations of how such scenes

---

[*] Shoutcaster (aka caster): another name for a commentator, who will speak over the action to engage, inform and entertain the viewer (British Esports Association definition).

must look. In Eastern Europe, university halls were filled with both BA and PhD students, Thermos bottles of tea in hand, attempting to trounce each other over local area network (LAN) parties. Fighting games tournaments held in the back garden of one of the organiser's parents' houses is another example of this community, in contrast to business-driven events. The corporate insistence on the infantilisation of esports at a professional level is a conscious choice.

Localised stories, exploration of cultural differences and diversity are no longer seen as an exercise in losing capital. The very diverse multiplayer-shooter *Overwatch*, with its deliberately wide-ranging character cast, like the Rihanna-owned make-up brand Fenty Beauty and *Teen Vogue* magazine, which constantly churns out lefty content, have all proven that expanding the reach of a product brings in monetary rewards. New kinds of representation create new communities and ways for people to relate to one another. For me, that gives them a possible relation to politics, if only at a level of forging communities among the already like-minded. While one-sided products are usually a response to a particular political reality, communities that form around them have the opportunity to share the reality of the future.

While this book describes the intersection between videogames and politics, in sports (football, for instance), political expression has a long history. The St Pauli Football Club (FC) in Hamburg was a progressive response to skinhead-led, right-wing football hooliganism. Anti-fascist organising became a key tenet of the club's existence and has inspired many sister clubs around the world. The St Pauli FC, the Glaswegian Celtic FC and my own beloved Clapton Community Football Club in London have established, or are enthusing about creating, electronic sports teams under their brand to maintain and support an anti-fascist presence within the digital realm, too. These clubs are not there necessarily to change minds, but by god are they a great space for a respite after a hard day's work building a better tomorrow.

To those in the know, esports is a dazzling, delightful part of games, thrilling in its creativity and sportsmanship. Watching a professional *League of Legends* player navigate a keyboard like a grand piano, with subtlety and prowess, is a sight to behold! The magnificent banter and beautiful connections made through independent matches in fighting games, for instance, are a component of humanity worth cherishing. Wholesome stories within the field are numerous. In a tiny local restaurant called Yumine in Seoul, the parents of a famous *League of Legends* player, Han 'Peanut' Wang-Ho, transformed the space into a proud shrine to their son, with the memorabilia for the team covering most of the walls. This serves as an inspiration and a visiting place for many beginner esports players attempting to convince their sceptical parents that they are making a serious career choice.[36] *Overwatch*'s Homestand Weekends are learning from analogue sports to embrace community-building within a physical area and are organising tournaments in arenas close to where the players grew up, adding city-specific activities and celebrating local culture. Teams like Silver Snipers, composed of *Counter-Strike* players above the age of sixty, are a lovely redefinition of who video-games are for![37]

At present, though, this great source of entertainment is increasingly lacking in creativity and a creative source of direction. It is untrue that esports have not found their own identity yet, it's just that the prevailing identity is so lazy and tedious. Run by crypto-related transactions or other investments lacking in transparency, the look and reputation of esports definitely reflects that shadiness. It does not have to be this way, but again, unless there is resistance to the current political and practical modus operandi, the medium will end up stifled rather than liberated and engaged with as creatively as it deserves to be.

The winds of change may be blowing in a different direction soon, however. Now that many venture capitalists are seemingly exiting the space, perhaps esports will find healthier, more organic ways to grow. For instance, the Saudi Arabian sovereign fund that invested heavily in esports decided in 2023 to pivot to supporting a games industry in Ryadh, and investing a staggering $38 billion (or 20 per cent of the overall games industry size) to develop, publish and acquire top-tier games.[38] So the future of gaming is not only stuck with the bulk of current problems and injustices, but parts of it will now also be at the behest of regions that jail dissenters for decades for the crime of posting a tweet.

Cryptocurrency? To be honest, few industries didn't tie themselves to this bizarre boom in one way or another. Crypto ads were heard during Super Bowl games, and celebrities such as Matt Damon and Tom Brady sang their praises. Even the travel sector was accepting crypto payments during the short-lived cryptomania of the late 2010s and early 2020s. In games, they are mostly encountered as a form of micropayment. Non-fungible tokens, or NFTs, also made their debut in games, the crassest example of which is *Dookey Dash* (2023), where the player is tasked with swimming through – you guessed it – digital excrement to find a key in a Bored Ape's bum. Bored Apes are a famous example of NFTs, a trademarked, randomly generated asset group portraying an animated ape. The apes appear with different accessories and surroundings. As a digital art asset they went viral in 2021, with variations owned by A-list celebrities like Justin Bieber and Paris Hilton. Only the lucky few who possess a Bored Ape or Mutant Ape NFT are eligible to obtain the 'sewer pass' that grants them entry into *Dookey Dash*. Despite the exclusivity, the game has already raked in nearly $40 million.[39]

In fact, there is vocal opposition to the introduction of NFTs into the gaming sphere. Social media posts boycotting titles or entire studios including NFTs and other cryptocurrency products in their games regularly went viral during their peak popularity in 2021. It appears that all sides of the political spectrum are finding reasons to loudly protest. The progressive community in games detests the speculative nature of NFTs and their staggering contribution to CO_2 emissions – at the time of writing, the global Bitcoin-mining CO_2 emissions (excluding other cryptocurrencies) per year were nearly as high as those of Greece – a country of more than 10 million people.[40] Libertarians and right-wingers object to yet another way their rights as consumers are being toyed with, by employing microtransactions, so it appears that everyone is upset with the crypto world attempting to dock in games.

The paths of cryptocurrencies and gaming also converge in how parts of them are produced. The rising popularity of microtransactions to wring revenue from otherwise free games has spawned an industry in click farms. These are real-life spaces, predominantly in the Global South and Eastern Europe, where low-paid workers are expected to click through thousands of combinations on computers and mobile phones. For other industries, this practice can be used in manipulating website traffic, posting and liking comments and giving a semblance of life to otherwise senseless bots. In games, it can be in the service of 'mining' loot boxes.

Some games encourage players to buy loot boxes – in-game items that at random generate (or don't) certain rewards – an unregulated gambling mechanic. Click-farm bosses make their workers open tens of thousands of such boxes each day in order to then sell any loot directly to wealthy players online. There is a similar market for buying artificially boosted player statistics: more gold results in higher ratings and so on. Some MMORPGs require hundreds of hours in order for players to 'level up', sprouting secondary-market click farms where workers play a game without a break, improving the position of a paying account holder, who will then perhaps sit down for an hour a night simply to enjoy the spoils of the conquest made by others on their behalf.[41]

Similarly, the entire economy of cryptocurrencies has armies of workers synthetically boosting the hype for this industry, facilitating pump-and-dump schemes and generating fake transactions and scarcity. Click farms – an unregulated and secret part of our everyday digital worlds – are shadowy and annoying at best, and part of human trafficking, slavery and torture networks at worst, with numerous accusations of brutal work conditions in Cambodia and the Philippines. This is nothing new. As early as 2013, Microsoft and Symantec shut down a botnet of nearly 2 million personal computers that were being used to generate an average of 3 million clicks per day for various purposes of upvoting, recommending and similar.

By 2023, click farms had become common, even in war operations. For example, the Russian paramilitary Wagner Group used a bot factory to achieve their goals. Few leaks from the sites and people engaged in this work exist, but investigative journalists report brutal conditions and abysmal pay, even while the profits for the people setting up click farms are soaring.[42]

Weapons industry? Videogames are there, too. Arms manufacturers and computer games with realistic weaponry are engaged in a symbiotic, mutually beneficial relationship. Suppose a game depicts or allows the player to engage with a realistic-looking branded weapon, as many do. In that case, the manufacturers are entitled to a licence fee for brand placement. A single game like *Call of Duty* could have hundreds of such licences, meaning that a purchase of this videogame will likely profit numerous real-life weapon manufacturers.[43] As mentioned in the Tutorial, game makers have had prolonged partnerships with the arms industries, directly or indirectly receiving obscure funding from state departments interested in games that promote their military agenda. Similar licensing deals are maintained with the car industry or sports organisations licensed within games. FIFA, the NFL and superstar skateboarder Tony Hawk all boast lucrative gaming deals, but it's important to establish a sliding scale as to how nefarious these can be.

Gamification – another buzzword to explain the conditions around us – is also a process, informed by videogames, that has now extended into many parts of our lives. Gamified methods of encouragement like badges and awards originate in the military or Scouts movements, but games have truly brought this trend into a digital age. Apps for language learning or exercise have clear gamified objectives and rewards. Point-collecting systems will get users discounts with, say, Starbucks or Nike. More alarmingly, Amazon uses gamification in its warehouses to have employees 'improve their efficiency' and compete against others for digital rewards such as virtual pets.[44] Uber presses its workers to reach goals and has crafted an interface of comparison for all drivers. This encourages them to spend more time at the wheel without taking breaks, leading to concerns about driver welfare and safety. The financial speculation app Robinhood also employs game systems, promising bigger wins to get users to spend more money.[45]

Culture? Apart from the highbrow galleries now curating respected exhibitions dedicated to the craft of making games or even to the skill of playing them and social affinities around them, a more mainstream, all-encapsulating trend of gaming is also taking shape. NPC streaming is netting its creators thousands of dollars a day. In this subculture, the (almost always) good-looking performer will swing in a particular manner, up and down, or sideways, recreating the aesthetic of the awkwardly positioned and cheaply animated non-playable characters that can be encountered in most videogames.[46] Cosplay (short for costume play) has fans recreating every stitch and surface of an existing fictional character costume, usually highlighting the sexual undertones of the character at the same time.[47]

All this influence, all these trillions of hours spent by billions of people gaming, forming communities, getting inspired to change the world for better or for worse – all of it stands on incredibly flimsy foundations. The infrastructure of the World Wide Web on which this huge industry relies is relatively fragile and unpredictable. A very few landlords own the vast majority of the edifice on which this entire domain is built. The researcher Daniel Greene has presented extensive evidence of the underbelly of data-centre logistics holding the internet together.

Although some top players in the software industry, such as Google, Amazon, Meta, Alibaba and Microsoft, have built their own data centres or bought them out, the majority of the internet is owned by a network of corporations with questionable stability. According to Greene's extensive research, the physical assets at the core of the internet, the warehouses that store the cloud's data and interlink global networks, are owned by commercial real-estate barons who compete with malls and property storage empires. 'Under their governance, internet exchanges, colocation facilities, and data centers take on a double life as financialized real estate assets that circle the globe even as their servers and cables are firmly rooted in place.'[48]

Equinix, Digital Realty, NTT Global Data Centers, OneAsia, 165 Halsey Street, Eurofiber and another 250 such companies are the more silent owners of the flimsily assembled tapestry that is the World Wide Web. Almost without exception, videogames, big or small, are automatically clients of these digital landlords – indebted, commercialised, bent towards a disaffected, alienating relationship from the outset.⁴⁹

The thickening lines of fibre-optic internet cables bringing the speed, the ever-smaller hardware delivering ever-more powerful image and performance capabilities are inevitably pushing this industry towards grander, hyper-realistic graphics. But do these graphics elevate the play experience? Or are they merely serving business interests? It is debatable if any other fighting game has had a bigger cultural impact than the relatively basic-looking (but complex in mechanics) *Street Fighter II* all the way back in 1991. Shooter games from the 1990s such as *Doom* and *Quake* continue to be influential. At no more than a couple of hundred megabytes in size, they are a thousand times smaller than some of the largest, heaviest game releases today, with one title, *Call of Duty: Black Ops* (2010), reaching a quarter of a terabyte.

This bleeding-edge highest-possible-definition realism, the fight to cram the maximum amount of pixels into the digital experience – one more eyelash can always be added to a character – is a chase that can never end. Enhanced visual fidelity creates an opportunity to increase a game's price tag, with some now costing upwards of £120. More visual and game design tricks call for more capable (and expensive) hardware with more complex chips, running the games on more power. Mobile gaming and more democratic sharing of games among PCs have allowed games to be more accessible than just the middle-class signifier of having a console at home, as it was in the 1980s, but justification and audience for merch or collector's items are also booming.

Steve Jobs himself, upon introducing the 2010 Retina display, said that 'the magic number for optimal perfect digital display is 300 pixels per inch, that's when you hold something around ten to twelve inches away from your eyes, is the limit of the human retina to differentiate the pixels.'[50] But these biological limitations do not stop hardware manufacturers from selling us 8K displays and raking in the profits from the price tags that come with them.[51] Buying hardware that would be able to run the latest hyped title is inconvenient to the consumer, who probably would have been happy to pay less money for a game with simpler graphics but with a rich story that felt meaningful, and is now having to throw eighty quid at a similarly impactful story with better graphics. The sectors of the industry that are having the best time with that are, of course, the hardware manufacturers – the true underbelly of the gargantuan videogames industry.

Destruction

No single factor in the production, circulation and consumption of the global videogames industry is as crucial and as harmful as the centre of it all – the physical devices on which we get to make them, enjoy them, critique them. The truth is that the conception of a videogame begins well before a game engine software is booted up on a screen. It's the piece of hardware onto which one is about to craft a game that carries the heftiest of politics within it, dark secrets that underpin and reinforce so much of the brutality of current capitalist landscapes.

This sin, this fundamental injustice and crime begins in the south of the Democratic Republic of the Congo (DRC) – in the Lualaba and Haut-Katanga Provinces, or the so-called Copperbelt. The mines of this region are the world's primary source of several rare metals that are essential to the manufacturing of high-end electronics. Siddharth Kara, author of the crucial book *Cobalt Red: How the Blood of the Congo Powers Our Lives*, evocatively describes the conditions experienced by people in and around these mines:

Hundreds of thousands of people have been displaced because their villages were just bulldozed over to make place for large mining concessions. So you have people with no alternative, no other source of income, no livelihood. In many cases, armed forces are pressuring people to dig, for a dollar or two a day, parents having to make a painful decision, 'Do I send my child to school or do we eat today?' So in the 21st century, this is modern-day slavery.[52]

Mass casualties of collapsing mines, child trafficking and sexual terror, rife across the region and in the mines themselves, are all accepted as normal. These constitute an unforgivable, undeniable and yet completely normalised part of videogame and tech production. The silence around it is staggering. These mines are the key to the trillionaire success of the contemporary tech conglomerates. They are established with recourse to local militias that do the dirty work for the establishment and provide the upkeep for resource extraction. Valuable and toxic minerals are pulled out of the ground with bare hands for pennies and sold to the companies, which then transport the goods to the manufacturing plants where this corrupt, brutal business enters the next stage. The DRC should be one of the wealthiest countries in the world thanks to its mineral-rich soils, but local and international corruption is sure to keep the prices of these indispensable extracts low, costing thousands of lives and creating endless human misery in the meantime.

The crux of the matter is that no other cultural medium as influential as games has its roots so deep in the blood-soaked soil of this extractivist, evil supply machine. To be sure, films are now increasingly shot on digital rather than film cameras, increasingly enjoyed on laptops rather than in cinemas, and much postproduction is done on computers, but there are still alternatives. Films can be shot entirely on relatively low-tech devices or using sustainably levied visual effects. In the culture of cinema, change is easier to imagine because there are precedents in the medium's history. The same goes for music. These minerals are indeed found in aspects of music hardware, production and reproduction, but again it's not utterly pervasive, there are ways to escape. For videogames, however, this has been the mode of operation since their cradle days, and it's getting more relentless. Few speak up about the dirty, dark implications of it all.

The heinous production line of modern hardware continues with the extracted raw materials being assembled into the devices we use and cherish, in invisible, barely regulated, gloomy mega-factories in another part of the Global South. In 1974, Taiwanese Terry Gou, aged twenty-four, borrowed $7,500 (the equivalent of $45,000 today) from his mother to start a business. Foxconn was born.[53] The company, first based in Guangdong Province in China, but now with factories all over the world, has been manufacturing tech for Western clients since the 1980s. But it was its collaboration with Apple in the late 2000s that caused an explosion in size and influence. When Foxconn began its operations in the 1970s, Shenzhen was a fishing port outside Hong Kong with a population of 300,000. Today, it is a megalopolis of 12 million people that produces 90 per cent of the world's consumer electronics. Pretty much all gaming hardware companies have or have had a relationship with Foxconn – Atari, Dell, Hewlett-Packard (HP), Microsoft (Xbox consoles), Nintendo, Nokia, Samsung Electronics, Sony (PlayStation consoles) – and all are assembled under questionable conditions.

The commute to and workday at a Foxconn factory do not follow the usual schedules; the work hardly ever stops. Foxconn is known for building entire cities – housing some 300,000 people – in order to satisfy the demands of its production. Workers are brought in from surrounding towns and villages, some from as far as 700 kilometres away, to live in one of these mega-factories for weeks on end, sleeping in large dormitories, eating and socialising in these facilities. The work hours average at eleven a day, with shifts sometimes lasting from 6 a.m. to 10 p.m. in the windowless, loud assembly halls. Weekends and holidays are not a thing. The workers are granted just a day off every month, but in the peak season they may go several months without one.[54]

Vertical integration – the technique of production that Foxconn is revered for and the reason for it getting all these contracts – consists of thousands of workers each engaging in a tiny task, repeatedly. Workers may be asked to simply insert or tighten a single screw, then the product moves along the assembly line and the next tiny job gets done by the next worker. A lot of devices can be made very quickly this way and crucially cheaply, as the labour costs are negligible. In the mid-2010s, Foxconn workers were earning as little as just over $1 an hour, or about $200 a month.[55]

Contrary to what their PR might parrot, the genius of Apple and the driver of its profits is less in its elegant design than in the clever outsourcing of the manufacturing process that actually builds their products. The profit margins are stark. Research shows that an iPhone retailing for $1,000 costs between $150 to $455 dollars to make; the rest are Apple's outstanding profit margins, placing the company as the most valuable in the world.

By the 2010s, it began to emerge that not all that may be materially genius is necessarily ethical. PR cracks were showing up. Before 2010, two workers took their own lives at the Foxconn campuses. Mr Hou hanged himself in a company bathroom in 2007.[56] In 2009, Sun Dan-yong threw himself from an apartment building after he lost an iPhone prototype. Before death, he reported that Foxconn employees had beaten him and searched his residence. In 2010, fifteen Foxconn workers attempted suicide, with two of them remaining alive; details about three of them were never released to the public. All but a few jumped off the buildings of the workplace. The company has since installed extensive netting systems around its premises to prevent others from following suit. Seven more suicides are known to have occurred since the peak of 2010.[57]

Outrage reverberated across the world. Even some of the tech companies had to justify their collaborations with Foxconn, although of course none severed their contracts. In response to the pressures by unions and protests, mostly in Hong Kong, Foxconn bumped the salaries of their Shenzhen workforce and brought in Buddhist monks to conduct prayer sessions. They also swiftly demanded that employees sign no-suicide pledges, preventing their families from suing in case of a death. Unverified reports also persist that Foxconn uses forced labour from the Uighur people.[58]

Riteng Electronics factories in Guangzhou are even worse offenders. On average, Riteng workers are on the job for nearly twelve hours a day for an average hourly wage of $1.30, well below the still-meagre average hourly wage of Foxconn workers of $1.62 in the early 2020s.[59] Half of Riteng workers rated the company's safety and health provisions as 'bad', compared to just 2 per cent of workers giving this rating to the Foxconn factory.[60] Notably, Riteng are the main mass manufacturers of modern arcade cabinets, fighting game sticks and other gaming paraphernalia. So, the assembly line for gaming gear is even more brutal and has fewer protections in place than equivalent item production in mixed technology sectors.

The trendy, well-off game devs of the Global North are seemingly the only cohort considered to be worthy of the prestige, security and salaries that come with working in games; the silenced populations of gaming hardware manufacturing workers, whose blood, sweat and tears enable game creators to enjoy their hip and profitable careers, are systematically overlooked. Even in the incredibly important game workers unionisation movement, few express solidarity with and recognise the crucial contribution made by the teams of people in mines in DRC or factories in Foxconn – as the colleagues who deserve our support and attention – not to mention take any action to collaborate with them in unionisation efforts.

Although underreported by the Western media, resistance towards these awful conditions is widespread. Instances of industrial action (i.e., factory strikes) were being counted in the hundreds in the first half of 2022. Thousands of protests take place in China every year. Unions are working under incredibly difficult conditions, but victories are achieved. In 2012 and 2013, after protests at Foxconn factories that manufacture Xbox and PS4 consoles, an improvement of the conditions from absolutely abhorrent to slightly better ensued.[61] Wages are increasing in the China-based Foxconn factories, but the improvement in conditions is unstable. Reports of stripped wages and benefits come in regularly.[62] Capital is sensing weaknesses in the business model, though, and assembly lines are being moved to Taiwan and India, where they can get away with even lower pay.

With the news that Foxconn manufacturing plants will now be opened in the US, too, it's tempting to believe that better conditions are on the way, but as long as profit-making is placed above the manufacturing workers and their well-being, little hope remains for a substantially better future, unless we entirely rebuild our industry. Besides, one only needs to look at the treatment of workers at America's Amazon warehouses distributing gaming hardware to know that the story there is barely better.[63] If we want to enjoy our beloved hobby of gaming guilt-free, the entire production line has to be abolished and rebuilt from scratch.

All this gaming tat ends up somewhere. The games industry is also responsible for an enormous amount of plastic and electronic waste, from consoles, PCs and subsequent paraphernalia. Ben Abraham wrote a book all about the games industry's carbon impact and carried out other investigations in the same realm. His estimation boggles the mind:

> For the three main living-room consoles we have data for, the weight of just the plastic game discs from 2000 to 2018(ish) comes out to 97,301 metric tons. For a sense of the scale of that, a fully laden 747 weighs around 412 metric tonnes. So that's plastic game discs equivalent to 236 fully loaded Boeing 747s planes. That's just plastic discs! How tall would a stack of those discs be? With each one 1.2 mm tall, our hypothetical stack of over 7.4 billion discs would be almost 9 kilometres tall (5.6 miles). Granted, it's a skinny stack, but yowza. The Burj Khalifa is only 892 metres tall, so our stack is over 10x taller than the tallest building on the planet. And what about the plastics in game consoles? Keeping in mind that this is a much less accurate estimate, it came out to a similarly impressive 251,817 metric tons of plastic. Not quite an Empire State Building worth of plastics, but close to 2/3rds.[64]

The production of all these items – ephemerally played with, so much of it quickly ending up in landfills – adds up to another wave of violations this industry is imposing on the world around it. The games industry's carbon footprint is barely calculated and considered by the industry as a whole, but it's no doubt growing at alarming rates. Few journalists and researchers are interested in taking on this work, and even fewer are funded to do so. Lewis Gordon, who writes for *The Verge*, is one of a handful of people tackling the topic. He cites that the electricity use of gaming devices themselves is estimated to sit at thirty-four terawatt-hours of energy each year, or the equivalent of 5 million cars. That is the equivalent emission of all cars in Austria or Saudi Arabia, just from gaming devices.[65] Here is another illustration of this stark statistic, from Alex Hern writing for the *Guardian*:

> Take *Elden Ring* (2022), the current star of the zeitgeist. According to analytics site SteamSpy, the PC version has between 10 and 20 million owners, with an average total playtime of 77 hours, drawing (let's say) 500W per player. That means the game has consumed, in its first six weeks on sale, between 385GWh and 770GWh of electricity. Just on the PC version: it's also out on Xbox and PlayStation. For comparison, in the same period, Hornsea One, the largest offshore wind farm in the world, can output 1,200GWh of electricity – if the wind is blowing just right the whole time.[66]

In conversation with Lewis Gordon, this time for *Wired* magazine, Ben Abraham tells it as it is: 'This is the only game in town now. How do we prevent our planet from being boiled alive?' He says that industry insiders must agitate for change, but that we also need more direct action, protests and substantial grassroots pressure to turn things around.[67] It is astonishing and utterly depressing that for a cause so important – the survival of the planet Earth – only people like Gordon and Abraham are ringing alarm bells.

There are undoubtedly some green initiatives here and there. But they amount to trying to soak up the sea with a towel. For example, the United Kingdom Interactive Entertainment (UKIE – a British industry lobby organisation) Green Games Guide delivers well-meaning, but ultimately futile, symbolic advice for games studios that would like to be greener: reduce waste and recycle, reduce staff commute and business trips, optimise games, consider offsetting your CO_2 emissions.[68] In the meantime, post-climate-disaster fictional scenarios and the survival skills that will be necessary for living through them are becoming popular aspects of contemporary games. UKIE also suggests, not at all cynically, making games with climate change themes in them as a method of resistance to said climate change.[69]

So we're at a full-circle moment. The games industry – a giant polluter and a substantial factor in the climate upheaval – is now profiting from the emergent themes around it. Lewis Gordon writes astutely for *ArtReview* about the *Battlefield 2042* game in 2021:

> A game that simultaneously utilises the climate crisis as a gameplay hook while perpetuating intensive resource extraction and energy consumption (including the electricity used to actually make and play it). The kicker is that its weightless take on extreme weather, which will set computer fans whirring across the world, is so inconsequential that it ends up as nothing more than a graphical showcase. *Battlefield 2042*'s spectacle isn't just hollow, it's also deeply cynical.[70]

In Level III, I suggest that games with politically engaging topics can certainly inform an already interested gamer and play an educational role, but whether they have the power to convince a climate denier into suddenly springing into action to save our world is debatable.

As Ben Abraham points out, it is unlikely that the necessary reduction in the CO_2 emissions in the games industry will come from the software development field.[71] Yes, optimising and contraction of the decadent energy consumption in games studios will have to take place, but they're a lesser culprit – most of the toxicity emitted by the industry sits within the hardware. The crux of the problem is, sadly, that the big manufacturers of the games hardware – Sony, Microsoft and Apple, to an extent (mobile gaming is massive, after all) – are also the big funders of games publishing deals, the two hugely interlinked. Xbox, PlayStation and Apple Arcade subsequently offer lump sums to game studios to produce

games for them and their hardware. Imagine if the vast majority
of all films were funded by companies making cameras or owning
cinema chains – the ability to enact change in such an industry
would prove that much more complex.

So expressing an opposition to the money-making exercises of
the companies of which studios are then asking said money from
is currently not the wisest plan. Crucially, companies like Nvidia,
which just hit a valuation of $1 trillion, are being boosted by a new
surge for chips driven by the artificial intelligence industry, and
have little incentive to change their practices.[72] It may be all too
easy to believe that gaming is only a small fraction of overall computational hardware production, but experts would disagree.
According to *The Verge*, which comprehensively covers this theme,
there has been a huge increase in gaming gear at the consumer
electronic shows (CES and others). They are predominantly
gaming hardware shows with other utilities attached.[73]

As this Level demonstrates, as much as progressive game
makers may desire to make a difference and convince their players
of a better tomorrow, the fundamental gluttony that underlines
much of the games industry tends to win out and overshadow any
positive change. The acts of resistance and political engagement
within the games themselves, or even among their communities,
are trumped by the sheer weight of the annihilation of lands, communities and livelihoods.

We are allowed to pour attention into games and enact our
fights within the safe corner they create, but all of it is so utterly
irrelevant, given the size of the problem. Even if our videogames
were all built around some fictional Barbie Land where everything
is peaceful and everyone agrees with each other and is kind, empathetic and generous – in game and out; even if we abolished all of
the violent, sexist, xenophobic and highly addictive videogames,
even then, the carnage would be barely lessened. It is paramount

that we not get distracted by in-game intrigues and injustices – as important as they can sometimes be – but instead focus on the big prize of abolishing this guilty, calamitous material reality which is flourishing right now, and rebuild something much less reprehensible.

Final Boss: Conclusion

In 1958, the economics educator Leonard E. Read wrote an essay titled 'I, Pencil', which chronicles all that goes into the making of a single pencil – the laborious timber-felling, shape-cutting, graphite-acquiring and glueing processes; the numerous countries, factories and dozens of materials required, including cedar, lacquer, graphite, ferrule, factice, pumice, wax and adhesives.[1] This complicated choreography results in complex chains of operations to source the components and a huge amount of labourers, including a sweeper in the factory and the lighthouse keeper guiding the shipment into port. In 1996, the essay was reprinted with a foreword by the neoliberal economist Milton Friedman championing unfettered free trade, ignoring the labour and climate disasters created by such unregulated, unsustainable global trade systems.[2] Although these industrial procedures should be seen as a marvel of cooperation and innovation, under the current circumstances, they are a monument to waste and exploitation.

A single modern videogames console, or a game itself, is a product a thousand times more complex than a single pencil; consequently, these products contain that many more spaces for negotiation. The industrial design of a game console – sketching and 3D modelling, picking out specs – is done in shiny headquarters, served by corporate benefits, with Michelin-starred canteens and assistants galore. The user interface and software architecture are crafted by highly remunerated engineering teams with corporate gym subscriptions and in-house masseuses. The most important items within these products are chipsets – CPU (central processing unit), GPU (graphics processing unit) and other crucial chipsets, such as ones used for power management, video and audio decoding, or for connectivity to wi-fi or Bluetooth. Most of these contain minerals obtained from poor states under appalling work conditions.

For instance, the semiconductor contractor for the PlayStation 5, AMD (Advanced Micro Devices, Inc), outsources the manufacturing process of the chips to TSMC (Taiwan Semiconductor Manufacturing Company Limited), which owns factories around the world that have varying levels of labour protections. The locations and processes of these plants are also subject to ongoing power shifts and geopolitical manipulations, with trade wars and sanctions distorting the field. In hermetically sealed, sterilised rooms, ultra-pure water, air, argon and nitrogen are ferried around through tubes and pipes for the procedure of crafting chips.[3] The toxic waste and pollution caused by these manufacturing processes are immense. Electromechanical components, such as cooling systems, power supply units, hard drives and structural components involving plastic casing and metal shielding, screws and fasteners, are all made with components such as oil that are harmful to the environment.

Furthermore, the human trafficking of the labour force is so widespread within the field that gaming corporations are having to issue statements decrying it. HDMI, USB, Ethernet, and other ports, buttons and LEDs, cables and connectors are all assembled, installed and soldered into a piece of hardware by armies of workers who labour for poverty wages. The units are tested, packaged, sent off, driven, placed into warehouses and shops and sold by a huge, alienated workforce, who are pressured to refrain from unionising and are otherwise abused. In an age of unprecedented decadence, gaming is yet another industry that has built itself on the back of powerless, muted populations subjected to ever-deepening misery. Behind every shiny game studio in Los Angeles, London or Shenzhen housing top-end developers, there exist armies of workers in mines outside Kolwezi in the Democratic Republic of the Congo, in warehouses in Longhua subdistrict in China and in click farms in Phnom Penh, Cambodia, or in the Russian provinces.

The process of making a videogame involves a wider range of conditions. The majority of game studios make hyper-casual, casino-style games, with intensely data-driven approaches and addictive mechanics that require minimal creativity, and generate swathes of low-paid, dead-end jobs. On the other end of the spectrum lie art-house, boutique and independent videogame studios that invest in their workforce more, but are trumped in influence by major AAA studios, where work conditions are tough and insecurity almost constant.

Even if you're lucky enough to be able to develop your own game independently, you'll still struggle to bring it out, not to mention to make a living from its publication. With publishing deals and store space in the hands of only a few important decision makers, unless you work for one of the hardware-wielding giants like Microsoft, Sony or Nintendo, precarity is the norm. The time frame during which developers have the funding to craft the now-obligatory bloated productions has grown shorter and shorter, and few games succeed. Those that succeed and also hold some true cultural value are exceptional.

Artificial intelligence, which is likely to define much of arts and production in the next century, is seeping into the game development process with unstoppable speed. In China, jobs related to game creation are already being axed and replaced with machines.[4] Artists in two-dimensional art, voice acting and no doubt more disciplines are being replaced; unless substantial protections come into effect immediately, this chipping away of labour costs and consequent increase in mediocrity will only continue. While automating certain repetitive, mundane tasks like level blocking or asset creation for marketing campaigns can free workers to learn and pursue more complex, creative, strategy-building tasks, managers tend toward short-term thinking in the form of cost saving and headcount reduction.[5] In this climate, the positions of even software engineers, programmers and top artists begin to look precarious. Who will fight for the level designers, producers, and staff working in quality assurance, localisation, community management and distribution? Or the people cleaning their offices? AI is killing the game experiences themselves, too, with bots outnumbering real players on servers in multiplayer games, creating a loop of artificiality and eventual rejection by real communities.[6]

Games are then branded and advertised to reach audiences that often create unmoderated communities of hate and exclusion. In 2019, a self-proclaimed gamer massacred fifty-one people and injured forty in Christchurch, New Zealand, with a weapon clad in gaming meme stickers, referencing PewDiePie and leaving behind a manifesto with numerous gaming references and jokes.[7] A racist attack at a Walmart in El Paso, Texas; another in Bærum, Norway; an aborted synagogue shooting in Halle, Germany; a devastatingly effective one in Poway, California – all were perpetrated by people employing videogame references and elements, and all occurred within a few months of each other. No doubt there will be more. Game companies, incentivised by profit and little else, make minimal efforts to curb far-right organisers who prey on and cultivate gullible communities to create division and encourage heinous acts. And these behaviours are on the rise – the proportion of players encountering toxic behaviour increased from 68 per cent in 2021 to 74 per cent in 2023.[8]

In digital spaces, which until recently were void of any progressive links, the task of energising disillusioned populations and galvanising a political project has grown easier. While the Arab Spring of the early 2010s demonstrated the importance of social media in political organising (a lesson that the Western left soon picked up, with Occupy demonstrations in many cities across the world), gaming spaces, where political disillusionment is expressed, were left to be groomed by reactionary influencers. Progressive organisers and collectives, usually quick to branch out to new social and logistical spaces, somehow managed to ignore this one, with excuses ranging from 'this technology is irrelevant' to 'this technology is evil', until the results began dictating the rules themselves.

In the absence of robust opposition, much of gaming has become a tool for the darkest part of the capital accumulators to entrench their influence – this is where crypto bros launder money and arms manufacturers fill their coffers. It's a space for testing political communications methods on millions of unassuming players, leading to those communication methods gaining influence in the wider digital world and producing real-life effects.

Culture now abandons aspirations to innovation and puts itself in the corner of conformism and profitability. Amusement under late capitalism is the prolongation of work. It is sought as an escape from the mechanised work process, to regain one's strength and be able to cope with work again. Culture, as it is now conceived of, exists because freedom does not.[9] Even the once relatively private and innocent activity of play has been commodified beyond recognition. Every possible activity is now commercialised, consumed and sold for the benefit of the owner. Images and gesticulation take precedence over the real, creating a pseudo-reality contrasting with the real one.

These forces may appear unstoppable, unchangeable, too large to comprehend and influence. And yet, in the words of the late David Graeber, the ultimate hidden truth of the world is that it is something we make, and could just as easily make differently:[10]

> If we can extricate ourselves from the shackles of fashion, the need to constantly say that whatever is happening now is necessarily unique and unprecedented (and thus, in a sense, unchanging, since everything apparently must always be this way), we might be able to grasp history as a field of permanent possibility, in which there is no particular reason we can't at least try to begin building a redemptive future at any time.[11]

Games don't have to be this way. In fact, in many parts of the industry, a movement toward real change is stirring. Now is our opportunity to strengthen it.

I am inspired by how an alternative could look, in a miniature way, when an online acquaintance sends me pictures of their set-up of a solar-powered Raspberry Pi (an ethically sourced and manufactured computer).[12] What would a mass version of such manufacturing ethics look like? How could we have computer operating systems and other software that would somehow not perpetuate capitalist practices? These are momentous questions without easy answers; the aim must be to shift gaming and many other digital practices away from their participation in the whirlpool of harm.

The scale of the problem only creates a wealth of openings for involvement. If, in the making of a pencil, there exist numerous parts of production and hence numerous points for sabotage, in games and their cursed hardware, there are that many more! The avenues for impact, revision and subversion are ample, and many are revelling in them.

Glimmers of hope exist in the hardware manufacturing business. In 2023, Namibia announced a policy which may bring about a sea change: a ban on exports of unprocessed lithium, cobalt and other minerals crucial for the manufacturing of electric batteries. Together with Zimbabwe, Namibia is beginning to profit from the growing global demand for metals used in clean energy technologies, instead of sending all profits to the owners of the private companies operating within them. Processing these metals at home, regulating better conditions in the mines and taxing the sales of essential minerals may turn around the brutal practices existing in these industries today.[13]

The US Inflation Reduction Act (2022) may also bring a wind of change to the industry. The act ushers in subsidies for manufacturing computer chips in America, diversifying where and by what means the chips can be obtained. This may make hardware manufacturing processes easier to initiate in economic areas with higher wages. Of course, one should not be fooled – such policies obey protectionist imperatives, not a concern for the greater good. They will still benefit the oligarchs who own the local means of production and proprietary barriers will go even higher. Still, the current bottom-of-the-barrel production processes are perhaps about to be overhauled.

Toxic modes of production have led to toxic brands. Hardware companies are beginning to take notice that their current way of operating requires paying lip service, at least, to the contrary. In 2019, the United Nations Environment Programme founded an initiative titled 'Playing for the Planet Alliance', which saw twenty-one major game companies, including Sony and Microsoft, promising to share best practices for becoming more environmentally friendly. While laudable, the initiative thus far displays slow progress – its crowning achievement was securing commitments from 60 per cent of the Alliance to achieve net zero or carbon negative status by 2030, a goal unlikely to be met.

We can deplore this UN initiative as the space where all substantial conversations about climate change and games get sucked in and processed into nothing. However, it is important to note even the emergence of this discourse. The fashion industry, for instance, has gone way further in approaching sustainability and manufacturing processes, at least at the high end, but the shift took time. Thrifting, faux leather and fur goods and entire micro industries centring around sustainability are now a cornerstone of the Fashion Week experience.

Under increased pressure from the gamer consumer base and caring individuals within the industry, with further transformation of the overall geography and incentives in the assembly lines, perhaps change will gather pace and the recycling process will involve more than just plastic, for starters.

On a modest scale, this is already happening in gaming. The Finnish Game Developers' Association, for instance, built a model for Finnish game companies to estimate their carbon footprint.[14] The Danish indie company Die Gute Fabrik provided a carbon footprint report as part of their 2023 release, *Saltsea Chronicles*.[15] Such examples will change the status quo.

The global trade union movement is providing plenty of reasons to be optimistic. These bodies will push for modifications in how games and their hardware are made. Healthy game worker unions exist in the UK, South Korea, Australia, Brazil, Argentina and many EU countries, and they are springing up in China, India and parts of Africa. In the US, the Campaign to Organize Digital Employees – a branch of Communications Workers of America (CODE-CWA) – have been unionising numerous companies, winning them compensation and ensuring dignity at work. With more than 4,000 members nationwide across many different technology and gaming sectors, the union has built an impressive and sustainable foundation for challenging oppressive company structures.[16]

For example, with the union's support, Raven Software quality assurance employees (testers for games like *Call of Duty*) built a Game Workers Alliance with the following goals:

> [We] focus on improving the conditions of workers in the video game industry by making it a more sustainable, equitable place where transparency is paramount. Additionally, we advocate for our disenfranchised and minority workers by creating a diverse space to let their voices be heard in solidarity.[17]

Studios that have reached collective bargaining agreements are appearing like mushrooms after rain, and there is now no question that our industry will finally have the strong union structures it deserves.

Also in the US, the powerful SAG-AFTRA screen workers union announced in 2023 that they will work to secure better contracts for their colleagues in the videogames voice acting industry.[18] Warehouse handlers of the American gaming hardware company Corsair have formed into a union, hopefully influencing their manufacturing plants in Taiwan. What if they follow suit? Board game workers are unionising.[19] Escape room workers are unionising.[20] Wonderful collaborations and solidarities exist between the game worker chapters of a union supporting a cleaners union or being supported by sex workers union branches, and so on.

An exquisite ecology of solidarity and cooperation is blooming with the help of the industry unionisation efforts. The message is loud and clear – no game worker is alone. Increasingly, game workers are seeing themselves as economic subjects and by extension educating their fans – the players – to understand that our material conditions should be improved by collective organising rather than by othering and oppressing already vulnerable communities. A network of resistance is being created to curtail the current vertical studio structures and the practices they impose on the workforce.

Some firms are pushing the organisational structures of game making even further. The hugely popular rogue-like platformer *Dead Cells* (2018) was made by the French studio Motion Twin, who describe themselves as an anarcho-syndicalist workers cooperative with equal salaries and decision-making powers.[21] Games by the studio are incredibly well received and have won multiple awards, proving that great-quality games can be successful when made under alternative formations to top-down, profit-extracting structures. Matajuegos is an Argentinian cooperative games studio formed in 2021 during the pandemic that has been releasing beloved titles. Imagine an industry with producers of expertise, rather than mere managerial hierarchies. That is not to say that cooperatives are the only answer – of course, toxic work practices can emerge even there – but the diversity of experimentation with work forms currently underway in the games industry illuminates a path forward to a bright future. Notably, games companies are also pioneers in the four-day work week proposition thanks to numerous studios large and small (including Crow Crow Crow, Kitfox Games, Splash Damage and Blackbird Interactive). With multimillion-dollar budgets, these not-insignificant players are demonstrating what a more humane work–life balance could look like.

Noma, the Copenhagen-based three-Michelin-star restaurant, announced it would close its doors at the end of 2024. The owners will run a high-end culinary products business instead. How could this closure possibly be related to the tendencies in the games industry, you ask? Four months before the announcement, Noma (where dinner for one could set you back $1,000) started paying its armies of interns for the first time. This was presumably driven by an important exposé in the *Financial Times* about the toll of high-end dining on its staff, who experience bullying and burn-out.[22] Similarly to gaming employees, people working in fine dining are exploited due to their general passion for the craft. We are now reaching peak game-making team sizes, peak complexity of mechanics and peak graphics fidelity, and thankfully the welfare of game devs is more scrutinised than ever, with sites like *Polygon* and YouTubers such as Jimquisition doing investigative work and critiquing labour practices. Now, will high-end AAA studios finally decide to scale down and work on smaller, more sustainable projects? Who knows? One can only hope, but the end of the baroque in games would be welcome.

Policy makers are slowly familiarising themselves with the loopholes that enable the more pernicious consumer-related practices within the industry. In 2023 alone, the Dutch government began looking into banning loot boxes, equating them to gambling; Microsoft, EA, Activision, Ubisoft and Epic Games faced game addiction lawsuits from plaintiffs in the United States; arrests were made in France regarding sexual harassment investigations at Ubisoft; pressure and calls for robust contracts with esports competitors grew; and the South Korean government charged the Game Rating and Administration Committee with embezzlement.[23] Predatory practices are increasingly challenged, and pressure from the game makers and the people enjoying them is set to continue.

Perhaps a new conceptual framework could appear in which we reject splitting media according to their genre and instead embrace grouping them according to their mode of production. The operations of an independent film production company such as A24 have much more in common with those of an artistic games studio like The Chinese Room or many of the gems that Annapurna Interactive publishes than with the studios that make Hollywood action blockbusters and lowbrow reality television. Mobile games stuffed with micro-transactions, addiction-inducing mechanics and stupefying writing are on a par with C-list Russian propaganda films or the senseless television series churned out by mediocre streaming services.

In terms of intentionality or quality of engagement, somebody loading up *Candy Crush* or another casual game will receive the same reward as someone loading up a deliciously tawdry reality series. A reactionary streamer upset by the option to choose one's pronouns in a game is the equivalent of a prejudiced football hooligan; similarly, there should be a kinship between an indie game connoisseur and an indie film buff. Still, as long as all games and their hardware are made under the current conditions of exploitation, such a recalibration of categories will not be enough to halt the crimes committed by the games industry's way of operating.

Many have written of the beauty and necessity of videogames, even those made under the current venal conditions. Simon Parkin wrote this about *Elden Ring* in the *Guardian*, underlining the best of gaming:

> Video games can be all kinds of different things, representing all manner of artistic ambitions. Most, however, share a common goal: to conjure a compelling fictional reality, filled with beckoning mysteries, enchanting secrets, and enriching opportunities to

compete and collaborate. They aim to provide a liminal space in which a determined player can fix that which is broken, order that which is chaotic . . . Its final gift is the assurance that, whatever monsters lurk in a broken world, with perseverance and cooperation, they too can be overcome.[24]

According to the videogame artist and researcher Mary Flanagan and the media theorist Helen Nissenbaum, 'All games express and embody human values. From notions of fairness to deep-seated ideas about the human condition, games provide a compelling arena where humans play out their beliefs and ideas.'[25] Many of us engage with videogames to a smaller or larger extent, many are curious, and many understandably don't want to touch them due to their ethically compromised ways.

And yet games can inspire the best in us. They portray and reflect values that shape and construct our collective identities. Games save lives, sometimes from helping players find meaning in their content or commonalities with millions of other people who enjoy the same pastime. With enough ambition and ingenuity, the design of a game can prevent fatalities, quite literally. *Foldit* (2008), available online, is a digital game focused on the intricacies of protein configuration. Originating from a pioneering research initiative by the University of Washington's Center for Game Science and its department of Biochemistry, *Foldit* invites players to meticulously arrange given protein structures using gamification-inspired tools. Researchers evaluate the top-performing arrangements to identify any natural structural patterns that could be applicable to actual proteins. Insights from these arrangements have assisted scientists in addressing diseases and developing biological advances.[26]

Games allow us to face our biggest fears. In *Still Wakes the Deep* (2024), players confront themes of isolation and losing loved ones in a Ken Loach–inspired 1970s Scotland.[27] On the flip side, titles like *Unpacking* (2021) sprinkle magic on the mundane, turning the act of unpacking into a playful journey, interspersed with a subtle narrative that deals with personal growth and toxic relationships. Life-simulation games such as *The Sims* help players give their daydreams more concrete shapes, allowing them to touch on ecstasies that may be denied to us in real life, if only in a brief, synthetic manner. Russian avant-garde gaming auteur Vasily Zotov's nightmare-inducing, actively and refreshingly *ugly* games explore the darkness of Hollywood, the hypnotisation of police officers, eight-sided eyeballs in psychiatric wards, a romance between an actress and a yeti, and the destruction of a courtroom by a fascist with a rocket launcher.[28] These weird, eccentric, truly outsider gems exist, but are not easy to come by, and are held at the margins of the industry with few accolades to their name.

It is only a matter of time until we find out what it means to have games done in the style of Fluxus or the Gutai Art Association. A punk-zine equivalent of a videogame with DIY production, hardware included? Some revoltingly wonderful Viennese Actionism games? Or Banksyesque games – found unexpectedly? A Sagrada Familia of videogames – an experience so profound it stops you in your tracks? These are all coming. What would it mean if games became tools for changing our lives, rather than mere signifiers of the status quo? What would gaming look like for us, the post-work-inclined? No longer would games be all about accomplishing missions or winning; they could wash over us effectively with minimal input from the creator, a sort of Malevich of videogames? What would it mean to have games made ethically and organically? Not just tiny mods in AAA games or art projects in Berlin. What would it mean to make this industry a source of renewable energy, rather than a draining force? But even within the current constraints, the creativity within our medium is unparalleled.

Games kindle a gamut of emotions and confront us with unexpected scenarios. *Pokémon Go* filled the streets with crowds of inadvertent Situationists involving themselves in *dérives* – a reimagination of the city. The Obscure Game Aesthetics Twitter account leaves one in awe at the wonderful, weird and surreal visuals that videogames can contain. Sometimes these qualities are crafted by gamers themselves when they tweak and bend somewhat standard games into weirdness. A wave of joy and giddiness washes over one before a fan-made mod of the popular fantasy game *Skyrim* (2011), which turns a flying dragon descending on a medieval village into Thomas the Tank Engine – train sound effects included.[29] Mattel, the owners of the blue locomotive's intellectual property and brand, were apparently less charmed and sent their corporate lawyers after the modder who built it.[30]

Videogames are being made about period cycles (*Tampon Run*, 2014), sixteenth-century Bavarian monks (*Pentiment*, 2022), post-apocalyptic Shropshire (*Everybody's Gone to the Rapture*, 2015), a 100-metre-tall policeman overlooking a gloomy industrial Russian town (*Militsioner*, TBA), dating in high school (*Raptor Boyfriend: A High School Romance*, 2021), and metro and highway systems (*Mini Metro* [2014] and *Mini Motorways* [2019] series). There are *Inception*-like scenarios of playing a game within a game (*Inscryption* [2021], children's doodles turned into entire levels (*Pedigree Tactics* [2023], and the nature of existence, the purpose of life and the repercussions of endless conflict (*NieR: Automata* [2017]). Studio Oleomingus in India created gorgeously surreal post-colonial videogame adaptations of the works of the fictional poet Mir Umar Hassan, while the American game studio Cardboard Computer featured the installations and theatre plays of fictional avant-garde artist Lula Chamberlain. Set in the 1960s, *Detention* (2018) by the Taiwanese studio Red Candle Games explores the horrors of the White Terror regime through the metaphor of a folk ghost story. *Atuel* (2022), by the Argentinian cooperative Matajuegos, documents the connections between people, animals and the changing natural landscape while players fly along a digital recreation of the eponymous Atuel River. In 2018 Robert Yang gifted the world the little queer masterpiece that is *Rinse and Repeat* – a tender, sensual, surreal opportunity to embody a stranger intently rubbing and scrubbing another man in a public shower. The geniuses behind the nightmare-inducing little game *Paratopic* (2018), a small studio called Arbitrary Metric, are releasing a philosophical and psychedelic detective mystery experience with *Roman Sands RE:Build*, in an aesthetic borrowing from both anime and vaporware. Sam Barlow created deep, haunting wonderlands in his *Mulholland Drive*–inspired game *Immortality* (2022) that have sparked more than one exquisitely erotic dream in this writer's mind.

Videogames are an incredible art form in urgent need of liberation from the draconian modes of production that entangle them with the darkest, most corrupt practices of the modern era. What needs to be fought for, what needs to be won, is for gaming to divorce itself from harm.

Claire Bishop's parting words in *Artificial Hells* offer poignant conclusions for this fight:

> The 'political' and the 'critical' becoming shibboleths of advanced art signals a lack of faith both in the intrinsic value of art as a de-alienating human endeavour (since art today is so intertwined with market systems globally) and in democratic political processes (in whose name so many injustices and barbarities are conducted) . . . The task today is to produce a viable international alignment of leftist

political movements and a reassertion of art's inventive forms of negation as valuable in their own right. We need to recognise art as a form of experimental activity overlapping with the world, and – more radically – we need to support the progressive transformation of existing institutions.[31]

There are so many facets to unpick, underline, revolutionise. The actors are numerous and the alliances diverse. This arena is bursting with politics – from the code written, to the theme portrayed, to the human cost of the objects on which games are played. Nothing short of an international worker-led takeover of this industry will suffice to save it, and the planet, from its own greedy, destructive tendencies. Resistance will be fierce – from a brutal last squeeze of the existing extractive practices, to a debasement of the workforce, to attempts to whitewash status-quo gaming and depoliticise union-busting. For the people embedded in the industry, this change must take place to salvage what is to be enjoyed here, not to take it away.

And what can players do to help the people in the industry win the battle for the soul of gaming? Some solutions for more ethical consumption, of course, come to mind – check the source of a game's materials, the conditions in its factories and the sustainability of its components. Upon purchasing a videogame, consider seeking out information about its makers and their record of treatment of the game's devs – chances are, there will be stories on the internet. Support the good ones; there are plenty of them!

Follow games industry unions on social media and support their calls for action. Enjoy and encourage artistic experimentation in this field and support smaller creators. Do not dismiss political action within these spaces as isolated aberrations, but engage with them, give them merit, be curious. Those most precious of encounters – organising, assisting, critical play, archaeology, scheming or even just dilly-dallying together in the most surreal circumstances, the David versus Goliath battles, reciprocal altruism and solidarity – all these must be rewarded and encouraged. A broad gamut of leftist playing exists which can beautifully assist in the fight against the bosses, beyond games. People working in the games industry cannot be the only ones expected to improve it – their job security is at stake. While we can play our part in pursuing less destructive methods of producing the figurative pencil, solidarity with those making a difference has to come from outside of game spaces, too.

Yes, politics have traditionally been assigned to analogue spaces – streets, libraries, pubs, union meeting rooms and launderettes. Increasingly, though, virtual spaces are becoming territories for political organising and scheming, often affecting what happens in real-life governmental buildings. Instead of viewing gaming as some sort of deranged aberration and a distraction from real life, realise that, for millions, gaming represents a very real means of communication about key subjects in their lives and, without doubt, about the wider world. The space in between ranges from reactionary forces using their influence for harmful ends to enabling the purest, kindest sides of humanity. Even today, children's analogue games hint at that possibility, too, providing a clue as to what a more equitable society would look like.

The 2022 Venice Biennale art piece that moved me the most consisted of videos of children playing regional iterations of classic playground games. At the Belgian pavilion, Francis Alÿs showed children transforming ordinary objects, such as stones, coins, plastic bottles and car tyres, into magical universes that transcend national borders and cultural divides.[32] Played for their own sake, rather than as a means to a repressive end, games show the emancipatory potential in the slapstick and nonsense of farceurs, clowns and circus performers.[33] Games and buffoonery bear witness to how life could be – free of domination and based around principles where actions are carried out autonomously for their own ends, beyond the sphere of power relations.

Plenty of space for fooling around, or it's not my revolution, eh?[34] We must criticise the debased forms in which competition is manifested in today's capitalist society, but we can also valorise and defend the possible liberatory types of rivalry that could flourish in a future society devoid of oppression and power.

The Situationists, in their own time, proposed correctly that love is under siege, stripped of its meaning and used as an element of consumption. Today a similar diagnosis can be made about games. Play is under constant siege, reduced to an act of competition, of winning, to a dance between constant upgrades and sudden downfalls. Herein lies the heartbreak that the games industry inflicts – the medium is capable of modelling infinite capacities and possibilities for utopian worlds not yet lived, and still it insists on tapping into our weaknesses, emboldening antagonism and destruction. Spaces for cooperation, selfless generosity and solidarity are mostly carved out by the players themselves, rather than by the game makers.

We must refrain from diagnosing the problems in gaming in terms of their aesthetics, and instead fight for emancipation and improvement in the same way we'd fight for the betterment of any industry. The spectacle does not colonise everything. Boundless creativity is exuded by masses of people who live under the existing system of domination.[35] The action of play, of enjoying artistic creations, has always been a part of that. The mission before us is to uncover the methods and mechanisms for unshackling games from their current modes of production, freeing them from the necessity to compensate for bad deeds.

To quote my beloved Raymond Williams, 'to be truly radical is to make hope possible rather than despair convincing.'[36] The glimmers of hope in this industry must be taken as inspiration for its long-term overhaul rather than as a sign that it will all be okay in the end. Without resistance, the interests of capital will weave their way into every part of our existence and leisure. The ethical scale will not tilt towards equity if we do not employ force. A fight must take place for every beautiful relationship established by gaming communities. For every uplifting experience, every epiphany met through loading up a videogame. For every minute we allow ourselves to relax and escape, beer in hand, after a day at a dead-end job or caring for a loved one.

We must wrest gaming from the shark jaws of extractivism for every kid or adult who wishes to live out their most outrageous fantasies, for every worker killing time during their lunch hour or taking three days off to enjoy plunging into imaginary digital worlds and leaving their mark there. For its communities, for its art, for its clumsiness, endearing quirks and vast universes, it is everything for some of us, and it is becoming increasingly influential even in the lives of those who don't partake. Gaming deserves to be rescued from its self-destructive ways that poison the most visionary parts of this captivating field, to be unleashed from the thorny vines that are smothering it.

Above all, this book is a love letter. It's my way of voicing all the fears and problems I have with this relationship I have found myself in, with this medium that brings me endless joy and has brought me together with some of the most important people in my life, that has changed my class position and inspired optimism in me during the darkest of times. This relationship is marred by a sense of guilt and anger, an inability to truly champion and love this pastime, as so many parts of it are defined by well-disguised cruelty. I want to get rid of that feeling. I want for all of us to be freed from it.

There exists, on the horizon, a possible revolutionary future where all of us can lie on the beach, cocktail in hand, with few cares in the world, but to get there, we must first overcome the obstacles and win many fights, including those that manifest themselves on our myriad of black mirrors. And for those who prefer a session of *Elden Ring* to the beach, there is everything to be won by challenging the current crooked, bloated and monopolised methods of game making and distribution. In the era of non-stop productivity contests, when work seemingly never ends and leisure blurs insidiously into minting coins for others, we demand the right to be lazy. With pride!

How special would it be to cleanse something as innocent as play of all those considerations? It will not be easy, but nothing is when fighting the juggernaut of capitalism. Still, we're equipping ourselves with knowledge and a variety of methods for engaging in this battle. Our leisure time is on life support – it is not yet completely destroyed, but has been colonised into a profitable network of little destructions. If we don't reclaim it – either via major reforms, a series of small revolutions or a thorough break in its current modus operandi – the corrosion will become terminal. The future is not decided; it is ours for the taking. The stakes are high and, indeed, it's still anyone's game.

Acknowledgements

Listen, I may not be able to do another one of these again, so I'm gonna take my time! I guess this is the part where I'm meant to celebrate a bit, right? My shrink would be disappointed, but honestly, my immediate feeling on starting these acknowledgements is a bit of dread and almost sadness. The truth is that this is not my first attempt to work on a book project. I was exploring ideas with another publisher, but in summer 2020, I was overcome by depression so intense, I just couldn't do the work, so it fell apart. My mental health was at its lowest – game over, I thought. And yet these angels surrounded me, like in a videogame, indeed, and bit by bit injected me with enough kindness, or Health Points, that I was able to rebuild myself. To them, I'll be forever thankful.

Also, very importantly, a book like this one doesn't happen because of my own talent or whatnot. It's a curation of hundreds and hundreds of sources from authors who have collated all the facts and figures that illustrate the arguments I'm making. I have tried to create a picture out of them, but I do I implore everyone to check out the work of all the amazing people referenced in the endnotes. In the last few years, I've had an Airtable sheet which

I've been filling with all the little factoids that have piqued my interest. This book is a collection of all those thoughts, ideas and commentaries, obviously with my personal slant and so on, but still – I just need to make a grateful acknowledgement of all the brilliant writers and journalists who have informed my own thinking over the years. Okay, now back to the folk I am lucky to know.

To Leo Hollis – for giving me the opportunity to realise this, for your warm wisdom, meticulous edits, curiosity, guidance and interest in this field when so few within the left care! Your work across radical literature is outstanding, and I'm immensely proud to be part of the catalogues you're curating.

To Alfie Bown – you offered me a pint and a job when I was at my lowest and believed in me. You're a comrade I'll always be thankful to. Your work on videogames and politics has been pioneering, and I'm so grateful for the opportunities you have given me – the idea for this book, too!

To Aylon Cohen – huge thanks for being my test audience for the book, for your thoughtful comments and for being a soulmate through the highs and the lows of our strange lives. I want to grow old with you; some of my favourite memories in life have you in them. I hope for many more to come.

To Ed Daly – you changed my life and had faith in me at a very crucial moment. Many things in my life are better because our paths have crossed. Your style is great, and our team bloody brilliant. Thank you for everything. (I'm a Marxist, alright? It's very strange for me to be shilling for my boss, but what can I say? You deserve it!)

To James Poulter – the only person to the left of me, I think, ha! Finding you (way too late, mind) was such a revelation, and seeing you prosper, proper shine right now, is just the warmest feeling. We've seen a lot together, no doubt there's more ahead. Thank you for being there for me through it all.

To Galan – you appeared out of nowhere and made a huge difference: to my confidence, to how I understood this strange space we found ourselves in, full of righteous combat and victories and egos larger than life. Your moral compass is sturdy as a rock and your sensitivity divine.

To Katherine Neil – a rare gem in this strange history. Your story is one of powerful action, integrity, creativity and vigour. For years I admired you online and from afar. I feel blessed our paths have finally crossed and I'm able to pick your lovely brains on a variety of topics. You teach me so much, and your kindness when you didn't have to be, ah, it meant so much. Thank you.

To Laurynas Šedvydis – during my tender teenage years, you took me under your wing when you were a young lad yourself and allowed me to ask any silly question about politics, with no judgement or disdain, just empathy and great, great humour. How thankful I am! Others, I think, have had a much worse experience. You taught me so much; I'll always be in your debt. Thank you.

To Matt Cole and Frank Mace – Frank, you were the first one to believe that there was a book in me. I'll always remember that meeting we had at an Elephant and Castle Wetherspoons, ha! Well, since then I couldn't unthink it, but finally, here we are. And Matt, wow, we've seen some crap, eh? But we persevered through it all, and I'm so proud of us for that. Having a connection with you through it all was invaluable. Your and Frank's union is romantic, lush, profound and so filled with meaning. I am so excited about your next chapter with more rad folk in your wonderful family.

To Rosie Collington – my move to Copenhagen was great enough, but then it gifted you into my life. And wow, a fortune came my way! As the meticulous, brave, awesome author you are, you guided me through so much of how this entire process would be, you mentored me and inspired me. But – even more importantly and preciously – you invited me into your wonderful circle of friends and painted this lovely city with entirely new colours. Many more *hygge* times for us to come, please!

To Rowan Milligan – I just love you, okay? I just do, and I always will, and I'm tearing up now, there we go. I don't know what miracle brought you into my life, or by what magic I managed to keep you, but, wow, what a reward that all has been. You enriched me – materially (oh, God bless magical Norman!), spiritually. You held me through the worst, and we laughed our bums off through the most amusing, strange little bits of our delightful life together. I look forward to our silver years. We'll have fun.

To TheoryFighter – many people made this book happen, but by god you're the beginning of it all. My searching mind met your brilliant, generous knowledge and, most importantly, a judgement-free zone where I was able to ask anything. You're the one who ignited my passion for this field, who conjured up a fire in me to explore these spaces politically, to have empathy for them, to dig deeper. And you offered it all with sass and unmatched humour. Thank you.

To Tomas Marcinkevičius – the wonderful first pair of eyes on my ramblings here. You are more than just a subeditor as you gave me so many brilliant pointers and ideas. I'm deeply proud and in awe with all the work you're doing to make our lil' neck of the woods a warmer, better place.

To Artūras Rumiancevas and the entire LŽKA crew – you're crafting a fascinating games industry over in Lithuania. I'm so happy that it's under the guidance of your creative and ambitious minds. To Josh Sawyer for, well, being you. Miss you profusely. To Katha for support through the years. To Luan – the amazing owner of the cafe in the Sundby Library where I crafted this book. Your occasional cheeky free noon rakias relaxed me when I was at a dead end, and your smile combated any writer's block I had. To Gabbas Salyamovich Islamov – my magnificent roots in Bashkiria, your values and smile and the sweet smell of your bees will always follow me. To Martha Lauren for your beautiful laughter, which I hear IRL too little. To Joshua Baldwin for your attention to the text and great comradeship at our ship. To my brother and Valentinas, who showed me games first. To Simon Saunders for encouraging me to pursue these themes when I was just getting started; your work was always a huge inspiration. To Assem Khaled for showing me light when I thought there was none left. To Matija for our dreamy summers on the Adriatic coast – I hope there are many more to come. To the brilliant comrades at STJV and other radical game unions across the world – you do God's work and are implementing groundbreaking change. Thank you. To Dovilė Valiūnė. To Dan B – thank you for looking after me in my early twenties. To Kate N for housing me when I really needed it. To Yusef / Marsy / Joy Connors – your sacrifice was not in vain, you hero.

I want to make all of you proud, folks, as you've been all so generous with me. Negronis on me next time we're together, this side of the rainbow or the other, eh!

And, finally, to the two most important ones:

To my mum, Guzel Islamova – everything that is good in me is because of you, and my life's work is to get at least close to the splendour of you, to make you know how thankful I am for all that you have given me. You've had the toughest time, and yet, out of it all you built magnificent talents, courage, strength; you carry immense beauty and that wicked wonderful Soviet sense of humour. What a brilliant fortune it is to be yours, to have you calm me, inspire me, look after me, to whisper in my ear sweet nothings that wrap me with love. The universe expands with our affection, with our strife, with our passion for a better tomorrow.

To Shalev Moran – I love us in intellectual conversations, in our precious silences, in warm cuddles, in wondrous adventures. You had me bursting with energy and ideas when I first embarked on this wonderful project; you helped me with all the stumbling blocks, and got it all to sound just right. You diligently walked me through my woes during all those 'ah, this is crap' moments. Your charm, grace and kindness have me feeling like the luckiest person, and I'm always in awe of all your talents and elegance. I still cannot believe we're spending our lives together, it's so delicious (thanks to Tim Garbos and Rosa Carbó-Mascarell for effectively bringing us together, too!). My heart trembles when I think of you – I love you so much.

All I do is to make you two proud, our future a bit more secure and our world a little bit kinder. Thank you for everything.

If I can be arrogant enough to suggest a soundtrack to accompany this book, may it be 52 Commercial Road – the album *A Wreck Provides an Excellent Foundation*.

Thank you so much for reading this book. If you're interested in my views on current goings-on, please feel free to find me online. Such is the gift of the interwebs.

Notes

Introduction: Main Menu

1. Global Games Market Report 2019, *Newzoo*, 2019.
2. Online Nation Report 2021, Ofcom.org, 2021.
3. 'Global Video Game Market Size, Share and Industry Trends Analysis Report by Type (Offline and Online), by Device (Mobile, Console, and Computer), by Regional Outlook and Forecast, 2022–8', KBV Research, 2022.
4. J. Clement, '*Grand Theft Auto V* Total Unit Sales 2023', Statista.com, 10 November 2023.
5. James Batchelor, '*GTA V* Is the Most Profitable Entertainment Product of All Time', GamesIndustry.biz, 9 April 2018.
6. David Curry, '*Minecraft* Revenue and Usage Statistics (2023)', Businessof Apps.com, 9 January 2023.
7. Charlie Campbell, 'How Netflix Is Extending Its Tentacles across Asia in Search of the Next Squid Game', Time.com, 24 November 2023.
8. Keith Stuart, '*Minecraft* passes one trillion views on YouTube', *Guardian*, 15 December 2021.
9. 'Essential Facts about the Video Game Industry 2022', Entertainment Software Association, 2022.
10. Kevin Webb, 'More Than 100 Million People Watched the "League Of Legends" World Championship, Cementing Its Place as the Most Popular Esport', *Business Insider India*, 18 December 2019. In the text, 'onwards'

next to the release date indicates the game continues to be developed up to the present day, in contrast to single complete releases.

11. 'Super Bowl LIII Draws 98.2 Million TV Viewers, 32.3 Million Social Media Interactions', *Nielsen Report*, 2019.

12. Tiffany Holmes, 'Art Games and Breakout: New Media Meets the American Arcade', SIGGRAPH 2002: Art Gallery art paper, 2002.

13. Lewis Gordon, 'The Environmental Impact of a PlayStation 4', *Verge*, 5 December 2019.

14. Johan Huizinga, *Homo Ludens*, Boston: Beacon Press, 1955, 173.

15. At that time, we lived in Šiauliai, the fourth-largest town in Lithuania. So don't worry, nobody too influential.

16. This house was on Miškas Street in Kaunas, Lithuania. Shout-outs to my neighbours from back in the day!

17. Nick Dyer-Witheford and Greig de Peuter, *Games of Empire*, Minneapolis: University of Minnesota, 2009, 228.

18. Stuart Hall, 'Encoding/Decoding', in Stuart Hall, Dorothy Hobson, Andrew Lowe, and Paul Willis (eds), *Culture, Media, Language: Working Papers in Cultural Studies, 1972–1979*, London: Routledge, 1980.

19. Stuart Hall, 'Notes on Deconstructing "the Popular"' in John Storey (ed.), *Cultural Theory and Popular Culture: A Reader*, 5th edition, London: Routledge, 2019.

20. Joshua Green, *Devil's Bargain: Steve Bannon, Donald Trump, and the Storming of the Presidency*, New York: Penguin Press, 2017.

Tutorial: History

1. Mariana Mazzucato, *The Entrepreneurial State: Debunking Public vs. Private Sector Myths*, London: Anthem Press, 2013. Another fascinating example on this theme I found recently: Uber scrapes and integrates the publicly funded Transport for London data into its apps. Egregious! Chris Stokel-Walker, 'Uber's London Data Grab Hints at a Future Subscription Service', Wired.com, 1 May 2019.

2. Marlene Simmons, 'Bertie the Brain Programmer Heads Science Council', *Ottawa Citizen*, 1975, 17.

3. Mark J. P. Wolf, *Encyclopedia of Video Games: The Culture, Technology, and Art of Gaming*, Santa Barbara: Greenwood Publishing Group, 2012.

4. Steven L. Kent, *The Ultimate History of Video Games: From Pong to Pokémon and Beyond*, New York: Three Rivers Press, 2001.

5. Ibid.

6. Steven L. Kent, *The First Quarter: A Twenty-Five-Year History of Video Games*, Bothell: BWD Press, 2000.

7. Adjusted for inflation. Source: *The Coin Operated and Home Electronic Games Market Report*, New York: Frost & Sullivan, 1976.

8. Dale Bashir, 'Treat Yourself to a Coveted Retro Console with the Game and Watch: Super Mario Bros.', IGN.com, 4 August 2023.

9. Damien McFerran, 'Thanks to Switch, Nintendo Has Now Sold Over Half a Billion Handheld Consoles', *Nintendo Life*, 7 May 2021.

10. Damiano Gerli, 'A Discussion on the European Gaming Market in the 80s', *Genesis Temple*, 30 April 2022.

11. Jennifer S. Light, 'When Computers Were Women', *Technology and Culture* 40: 3, 1999, 455–83.

12. Emily Chang, *Brotopia: Breaking Up the Boys' Club of Silicon Valley*, New York: Portfolio/Penguin Random House, 2018.

13. Clive Thompson, 'The Secret History of Women in Coding', *New York Times*, 13 February 2019.

14. Ibid.

15. Scott Cohen, *Zap! The Rise and Fall of Atari*, New York: McGraw-Hill, 1984.

16. The award was swiftly withdrawn after an outcry on social media, mostly by Atari's previous women employees.

17. Adam Fisher, *Valley of Genius: The Uncensored History of Silicon Valley*, New York: Twelve/Grand Central Publishing, 2018.

18. David Kushner, 'Sex, Drugs and Video Games: The Untold Story of Atari', *Playboy*, 19 July 2012.

19. Robert Wieder, 'A Fistful of Quarters', *Oui*, 1974.

20. For an important contribution to this entire subject, see Cecilia D'Anastasio, 'Sex, Pong, and Pioneers: What Atari Was Really Like', *Kotaku*, 12 February 2018.

21. Andrew Boyd, 'The Video Game Crash of 1983', *Engines of Our Ingenuity*, 7 January 2016.

22. Tristan Donovan, *Replay: The History of Video Games*, Lewes: Yellow Ant, 2010.

23. Tracey Lien, 'No Girls Allowed', Polygon.com, 2 December 2013. *Polygon* is one of the largest American gaming entertainment websites, publishing blogs, reviews, guides, videos, and news primarily covering videogames. It is owned by Vox Media.

24. Time stamp 44:40, 'Coleco Presents the Adam Computer System', YouTube, 3 May 2016, posted by Computer History Museum.

25. The politics of anime could take up another book. It's an extremely diverse field with numerous artistic and societal expressions. Just take Studio Ghibli, one of the most famous anime animation studios. Their films include themes of environmentalism, pacifism, feminism, anti-consumerism and so on. Once again, just because the aesthetic may be unfamiliar to many (mostly in the West), it doesn't mean that it's not incredibly rich with meaning.

26. Amanda Hess, 'A History of Sexist Video Game Marketing', *Slate*, 4 December 2013.

27. Mary Kenney, 'A Generation of Gamers Started Out Playing Barbie Fashion Designer', *Harper's Bazaar*, 20 December 2022. This article is a beautiful ode to this delightful game.

28. Leslie Wayne, 'Atari Moving Most Production', *New York Times*, 23 February 1983.

29. Peter McNiff, 'Atari Workers Protest', *RTÉ News*, 7 January 1985, archived on rte.ie.

30. David Kushner, *Masters of Doom: How Two Guys Created an Empire and Transformed Pop Culture*, New York: Random House, 2003.

31. Nic Reuben, 'House Flipper 2 Review – Moreish and Meditative Fixer-Upper Fantasy', *Guardian*, 13 December 2023.

32. Carly A. Kocurek, 'Coin-Drop Capitalism: Economic Lessons from the Video Game Arcade', in Mark J. P. Wolf (ed.), *Before the Crash: Early Video Game History*, Detroit: Wayne State University Press, 2012.

33. Kyle Riismandel, 'Arcade Addicts and Mallrats: Producing and Policing Suburban Public Space in 1980s America', *Environment, Space, Place Journal* 5: 2, 2013.

34. See Corey Mead, 'Shall We Play a Game? The Rise of the Military-Entertainment Complex', Salon.com, 19 September 2013; Owen Good, 'US Army Investing $50 Million in Video Games', Kotaku.com, 23 November 2008; Peter Suciu, 'The Complicated Relationship Between the Military and Video Game Industry', Clearance Jobs, 27 Aug 2021. Dollar figures adjusted for inflation.

35. Adjusted for inflation. Source: Jim Edwards, '"America's Army" Recruitment Video Game Cost Taxpayers $33M', CBS News, 11 December 2009.

36. Paul Cockeram, 'America's Army Preview (PC)', *Games First!*, 8 June 2002.

37. Jason D'Aprile, *Israeli Air Force: Defending the Promised Land*, PCGame-Pro – Fly/Drive Reviews.

38. Jamie Woodcock, *Marx at the Arcade: Consoles, Controllers, and Class Struggle*, Chicago: Haymarket Books, 2019.

39. Steffen P. Walz and Sebastian Deterding (eds), *The Gameful World: Approaches, Issues, Applications*, Cambridge: MIT Press, 2014.

40. Meghan M. Biro, '5 Ways Leaders Win at Gamification Technology', *Forbes*, 15 September 2013.

41. Ian Bogost, 'Gamification Is Bullshit', *Atlantic*, 9 August 2011.

42. 'Nintendo Wii Lifetime Unit Sales Worldwide as of September 2023', by region (in million units), Statista.com, 2023.

43. Informa Telecoms and Media, 'Mobile Games Industry Worth US$ 11.2 Billion by 2010', 3G.co.uk, 19 May 2005.

44. Tom Wijman, 'New Gaming Boom: Newzoo Ups Its 2017 Global Games Market Estimate to $116.0Bn Growing to $143.5Bn in 2020', Newzoo.com, 28 November 2017.

45. Oliver Yeh, 'Candy Crush Players Spent $4.2 Million Per Day Last Year, Pushing the Franchise's 2018 Total Past $1.5 Billion Report', *Sensor Tower*, 2019.

46. Stuart Dredge, 'Why Is Candy Crush So Popular?', *Guardian*, 26 March 2014.

47. Juegoadmin, 'Deep Dive: How Does Candy Crush Make Money?', *Juego Studio*, 28 July 2023.

48. 'Mobile Gaming Market: Information by Monetization (In-App Purchases, Paid Apps), Platform (Android, iOS), Genre (Casual, Action), Gaming Vertical (Money Games) and Region – Forecast until 2030', *Straits Research*, 2021.

49. Annie Njanja, 'Game Studios Come Together to Grow Industry in Africa', TechCrunch.com, 23 February 2022.

50. 'Video Games – Africa', Statista.com, 2023.

51. Julia Carrie Wong, 'Germany Shooting Suspect Livestreamed Attempted Attack on Synagogue', *Guardian*, 10 October 2019.

52. Lizzie Dearden, 'Stephan Balliet: The "Loser" Neo-Nazi Suspected of Deadly Attack on German Synagogue', *Independent*, 10 October 2019.

53. Olga R. Rodriguez, 'Man Accused of Attacking Paul Pelosi with a Hammer Testifies He Was Drawn to Right-Wing Conspiracies by "Gamergate"', PBS News, 14 November 2023.

54. Ash Parrish, 'Activision Blizzard CEO Denies Culture of Harassment and Blames Unions for Company Problems', *Verge*, 1 June 2023.

55. EA Spouse, 'EA: The Human Story', LiveJournal, 11 November 2004.

56. Tim Surette, 'EA settles OT dispute, disgruntled "spouse" outed', Game-Spot.com, 26 April 2006.

57. Dave McNary, 'SAG-AFTRA Goes on Strike against Video Game Companies', Variety.com, 21 October 2016.

58. Allegra Frank, 'Pro-Union Voices Speak Out at Heated GDC Round-table', Polygon.com, 22 March 2018.

59. Jack Morse, 'Netflix Is Quietly Working on a Livestreaming Feature, Report Claims', Mashable.com, 14 May 2022.

60. Hawken Miller, 'Video Games Connect Chronically Ill Children Isolated at Home', *Hospital, Prader-Willi News*, 22 May 2020; 'Video Games and Dyslexia: Can Gaming Increase Reading Speed?', *Succeed with Dyslexia*, 26 March 2021.

61. Brian Handwerk, 'Video Games Improve Vision, Study Says', *National Geographic*, 29 March 2009.

Level I: The Theme

1. Hope Roberts, 'A Jump Cut in History: How *Breathless* Revolutionized Filmmaking', Cinemablography.org, 27 March 2023.

2. Emru Townsend, 'The 10 Worst Games of All Time', PC World, 23 October 2006.

3. Keith Stuart, 'Danny Ledonne on Super Columbine Massacre RPG', *Guardian*, 9 August 2007.

4. Brian D. Crecente, '"Super Columbine" game triggers uproar,' Rocky Mountain News, 2008.

5. Ian Bogost, *Newsgames: Journalism at Play*, Cambridge: MIT Press, 2010.

6. Joseph 'Jagwar' Asuncion, 'Mortal Kombat 11 Banned in Japan, Indonesia, and Ukraine for Gore', *ONE Esports*, 24 April 2019.

7. Kim Ghattas, 'Syria Launches Arab War Game', *BBC News*, 31 May 2002.

8. YouTube User @CheeseYourself, a comment left under 'Hotline Miami 2: Wrong Number Soundtrack – The Green Kingdom – 02 Untitled', YouTube, 2022.

9. NPCs (non-playable characters): characters in a computer game not controlled by someone playing the game.

10. Archived on Reddit by user salamiolivesonions, 'If male costumes were designed like female costumes', r/gaming Subreddit, Reddit, 5 November 2020.

11. T. V. Reed, *Digitized Lives: Culture, Power, and Social Change in the Internet Era*, New York: Routledge, 2014.

12. Paul R. Messinger, Xin Ge, Eleni Stroulia, Kelly Lyons, Kristen Smirnov, Michael Bone, 'On the Relationship Between My Avatar and Myself', *Journal of Virtual Worlds Research*, November 2008.

13. Linda Katherine Kaye and Charlotte Rebecca Pennington, *'Girls Can't Play': The Effects of Stereotype Threat on Females' Gaming Performance*, Ormskirk: Edge Hill University, 2015.

14. Nick Dyer-Witheford and Greig de Peuter, *Games of Empire*, Minneapolis: University of Minnesota, 2009.

15. Donna Goodman, 'Capitalism Breeds Violence Against Women', *Liberation Magazine*, 1 June 2005.

16. Stefan Schubert, 'Playing With, Not Against, Empires: Video Games and (Post)Colonialism', *US Studies Online*, 27 November 2020.

17. Dmitri Williams, Nicole Martins, Mia Consalvo, James D. Ivory, 'The Virtual Census: Representations of Gender, Race, and Age in Video Games', *New Media and Society* 11: 5, 2009, 815–34.

18. Ibid.

19. Lucas Pope, @dukope, Twitter, 9 August 2016; Lawrence Bonk, 'Indie Favorite "Papers, Please" Has Sold 5 Million Copies', Engadget.com, 9 August 2023.

20. Walter Benjamin, 'The Author as Producer', in *Walter Benjamin: Selected Writings, Volume 2: 1931–1934*, Harvard University Press, 2005.

21. In his collection of essays *Revolutions in Reverse* (London: Autonomedia, 2011), anthropologist and political theorist David Graeber expresses similar worries about politics in the fine arts.

22. Lai-Tze Fan, Kishonna Gray, Aynur Kadir, 'How to Design Games That Promote Racial Equity', *Electronic Book Review*, 9 December 2021.

23. Liz Ryerson, @ellaguro, Twitter, 12 May 2021.

24. Joe Dempsey, Daniel Hargreaves, Daniel Peacock, Chelsea Lindsey, Dominic Bell, Luc Fontenoy, Heather Williams, 'Pudding Lane: Recreating Seventeenth-Century London', *Journal of Digital Humanities* 3(1), 2014.

25. Lissa Holloway-Attaway, 'Interview with Stella Wisdom, Digital Curator at the British Library', *Gamevironments Magazine* 14, 2021.

26. Fernando Fernández-Aranda, Susana Jiménez-Murcia et al., 'Video Games as a Complementary Therapy Tool in Mental Disorders: Playmancer, a European Multicentre Study', *Journal of Mental Health* 21: 4, 364–74, 2012.

27. Hawken Miller, 'Video Games Connect Chronically Ill Children Isolated at Home', *Hospital, Prader-Willi News*, 22 May 2020; Sen Li, Yang Song, Zhidong Cai, and Qingwen Zhan, 'Are Active Video Games Useful in the Development of Gross Motor Skills among Non-Typically Developing Children? A Meta-Analysis', *BMC Sports Science, Medicine and Rehabilitation* 14: 140, 2022.

28. Sara A. Freed, Briana N. Sprague et al., 'Feasibility and Enjoyment of Exercise Video Games in Older Adults', *Frontiers in Public Health* 9, 2021; 'Video Games Made Me a Better Surgeon', *BBC News*, 21 October 2018; Christian Moro, Charlotte Phelps, Zane Stromberga, 'Utilizing Serious Games for Physiology and Anatomy Learning and Revision', *Advances in Physiology Education* 44: 3, 2020.

29. 'Video Games and Dyslexia: Can Gaming Increase Reading Speed?', *Succeed with Dyslexia*, 26 March 2021; Eleanor Jameson, Judy Trevena, Nic Swain, 'Electronic Gaming as Pain Distraction', *Pain Research and Management* 16: 1, 27–32.

30. Mark Fisher, *Capitalist Realism: Is There No Alternative?*, New Alresford: Zero Books, 2009.

31. Angela Ndalianis, *Neo-Baroque Aesthetics and Contemporary Entertainment*, Cambridge: MIT Press, 2005.

32. Jean Baudrillard, *The Transparency of Evil: Essays on Extreme Phenomena*, London and New York: Verso, 2009, p. 17.

33. Nick Dyer-Witheford and Greig de Peuter, *Games of Empire*, Minneapolis, University of Minnesota, 2009.

34. The following article has a few ideas: Paolo Pedercini, 'Gaming Under Socialism', Molleindustria's blog, 12 April 2017.

35. Jen Pan, 'Why Liberals Lose Their Minds over Hollywood Movies', YouTube, posted by Jacobin, 16 September 2021.

36. Adolph Reed Jr, '*Django Unchained*, or, *The Help*: How "Cultural Politics" Is Worse Than No Politics at All, and Why', NonSite.org, 25 February 2013.

37. Pan, 'Why Liberals Lose Their Minds over Hollywood Movies'.

38. 'Games Are Not Empathy Machines | The Last Guardian | Subtext Adventure', YouTube, posted by Samantha Greer, 12 December 2022.

39. Johannes Breuer, Rachel Kowert, Ruth Wendt, Thorsten Quandt, 'Sexist Games = Sexist Gamers? A Longitudinal Study on the Relationship Between Video Game Use and Sexist Attitudes', *Cyberpsychology, Behavior, and Social Networking* 18: 4, 192–202, 2015.

Level II: Communities

1. youtube.com/@TheoryFighter.
2. Beautifully retold here: Eliza Gauger, 'Breaking: Goonfleet Stomps Band of Brothers in Biggest EVE Takedown Ever', Destructoid.com, 5 February 2009.
3. 'DKP Is Market Socialism', YouTube, posted by Joshua Citarella, 28 January 2022.
4. 'Battlefield 1 Players Hold a Cease Fire on Armistice Day to Commemorate the End of WW1 Clip', YouTube, posted by Isolated Gamer, 12 November 2018.
5. 'Chinese Gamers Bid Sad Farewell to "World of Warcraft"', France 24, 23 January 2023.
6. 'Last Minute Before Shutdown of Chinese WoW Servers', YouTube, posted by Asmongold Clips, 25 January 2023.
7. 'Gamers Meet in Real Life at Bedside of Terminally-Ill Friend', *BBC News*, 29 September 2018.
8. Nathan Grayson, 'Elite: Dangerous Players Band Together to Save Cancer Patient's Expedition from Griefers', Kotaku.com, 31 January 2018.
9. '10 Times Gamers Came Together to Do UNBELIEVABLE Things', YouTube, posted by gameranx, 16 March 2019.
10. Nick Dyer-Witheford and Greig de Peuter, *Games of Empire*, Minneapolis: University of Minnesota, 2009.
11. Henry Jenkins, 'National Politics within Virtual Game Worlds: The Case of China', *Pop Junctions*, 1 August 2006.
12. Steve Henn, Jess Jiang, 'A 12-Year-Old Girl Takes On the Video Game Industry', NPR.org, 8 April 2015.
13. Tom Regan, 'Gay Weddings for Russia: How The Sims Became a Battleground for the LGBTQ+ Community', *Guardian*, 22 February 2022.
14. Aja Romano, 'Is J.K. Rowling Transphobic? Let's Let Her Speak for Herself', Vox.com, 16 March 2023; Dani Di Placido, 'The "Harry Potter" Anti-Semitism Controversy, Explained', Forbes.com, 5 January 2022.
15. Evgeny Obedkov, 'Hogwarts Legacy Hits $1 Billion in Retail Sales, Nearly 10% of WB Discovery's Quarterly Revenue', *Game World Observer*, 5 May 2023.
16. Ed Nightingale, 'Homophobic Players Upset at LGBT+ Toggle in Arcade Racer Buck Up and Drive', Eurogamer.net, 17 January 2022.

17. Zack Zwiezen, 'Two Massive Charity Game Bundles Have Now Raised Over $12 Million for Ukraine', Kotaku.com, 19 March 2022.

18. See the Games Done Quick funds tracker at their website.

19. Andrew Webster, 'Ubisoft Keeps Pretending Its Political Games Don't Have Politics in Them', *Verge*, 9 May 2019.

20. John Herman, 'The Sad Parents of #Gamergate', *The Awl*, 16 October 2014.

21. A slightly later but similar phenomenon that possibly has its roots in #Gamergate is QAnon. Groups such as reddit.com/r/QAnonCasualties support the loved ones of the lost 'Q's.

22. This popular internet meme originated from the side-scrolling shooter arcade video game *Zero Wing* (1989). The phrase became famous in the early 2000s for its humorous, poorly translated broken English, and was widely shared across the internet, often accompanied by visually manipulated images and remix videos.

23. Heejin Kim, 'Michael Burry Calls GameStop Rally "Unnatural, Insane, Dangerous"', Bloomberg.com, 27 January 2021.

24. Emily Stewart, 'The GameStop Stock Frenzy, Explained', Vox.com, 29 January 2021.

25. Shona Ghosh, 'Reddit Group WallStreetBets Hits 6 Million Users Overnight after a Wild Week of Trading Antics', *Business Insider*, 29 January 2021.

26. Jack Morse, 'Reddit's r/WallStreetBets Breaks All-Time Traffic Record', Mashable.com, 27 January 2021.

27. Matthew Goldstein and Kate Kelly, 'Melvin Capital, Hedge Fund Torpedoed by the GameStop Frenzy, Is Shutting Down', *New York Times*, 18 May 2022.

28. Stephen Gandel, 'Corporate Executives Reap Millions from Reddit Stock Frenzy', CBS News, 30 January 2021.

29. Joe Rennison, 'GameStop Frenzy Helps Fuel Sharp Gains for Morgan Stanley Fund', *Financial Times*, 3 February 2021; Niket Nishant, 'Black-Rock May Have Raked in $2.4 Bln on GameStop's Retail-Driven Stock Frenzy', Reuters.com, 27 January 2021.

30. 'When Did the WoW Community Get So Political?', a Blizzard Forums thread made by user Lithya, 6 December 2018.

31. Thiago Falcão, Daniel Marques, Ivan Mussa, Tarcízio Macedo, 'At the Edge of Utopia. Esports, Neoliberalism and the Gamer Culture's Descent into Madness', *Gamevironments Magazine* #13, University of Bremen, 2020.

32. 'Esports: General Law of Sport is approved in the Senate with rejection of the amendment on CBDEL', IRGlobal.com, 17 June 2022.

33. *Minecraft* is apolitical, except for the fact that its creator, Markus Persson (aka 'Notch'), has demonstrated numerous far-right, misogynist and homophobic tendencies.

34. Tristan Kirk, 'Teenage Neo-Nazi Jailed for Sending Out Bomb Manual Disguised as Minecraft Handbook', *Standard*, 7 February 2022.

35. YouTube Culture and Trends Report, 'One Trillion Minecraft Views: Exploring the Data Behind a Mind-Boggling Milestone for Gaming Creators on YouTube', YouTube, 2023.

36. Chella Ramanan, 'PewDiePie Must Not Be Excused. Using the N-Word Is Never OK', *Guardian*, 11 September 2017; Ben Gilbert, 'Ninja Tyler Blevins Apologizes After Accidentally Using Racist Term on Twitch', *Business Insider*, 29 March 2018.

37. 'Putin's Palace. History of the World's Largest Bribe', YouTube, posted by Alexei Navalny, 19 January 2021.

38. 'Putin's Palace in Minecraft 1:1', YouTube, posted by TeamCIS, 24 January 2021.

39. '*Строю дворец Путина в SIMS 4 Прямой эфир*', YouTube, posted by Glitch, 28 January 2021; '*Строю дворец неПутина в Симс4*', YouTube, posted by HoneyMelon, 6 February 2021.

40. Alice Finney, 'The Uncensored Library Gives Gamers "a Safe Haven for Press Freedom"', Dezeen.com, 17 August 2021.

41. Cyrus Farivar, 'Extremists Creep into Roblox, an Online Game Popular with Children', *Head Topics*, 28 August 2019.

42. Cecilia D'Anastasio, 'How Roblox Became a Playground for Virtual Fascists', Wired.com, 10 June 2021.

43. 'Myanmar: Facebook's Systems Promoted Violence Against Rohingya; Meta Owes Reparations – New Report', Amnesty International, 29 September 2022.

44. One of the main influencers in this space is the incredible streamer Xmiramira, who creates the most magical, chaotic, surreal set-ups in her *Sims* games. She is also a modder who pushed for diversity in *The Sims*, eventually becoming a consultant for Electronic Arts, the creators of the game. Be sure to check her out!

45. Nathan Grayson, 'Sims Players Hold Virtual Black Lives Matter Rally', Kotaku.com, 12 June 2020.

46. Maurizio Lazzarato, 'Immaterial Labor', in Paolo Virno and Michael Hardt (eds), *Radical Thought in Italy: A Potential Politics*, Minneapolis: University of Minnesota Press, 1996, 133–47; Michael Hardt and Antonio Negri, *Empire*, Cambridge: Harvard University Press, 2000.

47. Rob Walker, 'The Buying Game', *New York Times Magazine*, 16 October 2005.

48. Sam Parker, 'Ultima Online Volunteers Sue Origin', GameSpot.com, 20 September 2000.

49. Cale Michael, 'Nintendo Imposes Severe Tournament Limitations – and the Community Responds with Uproar', DoteEsports.com, 24 October 2023.

50. Shiburizu, 'Capcom's New Community License for Street Fighter V Tournaments Is a Dangerous Misfire', SuperCombo.gg, 1 March 2022.

51. Guy Debord, 'Théorie de la Dérive', *Internationale Situationniste* #2, Paris, December 1958.

52. u/isavino, 'Why the fuck am I outside my house at 1am in my underwear trying to catch a meowth?', r/gaming Subreddit, Reddit, 7 July 2016.

53. David Hambling, 'Ships Fooled in GPS Spoofing Attack Suggest Russian Cyberweapon', *New Scientist*, 10 August 2017.

54. 'Pokemon Go Players Banned for Cheating', *BBC News*, 21 February 2021.

55. 'Grand Theft Auto 5 Mod Lets You Watch a Deer Roam Los Santos', GameRant.com, 21 March 2016.

56. Logan Molyneux, Krishnan Vasudevan, Homero Gil de Zúñiga, 'Gaming Social Capital: Exploring Civic Value in Multiplayer Video Games', *Journal of Computer-Mediated Communication*, 2015.

Level III: Efficacy

1. Pierre Bourdieu, Loïc J. D. Wacquant, *An Invitation to Reflexive Sociology*, Chicago: University of Chicago Press, 1992.

2. Geoff Cox, Nav Haq, and Tom Trevor (eds), *Concept Store #3: Art, Activism and Recuperation*, Bristol: Arnolfini, 2010.

3. Maria Lind, *This Is Going to Be Really Funny: Notes on Art, Its Institutions and Their Presumed Criticality*, Bristol: Spike Island and Systemisch, 2004, 33–4.

4. Nav Haq, 'Declarations: The Polemics of Art Engaged With Conflict' in *Concept Store #3: Art, Activism and Recuperation*, Bristol: Arnolfini, 2010.

5. 'Art in Service of the Environment: The Ice Bear Project', WWF.org, 2009.

6. 'Gameplay Trailer for Recharge', Music for Relief, 2013; Christina Nunez, '"Recharged": Linkin Park's Efforts on Energy Poverty Get Brighter', *National Geographic*, 18 November 2013.

7. The game first premiered on Apple Arcade, Apple's video game service. Apple is also a major polluter, with gigantic ecological manufacturing costs and waste emissions.

8. Clark Boyd, 'Darfur Activism Meets Video Gaming', *BBC News*, 6 July 2006.

9. Claire Bishop, *Artificial Hells: Participatory Art and the Politics of Spectatorship*, London and New York: Verso, 2012, 13.

10. Jane McGonigal, *Reality Is Broken: Why Games Make Us Better and How They Can Change the World*, London: Penguin Books, 2010, 11.

11. Toke Lykkeberg, 'Political Commitment Is a Beginning, Not an End', Kunstkritikk.com, 19 September 2016.

12. Nicolas Bourriaud, *Relational Aesthetics*, Dijon: Les Presses du réel, 2002.

13. Malcolm Miles, *The Strange Relation of Art and Politics: Considering an essay by Jacques Rancière*, paper at Loughborough University, for Radical Art Radical Aesthetics, March 2012.

14. 'Santiago Sierra by Teresa Margolles', *Bomb Magazine* 86, 1 January 2004.

15. Collection Items, Whitney Museum of Modern Art, whitney.org.

16. Tania Bruguera, 'Political Art Transforms the Audience Into Citizens', *Texte Zur Kunst* 80, 2010, 133–5.

17. To find out more about where the rich hoard their vast collections, read about Geneva Free Port and Le Freeport in Singapore. The former hosts a collection three times larger, according to the *New York Times*. *Hosts* is a generous word – the facilities are simply high-end containers with access only for security and the owners.

18. Kolja Reichert, 'The Vacuum Cleaner Effect', *Arts of the Working Class*, 3 December 2019.

19. Ian Walker, 'After Being 98% Off for 5 Years, This Indie Game Is Going Up to $100 Forever', Kotaku.com, 16 October 2019.

20. Alec Meer, 'Grab a Free Dog Opera from The Proteus Musicman', Rock Paper Shotgun, 4 March 2019.

21. wally b kleeposting, @kleeposting, Twitter, 5 March 2023.

22. 'A Response to PMG's Disco Elysium Investigation', YouTube, posted by stushi, 12 June 2023.

23. Claire Bishop, *Artificial Hells: Participatory Art and the Politics of Spectatorship*, London and New York: Verso, 2012, 19.

24. David Graeber, 'The Sadness of Post-Workerism, or "Art and Immaterial Labour"' in *Revolutions in Reverse: Essays on Politics, Violence, Art, and Imagination*, London and New York: Minor Compositions, 2011, 98.

25. Theodor Adorno, *The Culture Industry: Selected Essays on Mass Culture*, edited by J. M. Bernstein, London: Routledge, 1991, 168.

26. Jennifer R. Whitson, 'Book Review: Graeme Kirkpatrick, Computer Games and the Social Imaginary, Cambridge, Polity Press, 2013', *Canadian Journal of Sociology*, 2014.

27. Ibid.

28. Walter Benjamin, 'The Author as Producer', included in *Walter Benjamin: Selected Writings, Volume 2: 1931–1934*, Cambridge: Harvard University Press, 2005.

29. Such as criticising the very close relationship between the corrupt Barclays Bank and the progressive parts of the UK's games industry.

30. Philip Oltermann, 'Post-Internet Artist Hito Steyerl on Refusing Honours, Buying Her Work Back – and Fighting Big Tech', *Guardian*, 13 June 2023.

31. *Walter Benjamin: Selected Writings, Volume 4, 1938-1940*, Cambridge: Harvard University Press, 2003, 270.

Level IV: Modes of Production

1. Sarah 'KZ' Zulkiflee, 'How Many People Play Genshin Impact in 2022?', Esports.gg, 1 May 2022; Ann Cao, 'Genshin Impact Bags US$4 Billion in Sign of Rising Power of China's Video Gaming Industry', *South China Morning Post*, 2 January 2023. Important to note – there is absolutely nothing wrong with waifus or husbandos as game characters! They also must be liberated and unshackled from the profiteering, addiction-inducing incentives that they are mostly associated with these days.

2. Lewis Rees, 'Which Five Mobile Hits Generated $7.2 Billion in Revenue in 2022?', Pocket Gamer, 18 January 2023; Owen Mahoney, Shiro Uemura, *Investor Presentation Q2 2023*, Nexon Co., Ltd., 9 August 2023, 33.

3. Although in mid-2023, CD Projekt announced a move to Unreal Engine for Cyberpunk, away from their in-house tools, further solidifying Epic's influence in games.

4. 'Are Game Engines the Future of Filmmaking?', Filmmakers Academy, 26 July 2021.
5. 'Game Player and App User Privacy Policy', Unity.com, 15 November 2022.
6. Charlie Hall, 'The Fury Over the Epic Games Store, Explained', Polygon.com, 5 April 2019.
7. EA Spouse, 'EA: The Human Story', EA Spouse LiveJournal, 11 November 2004.
8. Kate Brice, '"Rockstar Spouse" Accuses Dev of Pushing Its Employees "to the Brink"', GamesIndustry.biz, 11 January 2010.
9. Ben Gilbert, 'The Creator of "Fortnite" Reportedly Has a Brutal Work Culture Where Some Employees Have 100-Hour Work Weeks: "I Hardly Sleep. I'm Grumpy at Home. I Have No Energy to Go Out."', Business Insider, 23 April 2019.
10. *2019 Developer Satisfaction Survey*, International Game Developers Association, November 2020.
11. Nathan Grayson, 'Guild Wars 2 Writers Fired for Calling Out Fan on Twitter', Kotaku.com, 6 July 2018.
12. Shannon Liao, 'Since Lawsuit, Riot Games' Once All-Male Leadership Now Over 20 Percent Women', *Washington Post*, 10 August 2022.
13. Tom DiChristopher, 'Digital Gaming Sales Hit Record $61 Billion in 2015: Report', CNBC.com, 26 January 2016.
14. 'Court Approves EEOC's $18 Million Settlement with Activision Blizzard', US Equal Employment Opportunity Commission, 30 March 2022.
15. Nick Statt, 'Telltale Under Fire for Prioritizing The Walking Dead Conclusion in Wake of Mass Layoffs', The Verge, 25 September 2018; Alissa McAloon, 'Capcom Shuts Down Dead Rising Developer Capcom Vancouver', Game Developer, 18 September 2018; Liana B. Baker, 'Activision Blizzard Cuts 600 Jobs', Reuters.com, 29 February 2012.
16. Todd Spangler, 'Electronic Arts to Lay Off 800 Employees, 6% of Workforce', Variety.com, 29 March 2023; 'Electronic Arts Revenue 2010-2023', Macrotrends.net, 30 September 2023; Ashley Capoot, 'Unity Software to Lay Off 600 Employees, or 8% of Its Workforce', CNBC.com, 3 May 2023; Ash Parrish, 'More Layoffs at Another Embracer Group Studio', *The Verge*, 5 December 2023.
17. Ian Williams, 'It's Time to Talk About Labor in the Games Industry', *Giant Bomb*, 9 February 2016.
18. *2022 UK Games Industry Census*, United Kingdom Interactive Entertainment, Ukie.org, 2023.

19. Alex Fernandes, @oneferny, Twitter, 3 October 2021.

20. As of early 2022, the top 10 companies were as follows: Tencent (gaming revenue of $32.2 billion), Sony ($18.2 billion), Apple ($15.3 billion), Microsoft ($13 billion), Google ($11 billion), NetEase ($9.6 billion), Activision Blizzard ($8.1 billion), Nintendo ($8.1 billion), EA ($6.5 billion), Sea Limited ($4.3 billion). Jeffrey Rousseau, 'Report: Top 10 Companies Made 65% of Global Games Market in 2021', GamesIndustry.biz, 12 May 2022.

21. Tom Warren, 'Microsoft Completes Activision Blizzard Acquisition, Call of Duty Now Part of Xbox', *The Verge*, 12 October 2023.

22. Brady Langmann and Josh Rosenberg, 'Leslie Grace Says Batgirl's Cancellation Felt "Like Deflating a Balloon"', Esquire.com, 13 February 2023.

23. Wenlei Ma, 'Disney+ Production Nautilus Scrapped after Wrapping on the Gold Coast', *Guardian*, 29 August 2023.

24. *Mergers: Commission Clears Acquisition of Activision Blizzard by Microsoft, Subject to Conditions*, press release, European Commission, Brussels, 15 May 2023.

25. Jay Peters, 'Microsoft's Phil Spencer Says Acquiring Nintendo Would Be "A Career Moment"', The *Verge*, 19 September 2023.

26. J. Clement, 'Steam Gaming Platform – Statistics & Facts', Statista.com, 10 November 2023.

27. Ibid.

28. 'Live Nation Entertainment's Revenue from 2006 to 2022', Statista.com, February 2023.

29. 'PC Video Gaming Software Sales Revenue Worldwide from 2008 to 2025', Statista.com, August 2021; 'Console Gaming Revenues Worldwide from 2020 to 2026, by Type', Statista.com, May 2023; 'Mobile Games – Worldwide', Statista.com; David Curry, 'Google Play Store Statistics (2023)', *Business of Apps*, 2 May 2023.

30. Jeffrey Rousseau, 'Mobile Games Accounted for 66% of App Store Spending in 2022', GamesIndustry.biz, 17 May 2023.

31. Ibid.

32. 'DOTA 2 The International Championship Prize Pool from 2011 to 2022', Statista.com, November 2022.

33. Some wild stories here: Nicole Carpenter, 'Philadelphia Fusion Overwatch Player Sado Apologizes for Boosting', *Dot Esports*, 4 December 2017; Kevin Webb, 'A Gamer Tried to Go Pro Using a Fake Identity, and

the Scandal Could Have Big Consequences for Women in Esports', *Business Insider*, 9 January 2019.

34. Jeffrey Boxer, 'Doping in Esports: An International Solution to the Problem that No One Is Talking About', Medium.com, 9 May 2022.

35. Marijam Didžgalvytė, 'Esports *Could* Be Sexy, So What's Going On?', Medium.com, 21 November 2017.

36. Emily Rand, 'Rand: Finding the Meaning of Family Through League of Legends', ESPN.co.uk, 30 September 2019.

37. Andrew Webster, 'Meet the Counter Strike E-sports Team Where Everyone Is over 60', *The Verge*, 20 December 2017.

38. Cecilia D'Anastasio, 'Saudi Arabia Is Investing $38 Billion to Become a Video-Game Hub', Bloomberg.com, 23 June 2023.

39. Robert Hoogendoorn, 'Exclusive Dookey Dash Game Does $35 Million in Trading Volume', DappRadar.com, 23 January 2023.

40. A great website collating this information live is the Cambridge Bitcoin Electricity Consumption Index. It is collated by the Cambridge Centre for Alternative Finance, Judge Business School, University of Cambridge.

41. Clint Pumphrey, 'How Gold Farming Works', HowStuffWorks.com, 30 April 2015.

42. Lydia DePillis, 'Click Farms Are the New Sweatshops', *Washington Post*, 6 January 2014.

43. Ian Bogost, 'How Video Games License Guns', *Atlantic*, 20 August 2019.

44. Paris Martineau, 'Amazon Expands Effort to Gamify Warehouse Work', *The Information*, 15 March 2021.

45. Adrian Hon, *You've Been Played*, New York: Basic Books, 2022.

46. Wilfred Chan, '$7,000 a Day for Five Catchphrases: The TikTokers Pretending to Be "Non-Playable Characters"', *Guardian*, 19 July 2023.

47. I want to be completely clear – I find cosplaying an intensely fascinating project. The craftsmanship and technical prowess demonstrated by cosplay is outstanding! As the daughter of a seamstress, I find the talent of sewing together complicating materials truly remarkable. It is a technical skill, a craft, then, rather than a purely creative art of coming up with designs. IP rules are being followed most of the time. Still, what a feast for the eyes!

48. Daniel Greene, 'Landlords of the Internet: Big Data and Big Real Estate', *Social Studies of Science* 52: 6, 2022.

49. Ibid.

50. Ben Abraham, '4K & 8K Gaming and Energy Efficiency: How Many Pixels Is Too Many?', *Greening the Games Industry*, 17 May 2022.

51. Ibid.

52. Siddharth Kara, *Cobalt Red: How the Blood of the Congo Powers Our Lives*, San Francisco: St. Martin's Press, 2023.

53. Charlie Campbell, 'Foxconn Founder Terry Gou Wants to Be Taiwan's President – and a Go-Between for US and China', Time.com, 11 July 2019.

54. 'Beyond Foxconn: Deplorable Working Conditions Characterize Apple's Entire Supply Chain', *China Labor Watch*, 27 June 2012.

55. Ibid.

56. Bin Jiang, *The Foxconn Factory Site, Methods, and Procedure for Design Interventions*, Hong Kong: University of Hong Kong, 2021.

57. David Barboza, 'IPhone Maker in China Is Under Fire after a Suicide', *New York Times*, 26 July 2009.

58. Brian Merchant, 'Life and Death in Apple's Forbidden City', *Guardian*, 18 June 2017.

59. 'Beyond Foxconn: Deplorable Working Conditions Characterize Apple's Entire Supply Chain', *China Labor Watch*, 27 June 2012.

60. Jenny Chan, Ngai Pun, Mark Selden, 'Dying for an iPhone: the Lives of Chinese Workers', *China Dialogue*, 15 April 2016.

61. Han Tang, 'China's Young Workers Fight Back at Foxconn', *Labor Notes*, 13 August 2013.

62. Shannon Liao, 'Amazon and Foxconn Reportedly Strip Workers of Benefits and Pay Low Wages in Chinese Factory', *The Verge*, 11 June 2018.

63. Michael Sainato, '"They're More Concerned about Profit": Osha, Doj Take On Amazon's Gruelling Working Conditions', *Guardian*, 2 March 2023.

64. Ben Abraham, 'What's the Game Industry's Plastic Footprint?', *Greening the Games Industry*, 17 April 2023.

65. Lewis Gordon, 'The Many Ways Video Game Development Impacts the Climate Crisis', *The Verge*, 5 May 2020.

66. Alex Hern, 'TechScape: Will the Video Games Industry Ever Confront Its Carbon Footprint?', *Guardian*, 13 April 2022.

67. Lewis Gordon, 'How to Make the Video Game Industry Greener', Wired.com, 9 June 2022.

68. Offsetting is a corruption-ridden approach where a private company promises to do something, normally to plant trees, to offset the CO_2

emissions of a funding organisation. Notably, some game companies like Sumo Group, for instance, choose to offset locally, funding peatlands in the UK which lock in huge amounts of carbon. The results are then easier to verify and see with one's own eyes compared to other approaches.

69. *Green Games Guide*, Report, United Kingdom Interactive Entertainment, 2021.

70. Lewis Gordon, 'This Videogame Is Killing the Planet', ArtReview.com, 8 December 2021.

71. Check out more of Dr Ben Abraham's brilliant blog: benabraham.net.

72. Wes Davis and Richard Lawler, 'Nvidia Became a $1 Trillion Company Thanks to the AI Boom', *Verge*, 31 May 2023.

73. 'The TVs, monitors, and laptops of CES 2024 / Today on The Vergecast, it's screens all the way down', *Verge* podcast, 10 January 2024.

Conclusion: Final Boss

1. Leonard E. Read, 'I, Pencil: My Family Tree as Told to Leonard E. Read', *Irvington-on-Hudson*, New York: Foundation for Economic Education, 1998.

2. Ibid.

3. Lewis Gordon, 'The Environmental Impact of a PlayStation 4', *The Verge*, 5 December 2019.

4. Viola Zhou, 'AI Is Already Taking Video Game Illustrators' Jobs in China', *Rest of World*, 11 April 2023.

5. David Graeber, *Bullshit Jobs: A Theory*, New York: Simon & Schuster, 2018.

6. Laine Brotherton, 'Are Bots a Threat to Multiplayer Games?', *Michigan Daily*, 8 April 2021.

7. Anthony Cuthbertson, '"Subscribe to PewDiePie": What Did Christchurch Mosque Gunman Mean in Final Words Before Shooting?', Independent.co.uk, 15 March 2019.

8. *Toxicity in Multiplayer Games Report*, Unity, 2023.

9. Theodor Adorno, *The Culture Industry: Selected Essays on Mass Culture*, edited by J. M. Bernstein, London: Routledge, 1991.

10. David Graeber, *The Utopia of Rules: On Technology, Stupidity, and the Secret Joys of Bureaucracy*, New York: Melville House, 2015.

11. David Graeber, *Revolutions in Reverse: Essays on Politics, Violence, Art, and Imagination*, London and New York: Minor Compositions, 2011, 111.

12. Marijam Didžgalvytė, @marijamdid, Twitter, 8 March 2023.
13. 'Namibia Bans Export of Unprocessed Critical Minerals', Reuters.com, 8 June 2023.
14. 'Finnish Game Industry Model for CO2 Emissions Calculations – An Update', *Neogames Finland*, May 2023.
15. Sophie McEvoy, 'Die Gute Fabrik and the Necessity to Tackle Climate Inaction', GamesIndustry.biz, 26 October 2023.
16. Read more about all their brilliant victories on their website: code-cwa.org.
17. 'Mission Statement', Game Workers Alliance.
18. Gene Maddaus, 'SAG-AFTRA to Set More Talks with Video Game Companies in Hopes of Averting Second Strike', Variety.com, 16 October 2023.
19. Nicole Carpenter, 'Corsair's Warehouse Workers Make Pennies Compared to CEO's Millions – and Now They're Fighting Back', Polygon.com, 15 September 2023; Nicole Carpenter, 'Tabletop, Card Game Retailers Join the Game Industry's Burgeoning Union Push', Polygon.com, 9 November 2022.
20. 'Escape Room Workers Union Goes Public', Industrial Workers of the World (IWW), 2 July 2023.
21. Nathan Grayson, 'Game Studio With No Bosses Pays Everyone the Same', Kotaku.com, 25 July 2018.
22. Imogen West-Knights, 'Fine Dining Faces Its Dark Truths in Copenhagen', *Financial Times*, 2 June 2022.
23. Jeffrey Rousseau, 'Dutch Government Seeks to Ban Loot Boxes', GamesIndustry.biz, 3 July 2023; James Batchelor, 'Microsoft, EA, Activision, Ubisoft and Epic Face Game Addiction Lawsuit', GamesIndustry.biz, 8 November 2023; Ash Parrish, 'Former Ubisoft Executives Arrested After Sexual Harassment Investigation', *The Verge*, 4 October 2023; Jeffrey Rousseau, 'South Korean Government Charges Game Rating and Administration Committee with Embezzlement', GamesIndustry.biz, 5 July 2023.
24. Simon Parkin, 'Elden Ring Review – An Unrivalled Masterpiece of Design and Inventiveness', *Guardian*, 23 February 2022.
25. Mary Flanagan and Helen Nissenbaum, *Values at Play in Digital Games*, Cambridge: MIT Press, 2014, 3.
26. 'Foldit Players Beat Scientists in Determining a Protein's Shape', Graduate School of Arts and Sciences, Harvard University, 3 October 2016.
27. Full disclosure – at the moment, I work for the company making the title.

28. A highly recommended read – a beautiful interview with Zotov: Fuzz, 'Space Spy: Interview with Vasily Zotov', TigSource.com, 20 November 2009.

29. 'Skyrim – Thomas the Tank Engine Mod (HD)', YouTube, 12 December 2013, posted by lambo_96.

30. Patricia Hernandez, 'Thomas the Tank Engine Mod Got Skyrim Player in Legal Trouble', Polygon.com, 15 May 2019.

31. Claire Bishop, *Artificial Hells: Participatory Art and the Politics of Spectatorship*, London and New York: Verso, 2012, 284.

32. 'FRANCIS ALŸS: Children's Games 1999–2022', press release, Copenhagen Contemporary, 2022.

33. Max Horkheimer and Theodor W. Adorno, *Dialectic of Enlightenment*, Stanford: Stanford University Press, 2002, pp. 137, 143.

34. A reformulation of the famous quote, 'If I can't dance, it's not my revolution!', attributed to the legendary anarchist Emma Goldman.

35. 'Helmers and Hill Argue that Visual Rhetoric Is Particularly Essential in the Face of Globalization and Mass Media', insights from Ian Bogost, *Persuasive Games: The Expressive Power of Videogames*, Cambridge: MIT Press 2007, 21; John Clark, 'The Society of the Spectacle, Reconsidered', Fifth Estate.org, 1 June 2015.

36. Raymond Williams, *Resources of Hope: Culture, Democracy, Socialism*, London and New York: Verso, 1989, 118.

Index